THE COMPLETE IDIOT'S GUIDE™ TO

Microsoft® Excel 97,

Second Edition

by LauraMaery Gold and Dan Post

alpha
books
que®

A Division of Macmillan Computer Publishing
201 W. 103rd Street, Indianapolis, IN 46290 USA

The Complete Idiot's Guide to Microsoft® Excel, Second Edition

International Standard Book Number: 0-7897-1693-3
Library of Congress Catalog Card Number: 98-84859

01 00 99 98   8 7 6 5 4 3 2

Interpretation of the printing code: The rightmost number of the first series of numbers is the year of the book's printing; the rightmost number of the second series of numbers is the number of the book's printing. For example, a printing code of 98-2 shows that the second printing of the book occurred in 1998.

Screen reproductions in this book were created by means of the program Collage Complete from Inner Media, Inc., Hollis, NH.

Printed in the United States of America

Credits

Executive Editor
Angela Wethington

Acquisitions Editor
Jamie Milazzo

Development Editor
Robin Drake

Technical Editor
Patrick Blattner

Managing Editor
Thomas F. Hayes

Production Editor
Karen A. Walsh

Copy Editor
Margaret Berson

Indexer
Tim Tate

Production
Svetlana Dominguez
Mary Ellen Stephenson
Megan Wade
Pamela Woolf

Book Designer
Glenn Larsen

Cover Designer
Dan Armstrong

Cartoonist
Judd Winick

Contents at a Glance

Contents

3 Saving and Closing Documents   27

4 Help, Help   39

Part 2: Getting to Work   51

5 Shake, Copy, and Move: Filling Blocks of Cells   53

13 An Open and Shut Case 153

14 Customizing the Spreadsheet 167

xiii

22 The What-If Conundrum   273

Part 5: What Good Is Excel?   279

23 Tracking Your Life and Your Business   281

Introduction

Welcome to *The Complete Idiot's Guide to Microsoft Excel 97, Second Edition*. Faster than a speeding bullet, we promise! In minutes you'll be more powerful than the odor in the '49ers locker room, and find yourself leaping tall spreadsheets in a single bound.

If you want to become the office computer guru, consider another approach (three years in a seminary should do). But if you just want to dig right in and work with Excel, then buddy, you're in the right place. This book is for people like you who think angst-filled computer obsessions are a little unhealthy; people who prefer to have no more than a professional relationship with their machines.

In this book, you won't find yourself buried under mountains of techno-jargon. And we won't wax poetic about how computers are more dependable than your spouse. Instead, we've taken great care to assemble a book that is informative and heavily caffeinated.

So sit back and make yourself comfortable. We prefer the feet-on-desk/straddling-the-monitor work position... do ring the doorbell before you walk in on us that way, won't you?

How Do I Use This Book?

This is a guide book, so you can pick at it in bits and pieces. Read it in the bathroom, in fact—but don't get your computer wet.

Part 1, "Excel Over Easy," takes you quickly through a practice spreadsheet. When you've finished, you'll receive a gold-and-diamond-encrusted certificate assuring potential employers that you're Excel-savvy. Or maybe not. But you will know enough to jump around the rest of the book with the greatest of ease.

Part 2, "Getting to Work," tackles Excel's power features: Internet stuff, auditing, formulas, functions, and lots of other words nobody knows.

In Part 3, "Charts, Graphs, Maps, and Other Things," you get the fun stuff: charts, graphs, drawing tools, and even geographic maps.

Part 4, "Like a Database," bends and twists Excel like a pretzel into a powerful database. You'll work with databases, data consolidation, and changing scenarios.

In Part 5, just in case there is still some doubt, you'll sample "What Good Is Excel?"

Go straight to Part 6, "Stuff at the Back of the Book," if you need a quick reference to Excel functions or keyboard alternatives to mousing and menus.

In addition, we added some helpful hints in shaded boxes like these:

You don't *have* to know the stuff in these boxes, but it'll definitely impress the people you're dating! Memorize all of it, and you'll be tapped as a guest speaker at the International Geek Fest.

If you're one of the 200 bazillion people who've used older versions of Excel, you'll find helpful pointers like this to show you how it's changed in Excel 97.

When we've got a really cool secret tip or shortcut, we've placed it in a box like this. When you've finished reading the tip, tear it out of the book and eat it.

Acknowledgments

To another great team of editors and staff at Macmillan: Jamie Milazzo, Lisa Wagner, Robin Drake, Karen Walsh, Karen Opal, Patrick Blattner, and everyone else who contributed to this updated version. Our sincere thanks!

And thanks, most of all, to our kiddos, who once again spent altogether too much time on tiptoe. Pack up the cat, kids! We're going to Seattle!

Trademarks

We used lots of words in this book. Many of them are probably copyrighted, trade-marked, double-crossed, tick-marked, pock-marked, and hexed. The following words, for example, are trademarks and proper nouns, not to be messed with by amateurs:

dBASE

Intuit Quickbooks Pro

Lotus 1-2-3

Macintosh

Microsoft Excel

Microsoft Access

Paradox

Taco Bell

Donald Trump

Terms suspected of being trademarks or service marks have been appropriately capital-ized. We didn't, however, date the staff of the international patent and trademark offices, so don't regard our failure as a reflection on the validity of any trademark or service mark.

Part 1
Excel Over Easy

A wise man—or perhaps it was a mediocre screenwriter—once said there are three ways: your way, my way, and the right way. Obviously, he'd never heard of "Our Way."

In this section, you'll learn what a worksheet is, what a workbook is, and why professional accountants would rather you didn't have this information. Soon you'll be opening workbooks, mastering the cursor, entering data, printing, and saving your work. Also, sprinkled throughout, we'll note the significant differences between Excel 97 and older products.

Tick
Tick Tick Tick

Chapter 1

10-Minute Guide to Excel

In This Chapter

➤ Spreadsheets then and now

➤ In the beginning

➤ Introduction to the work area

➤ Old versus new

➤ An almanac of all-purpose advice

In the beginning there was stone—useful primarily for weapon making, cave art, and preventing your significant other from leaving. Back in the Stone Age, "fast food" referred to the speed of your prey. Ordinary people didn't have time to deal with numbers. They had other, more important matters to deal with—learning to shave with rocks, for example. Although stone tables are durable, they proved less than ideal for working out complicated mathematical formulas. Many a Stone-Age accountant went into apoplectic seizure when a layman questioned the figures on the stone tablet and asked, "What if we changed...."

The Spreadsheet Intro

The notion of an accounting spreadsheet didn't change much until the advent of the personal computer in the late 1970s. Even then, only a few visionaries seemed to realize that a revolution was under way—although there is always someone who will claim that Nostradamus first predicted Excel 97 way back in 1555. To people with less imagination, personal computers and spreadsheets were simply the thing that would forever protect them from the embarrassment of writing another bad check.

If you've used other software—word processors or databases, for example—you'll recognize some vague similarities between those programs and the Excel spreadsheet. The Excel spreadsheet looks something like a word processor, as viewed through the bars of a prison cell.

Cell. That's a word you'll see frequently throughout this book. A spreadsheet is a collection of *cells* arranged in columns and rows. Cells can hold numbers, text, or formulas. Each cell has an address, the point where the row and the column intersect. Figure out how to speak in spreadsheet cryptics, and you'll soon find yourself talking to your accountant in condescending tones, such as this: "It's simple. Cell B3 starts at column B as labeled across the top of the spreadsheet grid and continues down until it intersects with row 3, as labeled on the left side of the grid. That internal cell reference you see on the right is a trace to cell D5."

Ask What It Can Do for You

It's time to put away your abacus for good. A spreadsheet automates all the recalculating that has to be done each time you change a number. Remember that battered piece of scratch paper you used for algebra class in high school? Every problem on it had to be erased and changed at least twice, and every change meant you had to completely recalculate from top to bottom. At the time, it seemed as though your entire junior prom night might be spent running through the calculations "one more time."

A spreadsheet lets you do what you wish you could have done with that piece of paper (and your prom date): play around all evening and never make a permanent commitment. It does all the recalculating automatically without ever causing a bit of trouble. Let's stop the analogy here, before someone turns on the cold water.

In a spreadsheet, you write complicated formulas only once. Excel's spreadsheets, called *worksheets,* are something like those battered pieces of scratch paper from algebra class. Now imagine a notebook with as many as 255 of those battered pieces of paper. That notebook is what Excel calls a *workbook*.

So let's look at a real Excel workbook. There's no time like the present. (Actually, there've been seven or eight times like the present, but never mind.)

In the Beginning

There, wearing nothing but a pair of socks and a dirty T-shirt, is the Windows screen: a few *icons* on the left, and the all-important *taskbar* at the bottom. On the left end of the taskbar is the Start button, your access point for almost anything you want to do with Windows. Click the **Start** button, and the Start menu pops up.

Excel 97 icon

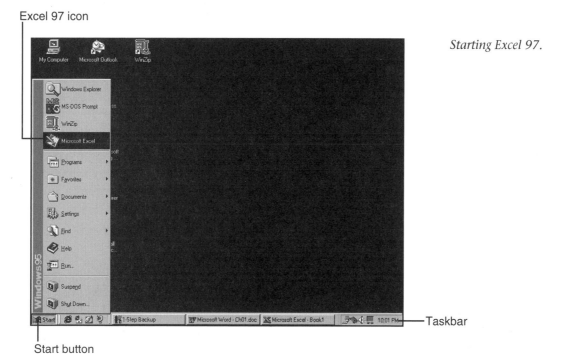

Starting Excel 97.

Start button

Taskbar

Move the pointer to the **Start** menu and position it over the Programs selection. The Programs menu appears to the right. Move through your folders until you locate the Excel 97 folder. You may find Excel 97 located in the Microsoft Office 97 folder if you installed it as part of that package. See the installation guide (Appendix A, "Installation and Technical Support") for details on Excel installations. After you find the correct folder, click the **Excel** option and make yourself comfortable while Windows loads Excel.

What's on the Big Screen

Let's try a quick run-through of what first appears on the main Excel screen. To help make it interesting, try getting through the next paragraph without taking a breath.

From top to bottom, the Excel screen features the title bar, main menu, standard toolbar, formatting toolbar, formula bar, and worksheet area. Across the bottom you find file-folder-like tabs for the worksheet pages, as well as the horizontal scrollbar and a status bar. At the far right of the screen is the vertical scrollbar.

Formatting toolbar

Standard toolbar

Excel main menu bar

Title bar

These buttons control the Excel window

Excel's opening screen.

These buttons control the document window

Formula bar

Office Assistant

Scrollbars

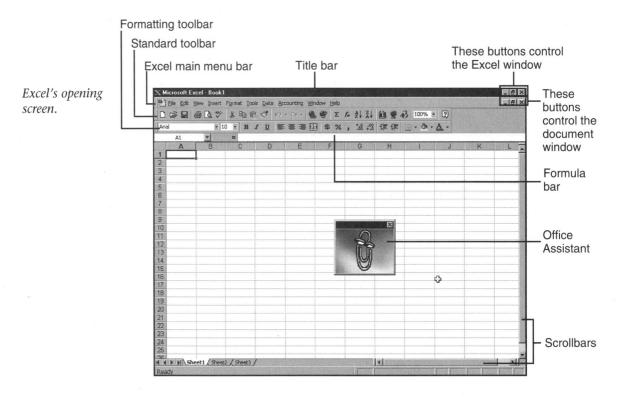

Whew! Now the details. Holding your breath through this section is for iron-lunged readers only.

Judging a (Work) Book by Its Title (Bar)

The trend today is to create computer software that is as simple to use as possible. This is accomplished by making things so complicated that most people give up on all the really cool features and just type.

To help you get your bearings, Windows displays a title bar across the top of every program window you open. The title bar tells you the name of the program you're running—Microsoft Excel, we hope—as well as the name of the file you're working on.

Menu, Please

Directly below the title bar is Excel's main menu bar, which breaks Excel commands into groups of related options. The commands on the menu bar are grouped under File, Edit, View, and so on. To the right are three more display buttons. The first reduces the workbook (not the entire program) to an icon within the Excel window. The second toggles between the full Excel screen and Excel window view. The Close button closes the current file, which Excel calls a *workbook*.

About That Toolbar in the Window (The One with the Waggily Icon)

Excel displays several rows of *toolbars*—ribbons of icons that are designed to simplify your work. Some of the icons have obvious meaning; others, however, are mysteries that rival the Sphinx. But no matter how mysterious, toolbar icons generally duplicate commands found on the menus. That means there are nearly always two ways to do anything. Excel has multiple toolbars, all of which are basically alike: a logical grouping of shortcut icons. For now, we'll concern ourselves with only the two that appear on the opening screen:

➤ The standard toolbar features shortcut icons for the most common commands you use in Excel; using these toolbar icons saves you from having to search through the menu items (as soon as you learn what they all mean).

➤ Next up (or down, as the case may be) is the formatting toolbar. The formatting toolbar bundles commands that affect the appearance of your text: font type, size, alignment, and other options. Turn to Chapter 14, "Customizing the Spreadsheet," for a discussion of these functions.

Check This Out...

What Does This One Do?

Confused by all the toolbar icons on your screen? You're not the only one. To find out what one does, position your mouse pointer over any toolbar icon. The room around you grows dark, thunder sounds in the distant plains, smoke wafts out of your floppy drive, and an explanation appears onscreen. Fear not. The explanation disappears when you move the pointer.

A Winning Formula

In the fifth position (below the formatting toolbar) is the formula bar. The formula bar gives you information about the *active cell*—the cell you're using now. You can enter and edit formulas in the formula bar. Chapter 6, "The Editing Test: Change the Contents of Your Spreadsheet," explains editing in general. Chapters 10, "The Winning Formula," and 11, "Fully Functional," explain how to use formulas.

Office Assistant

 The Office Assistant is helpful, bothersome… and always ready to tell you what to do. We explain the new Office Assistant help feature in Chapter 4, "Help, Help."

The Work Area and How to Work in It

And now the reason we're here: the *worksheet*. This collection of cells, very cleverly laid out in columns and rows, is where you do all the real work. Your *labels* (the titles you put at the tops of columns and the left of rows), values, formulas, or whatever else you might choose to slap down on a sheet of notepaper all come to life here.

The following figure shows the elements of a worksheet.

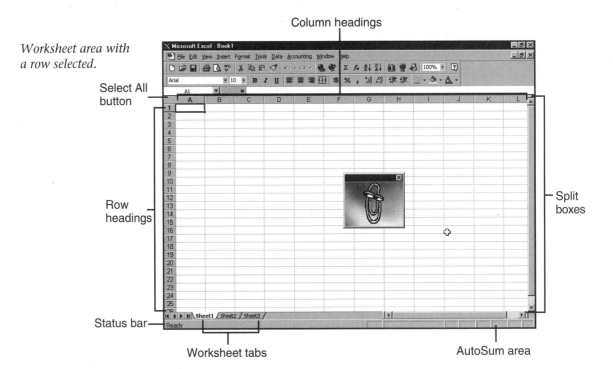

Worksheet area with a row selected.

Column headings

Select All button

Row headings

Status bar

Worksheet tabs

Split boxes

AutoSum area

Selection '97

Selecting—or highlighting—cells is a fundamental life skill, like walking, balancing your checkbook, or riding an escalator. Here are some different ways you can do the job:

➤ To select a single cell, click it.

➤ To select multiple cells, click at one corner of the block and drag your mouse diagonally across the rectangle of cells.

➤ To select an entire row or column, click its *heading*—the grayed-in number or letter at the left or at the top of the worksheet.

Navigational Tools

Below and to the right of the worksheet area, you see an assortment of scrollbars, arrows, and tabs. You use these to navigate around your workbook. Click a tab (or the arrows to the left of the tabs) to move to another worksheet in the same workbook. Use the scrollbars to move around the spreadsheet in great gallumphing strides. If you click and drag the Split boxes, you'll divide the screen into parts. We'll explain why you might want to do such a thing in Chapter 12, "Keep It Clean, Keep It Accurate, Keep It Safe," but in the meantime, if you do it accidentally, just double-click the split bars to make them go away.

Experiment with the navigation tools to get a feel for moving around the worksheet. As you do, you'll notice that the mouse pointer is a kind of changeling that assumes a different shape and meaning depending on its onscreen location. The following table shows the various forms the mouse pointer can take on.

Shape	Pointer Type	Description
↖	Regular Mouse Pointer	The standard mouse pointer appears when you point at command functions. Use it to select commands from the Main menu or the toolbars.
✛	Shaded Cross Pointer	The shaded cross pointer appears in the cell area of the workbook. Use it to select a block of cells you want to work with.
+	Black Cross Pointer	Appears over the *fill handle*, the black square in the corner of the selected cells. We describe uses of the fill handle in Chapter 5, "Shake, Copy, and Move: Filling Blocks of Cells."

continues

continued

Shape	Pointer Type	Description
ⓘ	What's This? Pointer	To find out the use of anything on your screen, use this pointer. It appears when you press the Shift+F1 combination of keys. See Chapter 4 for more information on Excel's help tools.
I	I-beam Pointer	The I-beam pointer appears in the formula bar or in any area of the screen where you can enter data. Point to the formula bar or double-click a selected cell to get this pointer.
↗ ↔ ↖ ↕	Double-Headed Arrow	The double-headed arrow resizes graphic elements: imported pictures, charts, maps, and drawings. See Chapters 16 through 18 for more graphics guidance.
‡ ⊹	Two-Arrow Beam	The two-arrow beam resizes grayed-in areas of the worksheet. Place the pointer next to grayed-in arrows, column headings, or row headings and drag them to a new size.

All Your Tabs Aren't Showing?

If you want to see more worksheet tabs and less scrollbar, position your pointer just to the left of the left scrollbar arrow. When the pointer changes to a two-arrow beam, you can resize the scrollbar and make room for additional tabs.

What's Your Status?

At the bottom of the Excel screen is the status bar. It displays information about your document and the currently selected (active) cell. (The status bar also displays the results of the AutoSum function, described in Chapter 8, "AutoPilot: Excel's Automatic Features.")

Do I Know You?

When you want to know what a menu command or a toolbar button is doing, look for an explanation in the status bar. You can turn off the status bar display from the View menu.

What's Changed from Earlier Versions

If you've used Excel before, you'll find lots to learn in Excel 97. A few minor things: There's the end of version number conventions—this should have been Excel 8.0, but it's not—and the introduction of icons on the pull-down menus.

Then there are the major things: the great Internet connection. New tools bring Excel 97 to the World Wide Web and vice versa. Animated Office Assistants gladly offer gobs of free, sometimes unsolicited information. The bottom line: There are plenty of changes in this upgraded package. The following sections outline several important features.

New Automated Functions

If you thought you were fast working in previous versions, you can now consider yourself turbo-charged. You'll wonder how you ever lived without these functions:

➤ *AutoShapes.* Great huge arrows, happy faces, hearts—your spreadsheets come alive with automatic drawing tools. We explain AutoShapes, as well as the other new Excel 97 drawing tools, in Chapter 16, "Graphics Workshop."

➤ *AutoComplete.* It'll make you crazy at first, but once you grow accustomed to having Excel think faster than you do, you'll love the automatic word completion feature. Another AutoComplete function enables you to pick a correct entry from a list Excel creates based on your previous entries. It's all explained in Chapter 2, "Getting Started."

➤ *AutoCorrect.* Yeah, we sometimes spell it "teh," too. That's okay. Excel 97 knows what you mean and corrects it before you know you've done it. You'll find a great tip for using AutoCorrect as a form of shorthand in Chapter 6.

➤ *AutoFilter.* You've seen the filter function in earlier versions. Well, it's been improved. Pick out the top 10 items from a list, or pick the bottom 10, or change the number of items it finds. Chapter 8 explains how.

➤ *AutoSum.* Excel has the capability to automatically sum, average, or count the items in any highlighted range. Turn to Chapter 8 for information on using this function.

Editing Made Easy

These new features give you Perry White–like powers over everything you edit:

➤ *Multilevel undo.* If you make a series of mistakes and you want to correct them all, this newest version of Excel lets you undo the last entry you made, and the entry before that, and the entry before that....

➤ *Drag-and-drop editing.* Drag cells and ranges to another worksheet or even to a completely different workbook.

➤ *Improved number formatting.* Why didn't someone think of this years ago? Telephone numbers, Social Security numbers, and zip codes have their own formats now, and right-button formatting simplifies the task. Learn all about it in Chapter 5.

➤ *Cell comments.* You've always known you really ought to document those obscure formulas and references. Now you've got no excuse because Excel lets you attach comments. Chapter 12 explains how you can finally do it right.

➤ *Scroll tips.* Navigation just got easier. As you use the scrollbars to get around a spreadsheet, a pop-up tip box tells you which row or column you're on. This, and other navigation information, is explained in Chapter 2.

Data Manipulation

Excel developers have found new ways to display and use data:

➤ *Small Business Financial Manager.* Make sense of the cents in your bottom line and see an excellent example of the power of spreadsheet computing. Check out Chapter 24, "Small Business Financial Manager," to learn what SBFM, as it's known among friends, can do.

➤ *Data Map.* Excel 97 graphically displays the distribution of data in a geographic map. See Chapter 18, "Mapping Your Future," for mapping information.

➤ *List sharing.* Networked users have the option of sharing files. To make that easier, Excel 97 allows multiuser editing, maintains a status sheet, and records a conflict history. Chapter 15, "Managing in Multiples," has the details.

Document Handling

The power of Windows extends to Excel 97, giving you new ways of handling the documents you deal with every day:

➤ *Document retrieval.* The new preview function gives you a sneak peak at the file before you open it, and content-based document searches provide a powerful way to track your files. Learn more in Chapter 13, "An Open and Shut Case."

➤ *Improved document management.* The Open dialog box (which appears when you open a file) has new options that will change the way you manage your documents. Click the right mouse button to call up a menu of options. A collection of buttons changes the way your files are displayed, and an indexing feature speeds up searches. We discuss all these improvements in Chapter 13.

The Least You Need to Know

In this chapter you learned the basics of Excel 97. You opened Excel and memorized the jargon words describing all the stuff on the screen. When you wake up in the morning, here's what you should remember:

➤ Spreadsheets are, essentially, nothing more than tablecloth-sized scratch paper.

➤ When you start Excel 97, you see a blank spreadsheet and a screen full of tools.

➤ The toolbar buttons duplicate menu commands. There's nothing new there.

➤ Even if you've used Excel in the past, there are enough new features in Excel 97 to fill a book. In fact, that's exactly what we've done: filled a book.

Getting Started

There are two good reasons for tossing coins in a fountain. First, there's the romantically optimistic hope that your wish will come true; second is the positive impression it can make on your girlfriend. On an evening when everything else has gone bust, this bit of romance could be the last chance you get to see your wish come true.

If you can suspend disbelief for a moment, entering data in a worksheet is a little like tossing coins in a fountain. You throw numbers on it in hopes that your dreams come true. Juggle enough numbers, and you might find enough spare change in your food budget for that Porsche you've always dreamed of. So let's get started—and be sure to honk as you drive past the girl who dumped you at the fountain!

Menus for Beginners

Before we launch into a discussion of Excel 97, there are a couple of skills you'll need to master: menus and dialog boxes.

The Main Menu

The menu at the top of your Excel screen lists the major groupings of Excel's commands. There you'll see groupings for File, Edit, View, Insert, Format, Tools, Data, Window, and Help.

There are two ways to access the contents of Excel menus: Use your mouse pointer to click one of the words, or hold down the **Alt** key on your keyboard and press the underlined letter of the Menu item you want to open. For example, to see what's on the Edit menu, you could click the word **Edit** or you could press **Alt+E**.

As you view each of these menu groupings, you'll see a pull-down menu with the commands for that feature. Under the Edit menu, for example, you'll see commands to Undo mistakes, Cut, Copy, Paste, and a few others.

The pull-down Edit menu.

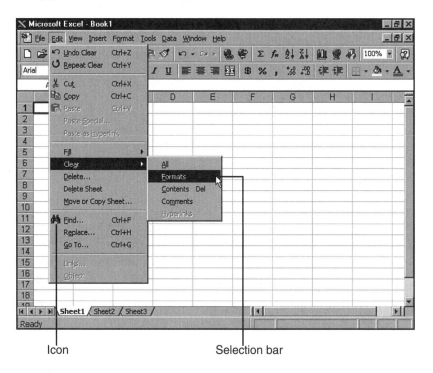

Icon   Selection bar

You can start a menu command in the following ways:

➤ Click the item with your mouse pointer.

➤ Use your keyboard arrow keys to highlight the command and press the **Enter** key on your keyboard.

➤ Type the underlined letter associated with the item.

➤ Skip the menu altogether and click the related toolbar icon.

New to Excel 97

Pull-down menus show the icons for many commands. It's an easy way to learn the icons and speed up your work!

➤ Use a keyboard shortcut. The key F7, for example, is the shortcut to the Spelling command.

Along with the menu command, you may see a few other things. Here's what they mean:

Icon
An icon may be located to the left of the command, as it is with Undo Clear on the previous figure. This is a good indication you could have saved a few steps by clicking on the identical icon in one of the toolbars.

Shortcut
Means that you may execute the command by pressing the shortcut keys (usually Ctrl plus a letter) at the same time. In the preceding figure, the Cut command can be executed with the Ctrl+X key combination.

Ellipsis
The series of three dots means that when you click the command, a *dialog box* will appear. (You learn more about dialog boxes in the next section.) In the preceding figure, the Delete command is followed by an ellipsis. Clicking **Delete** brings up a dialog box.

Arrow Head
When you select a command with an arrow head beside it, Excel displays a sub-menu with new commands. In the previous figure, the Clear command calls up a submenu.

Check This Out...

How Short Is It?
Keyboard shortcuts save time and potential mousing-related repetitive stress injuries. The downside is that you've got to memorize them to make them useful. Most short-cuts are listed to the right of the related menu command, but you'll find a complete list in Appendix C, "Excel Shortcut Keys," at the back of this book.

Grayed-Out Commands

When a particular command cannot be executed at the present moment, the command will appear in a different—usually lighter—color. In the previous figure, the Links command is grayed out.

No Symbol

When you select a command that does not have any of the preceding indicators (such as the Delete Sheet command in the previous figure), Excel executes the command immediately.

Dialog Boxes

Certain menu commands call up *dialog boxes*, windows in which Excel gives you several choices for how you want the command to operate. Most dialog boxes are far less complicated than the one in this figure:

Dialog box options.

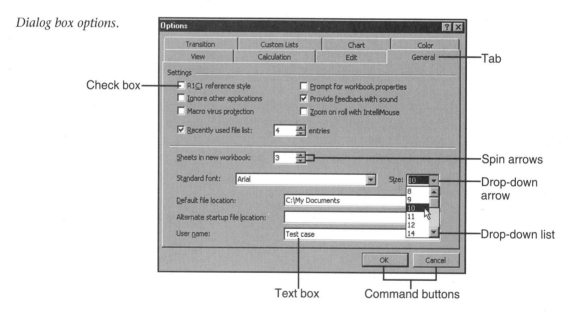

To select a tab, check box, command button, or spin arrow, simply click the button or box to choose it. To make a selection from a drop-down list, click the drop-down arrow and make your selection. A text box indicates that you should enter information. Just click the text box and type in your words.

When you've finished entering your choices in a dialog box, press the **OK** button to return to your worksheet.

All right. Menus, commands, dialog boxes. We've covered 'em all.

Navigation

A wise man once said that the best way to get someplace is to begin at the beginning and end at the end. And who are we to argue with a wise man? Navigation is the art of getting where you want to go from a place where you've already been.

I Get Around

When you open Excel, you find yourself on Sheet 1 of an empty workbook. You learned in Chapter 1, "10-Minute Guide to Excel," that *workbooks* are made up of a collection of worksheets, and that *worksheets* are made up of rows and columns. We call the intersection of each row and column a *cell*. To find cell C5, you start at the top of column C and go down until it intersects with row 5.

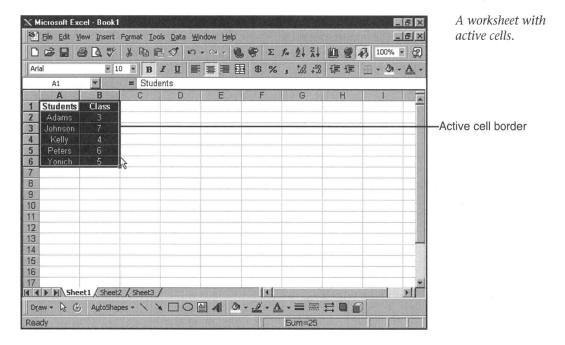

A worksheet with active cells.

—Active cell border

You can enter data into the *active cell* area only. A heavy border indicates which cell or group of cells is active. To change the location of the active cell, move the pointer (the shaded cross) to another cell and click, or simply use your arrow keys to move the active cell indicator. This section concentrates on working with single active cells. Chapter 5, "Shake, Copy, and Move: Filling Blocks of Cells," goes into greater detail about handling blocks of cells.

I Get Around and Around and Around...

In addition, you can use a command called Go To if you want to move to a specific cell or group of cells within your worksheet.

If, for example, you know that you need to go to cell N30 of your 1996 Expenses spreadsheet to find out what your gross income was (and see if you really did get that 10 percent raise they promised), you use the Go To command to jump directly there.

You can issue the Go To command in any of three ways: Open the **Edit** menu and choose **Go To**, press **F5**, or press **Ctrl+G**. To repeat the Go To command, press **Shift+F4**. When you do, the Go To dialog box appears:

The Go To dialog box.

Go to list

Special button

Reference box

Make It Active
When you move to another area of the worksheet using the scrollbars or any of the keyboard shortcuts, your active cell doesn't change. When you reach your destination, you must activate a cell by clicking it before you can enter or edit its contents.

When the Go To dialog box appears, select the destination cell from the Go to list, or enter a cell address—the intersecting point of the row and the column—in the Reference box. You can also click the **Special** button to select from a long list of other locations, including blank cells, formulas, last cell, and objects. Click **OK** to execute the Go To command.

Use the *Range Name box* (the box at the left end of the Formula bar) to go directly to a named range. See Chapter 9, "Home on the Range," for more information on ranges.

Entering Text

Remember that old saying, "You learn by doing"? Well, that's the approach we're going to take in this section where we begin to enter actual information in Excel. Feel free to follow along as we build a sample worksheet. We begin here with straight text entry, and graduate in the next section to numbers.

To start, click cell **B2**, type **Employees**, and press **Enter**. The active cell moves down a row. Your screen should look like the one here. Pretty simple, huh?

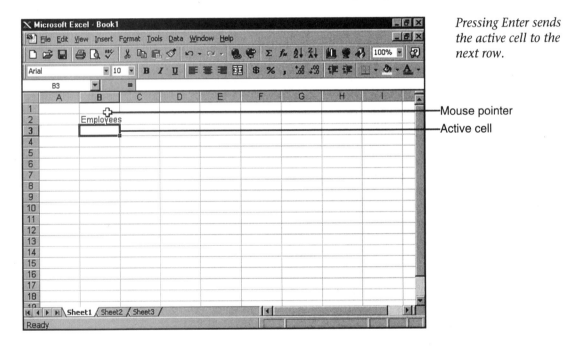

Pressing Enter sends the active cell to the next row.

Mouse pointer
Active cell

If you make a mistake, use your mouse or the arrow keys to return to cell B2, and retype your text. The following table lists some shortcut keys you can use to speed up the process of entering and editing data. For additional editing tips, see Chapter 6, "The Editing Test: Change the Contents of Your Spreadsheet."

Because you must follow different data entry rules when entering text and entering numbers, we'll look at each subject separately.

Text as Text, Nothing More, Nothing Less

To continue entering text, simply move the pointer to a new cell, click the cell, and type. For example, let's move to cell A1. (Put down that steak knife; A1 is simply a logical starting point.) Click the left mouse button to make cell A1, also called the *home cell*, active. In compliance with the law that states all examples must incorporate the word "widget," we'll name our company "Widget Inc." Type away.

Now, for no reason other than aesthetic considerations, move to cell B3 and begin listing the names of your employees. Enter a name and press **Enter**, and the next cell in the column becomes the active cell. Feel free to use any names you choose, but be sure to include the name "Hillary Clinton" in your employee list. There. Doesn't that make your chest swell with pride? List as many or as few employee names as you like. If some of your names are similar, you might notice Excel trying to complete them for you. Pay no attention. We explain the AutoComplete feature later in this chapter.

The employee list in progress.

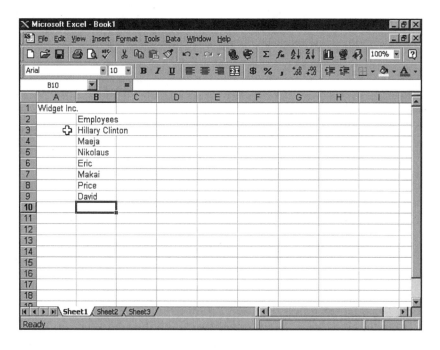

Let's look at a few of the simpler changes you can make to the text. First, move the pointer to the first cell containing a name (cell B3 on our sample worksheet). Then, in a sneak preview of Chapter 5, press and hold the left mouse button and use your mouse to drag the highlight to the bottom of your list of names. The names appear boxed. Release the left mouse button and right-click anywhere in the middle of the highlighted area. A shortcut menu appears with options related to the current function. Select **Format Cells**. In the Format Cells dialog box, click the **Alignment** tab. The Alignment tab (shown in the following figure) contains options for horizontal and vertical alignment and text orientation. For the sample worksheet, click the **down arrow** in the Horizontal box and choose **Right** alignment.

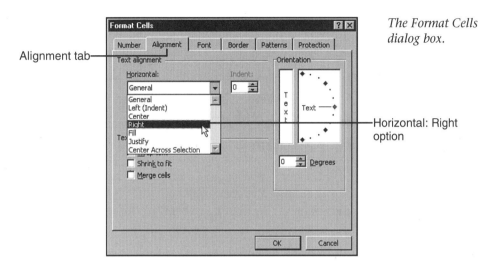

The Format Cells dialog box.

Now click the **Font** tab. On the Font tab, you can choose from the available fonts, font styles, font sizes, and other special features such as underline, color, superscript, subscript, and strikethrough (all of which are discussed in more detail in Chapters 5 and 14, "Customizing the Spreadsheet"). Right now, let's keep it simple. For the sample worksheet, click **Bold** to change the font style from regular to bold. Click the **OK** button at the bottom of the box to apply the formatting changes. To remove the highlight, click anyplace on the spreadsheet work area.

When 6 Means Six

Just as Excel has certain data entry rules for numbers and others for text, it also has different formatting rules for figures and text. Excel assumes that when you enter a number, you're going to use it in a calculation, and it formats the number accordingly: right-justification, decimal places, and anything else you've told it to do. (See Chapter 5 for an explanation of number formatting.) But suppose you want to enter a number as text instead? Say, for example, you want to compare a class of third graders to a class of fourth graders, and you want to label the first column "3" and the second column "4." If you simply enter the 3 and 4, Excel will treat your labels as numbers and format them all wrong. It will also mess up when you use great features such as AutoSum (see Chapter 8, "AutoPilot: Excel's Automatic Features").

Have no fear. The software is smart enough to make an exception for those times when you want a number to be a label and not a value. But it's up to you to distinguish whether you want Excel to treat the 6 you type as 6 (a number) or six (text).

23

The simplest way to indicate that Excel should treat a number as text is to type an apostrophe (') before the number. Take a minute to go back to the sample worksheet and add another entry to your employee list. Go to cell C3 and type in the department number for this employee: **2**. Hit **Enter**, and Excel displays the number 2 lined up at the right of the column. Wrong. Now go to cell C4 and type **'2**. This time, the 2 appears at the left of the column, just like your original text entries did. If you try to add this label 2 to another number, Excel ignores it. This is good.

Alternatively, you can enter the number 2 in the usual way, select the cell, right-click it, and select **Format Cells** from the pop-up Shortcut menu. In the Format Cells dialog box, click the **Number** tab and choose **Text** to reformat the number as text.

The AutoComplete Function

Like a significant other who won't ever let you... ahem... complete your sentences, AutoComplete works by matching the characters you type with existing text entries. Just as soon as it thinks it knows what you intend, wham! It fills in the remaining text for you.

Here's how it works. In the sample worksheet, you typed the name Hillary Clinton in the employee list in column B. Move to the bottom of that list now and type **H**. You should see the entire name appear in the box.

If AutoComplete doesn't work on your first try, try these tricks:

➤ *Continue typing.* If your column contains multiple entries with the same beginning letters, AutoComplete doesn't fill in the entry until you type enough characters to make it unique. For example, if your column lists Martha and Marie, and you type Mar, Excel is clueless as to what to do. The next letter should solve the problem.

➤ *Pick and choose.* If you really like AutoComplete, press **Alt+down arrow** after you start typing your entry. A list of all the possible entries (such as Martha and Marie) appears. Click the desired entry, or use the arrow keys to highlight it and then press **Enter**.

➤ *Make sure AutoComplete is turned on.* To turn on AutoComplete, open the **Tools** menu and click **Options**. In the Options dialog box, click the **Edit** tab. Click **Enable AutoComplete** to check the box. (An empty box means that the feature is not turned on.) Click **OK** after you make your selection. To turn AutoComplete off, repeat the steps and remove the check from the box.

There is a limitation to this incalculably significant feature. Excel chooses its AutoCompletions from your existing entries in the current column only. Items in column B, for example, would not AutoComplete in column C.

We can't say AutoComplete will actually save you time or effort, but it could provide hours of fun.

Entering Numbers

Excel is good with numbers. Unless your intention was to purchase a word processor, you're probably delighted to hear that. In this section, you'll add a few numbers to the simple sample spreadsheet you've been building. You have been following along, right?

Pick a Number, Any Number

Numbers are what Excel does best, and entering a number is every bit as easy as you would expect. Select a cell and type a number. Simple. Done.

Of course, life isn't always that simple. Sometimes those numbers should have several decimal places behind them or dollar signs in front of them. They could be negative numbers. Stay with us here. Excel accommodates them all.

The default number format (how Excel displays numbers by default) is called the General number format: unstructured numbers with floating decimal points and no commas. If you're dealing with other kinds of numbers, though, that format doesn't work out very well.

People from the old school of spreadsheets will remember a time when every number had to be entered in painstakingly correct form. Spreadsheet writers had to be careful to properly format every single cell. Of course, you're still free to do everything the proper way: Plan things out and select the format before you make your data entries. Or you can just wing it. You can enter a number in a valid format (numbers, commas, and decimals in place), and Excel recognizes the format and changes the cell accordingly.

Try it on the sample spreadsheet. Enter some dollar amounts in column C. Assume that you're the boss and these are hourly wages. Adjust your generosity accordingly.

Now pat yourself on the back. You're well on your way to spreadsheet fluency. In the next chapter, you learn how to save, print, and get out of your Excel spreadsheet.

The Least You Need to Know

There's just no doubt about it: If you've gotten this far, you can confidently give Excel a place on your résumé. (Maybe not a large place, but certainly above that line about the high school debate team.) Make sure you remember the following facts. There may be a test in the morning:

➤ You can enter data in an active cell only. The bold border indicates the active cell.

➤ Different types of data require different cell formats. If you format dates and times incorrectly, Excel misinterprets them as text.

➤ You can easily format cells by accessing the Format Cells dialog box. The simplest way to do that is to right-click a cell and choose **Format Cells**.

Saving and Closing Documents

A few decades ago a revolution swept across the great American plains. After almost 100 years of adhering to mindless rules, the American people emerged from under the great hoops of Queen Victoria's gown and declared themselves liberated. No longer would they bow to the convention that forced parents to name their children Tom, Dick, Harry, and Edwina. No, the names of new American children would represent the heart and soul of their Yankee parents. Thus were born names such as Buttercup, MoonBeam, and SocketWrench.

Once you've played a bit with your Excel worksheet, you'll want to name, save, and print your work and then close down the operation. This chapter shows you how to do all those things.

Saving the Document

When you save a document, you must do three things: Name it, indicate where you want it stored, and execute the save. The following sections give you the details on how to perform each of those steps.

What's in a Name?

Bet you wouldn't ask this question if your name were Chastity Sue. Names have but one purpose: To help distinguish one person, place, or thing from another. Sometime back in the middle ages, someone thought it would be a good idea if a name also gave an idea of what a person did (Brewer, Farmer, Cartwright, Walmart). The name fit the function.

Prior to Windows 95, MS-DOS computer users had to follow a similar naming convention when naming files; they tried to make the names unique yet descriptive. The big difference was that they were limited to using no more than eight characters followed by a three-character extension for a filename.

For years, this didn't seem to be a bad method. Give or take several thousand possibilities, there are approximately 3.51E+12 legitimate names a person could use under the filename.ext naming system. Problems arose, however, when people discovered that there were fewer than six ways to name a file in a way that would make logical sense several months later. By the time you got to the file named JOHNFILE.099 and you wanted to know what JOHNFILE.054 was, you were wishing you had used a better naming method.

With the introduction of Windows 95, the PC-compatible family of computers entered a new age in filenaming conventions. What had to be said in eight or fewer characters could now be stretched out across 255 letters and numbers.

Here are the requirements for choosing a Windows 95 or later filename:

➤ The complete path to the file (including the drive letter, the server name, the folder, and the word) can contain no more than 255 characters.

➤ Words cannot include any of the following characters: / \ > < * ? " | : ;

However, there is one catch to this new-found freedom. If you do any work in DOS mode, or if you exchange files with people who haven't yet upgraded to Windows 95, your long words are changed to fit the old filenaming conventions. For example, a file named JOHNSFILE 001 EXCEL EXPENSES 1997.XLS becomes JOHNSF~1.XLS when you view it from the DOS prompt or open it in a previous version of Excel. But don't let that stop you from using long words if it helps your productivity.

Save for the Web

You can now save your work as an HTML file. This feature, along with many other Internet and Web features, is covered in detail in Chapter 7, "Excel on the Net."

Save That Workbook

To save a file for the first time, click the **File** menu and select **Save As**. Alternatively, you can click the **Save** icon or press the **F12** key on your keyboard. Either way, the Save As dialog box appears.

Simple Save

Excel is pretty smart. When you click the Save icon, it knows whether you're saving a new file or an existing file. If you saved the file before, Excel saves it under this name again; if you have not saved the file under this name before, Excel displays the Save As dialog box.

Files and folders display area   Save in box   Drop-down list arrow   Display buttons

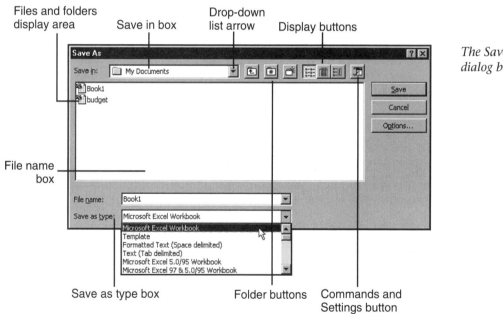

The Save As dialog box.

File name box

Save as type box   Folder buttons   Commands and Settings button

In the Save As dialog box, you see several options. The Save in box names the current or most recently used folder or subfolder. Unless you change this folder or drive, this is where Excel will save your new workbook. (See the discussion "Other Options Dialog Box Options" in Chapter 9, "Home on the Range," for an explanation of how to set up a default "Save" folder.)

Now They're Folders

In older versions of Windows and DOS, you saved your files in sub-directories. Now you save them in folders. Nothing's changed but the name.

To change to another folder or drive, click the down arrow at the right of the Save in box. A drop-down list appears, from which you can select the folder (or disk drive name containing the folder) that you want. To view other folders, double-click the name of the appropriate disk drive.

Next to the Save in box is a row of buttons. The first three are folder buttons. Click these buttons to move up one folder level, go straight to a folder named "Favorites," or create a new folder (from left to right, respectively). Moving to the right, the three display buttons control how Excel displays your files in the files and folders display area. Click these buttons to have Excel list your files and folders by name in columns, by name with detailed information, or by name in a list format (again, from left to right, respectively). The final button, Commands and Settings, accesses a menu that is of absolutely no interest when you're saving files. All its commands are explained in other, relevant, chapters.

The largest area in the Save As dialog box is the files and folders display area. There you see the names of the files and folders that already exist in the current folder. That's a hint, you know: Don't give your new file a name you've already used. Not to worry, though. If you ever do attempt to reuse an existing word, Excel is courteous enough to ask whether you're sure you want to write over the existing file.

To the right of the screen are three command buttons: Save, Cancel, and Options. Click Save only when you're sure all the information (the word and the folder to which it will be saved) is correct. Cancel lets you back out of the Save As command completely. Clicking the Options button accesses a dialog box you can use to protect and back up your file. If you share files with other users, take advantage of these options to prevent errant file changes (or just use them to annoy and harass other users, if you want). It's all explained in Chapter 13, "An Open and Shut Case."

In the File name box, you find Excel's suggestion for a word. Be revolutionary. Accept no defaults. Simply type over the suggested name with a clever name like "Why I Deserve a Raise." Excel adds the requisite .XLS extension automatically. (That's how Excel knows, in the future, that this is an Excel file—not a picture of your father's St. Bernard wearing a blonde wig.)

At the very bottom of the dialog box is the Save as type box. By choosing a different option from this list, you can save files in the format of other spreadsheets, word processors, or database programs (for example). So if you share data with people who use older versions of Excel, you need to convert your Excel 97 spreadsheets to their backward, ancient, outmoded file formats. (Be sure to remind them of that each time you swap disks.) Note: This can result in a loss of data for the file going backwards. THIS IS THE VOICE OF GOD SPEAKING. All that transfers is the basic spreadsheet. The fancy-schmancy Excel 97 stuff disappears.

Check This Out...

By Default

Excel 97 assumes you want to save your files in the Excel 97 format. If you're working with people who use different spreadsheets, or no spreadsheet at all, you might want to change that assumption by changing the default. Go to the **Tools** menu, select **Options**, and in the Options dialog box that appears, click the **Transition** tab. The first setting lets you change the way you save Excel files.

When all the information in the dialog box is correct, press **Save** to save the file and return to your worksheet.

Other Sorts of Saves

Suppose that you created a worksheet last week and saved it, and today you opened it and made some changes. You need to save it again with those changes, but you don't need to go through the process of naming the file and telling Excel where to store it again:

➤ To save existing worksheets or worksheets in progress, just click the **Save** icon, or hold down the **Ctrl** key and press **S**.

➤ To save the same worksheet with a new name, use the **File**, **Save As** command again.

➤ If you want to save just the settings of your current workbook, without any of the contents, open the **File** menu and choose **Save Workspace**.

Print the Light Fantastic

You'll miss the onscreen pyrotechnics of Excel when you print, but there are times when you really want a hard copy of your spreadsheet. This is particularly true if you work for a boss who still believes that if you can't weigh it, it isn't work. This section teaches you everything you need to know to print in Excel.

The Water's Fine

If you want to jump right in and print an open file, just click the **Print** icon. This method is quick and painless—and is perfectly viable if you like surprises and have plenty of paper. However, sometimes the printed worksheet is not what you expected.

Although Excel does an adequate job of printing based on its own default settings, you can control a number of printing variables. Take a few moments to play with Excel's print features, and you'll soon be producing eye-popping documents all by yourself.

Let's examine the entire printing process, which begins with setting up a page.

It's a Setup

Before you print for the first time, be certain that your page is set up properly with correct margins, scaling, page numbers, and other options. To set up your page, open the **File** menu and choose **Page Setup**. The Page Setup dialog box appears.

The Page Setup dialog box.

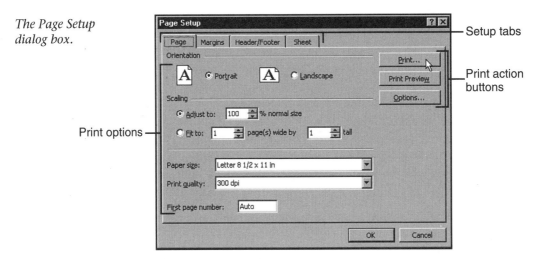

There are four tabs in the Page Setup dialog box:

➤ *Page.* The Page tab features settings that enable you to adjust for different paper sizes and change the paper orientation (portrait or landscape). In addition, you can use the Scaling feature to have Excel automatically print your spreadsheet on the number of pages you specify.

➤ *Margins.* This tab sets a margin for every occasion. From as wide as you like to as small as your printer allows, set the margins here.

➤ *Header/Footer.* This is where you set page numbers and set up *headers* and *footers* (lines that print at the top or bottom of every page of a spreadsheet). You can select a header or a footer from Excel's preformatted lists, which include lines with your name, your company name, the date, and page numbers in various formats. Or you can click the Custom Header or Custom Footer icons to open a dialog box where you enter your own information (page numbers, date, time, workbook title, or the name of your one true love) in the header or footer areas of your document. We explain headers and footers further in Chapter 14, "Customizing the Spreadsheet."

Name That Name

Your username and company name were recorded when you installed Excel 97, and they appear in the list of options for headers and footers. If you don't like the way you recorded your company name, you're stuck; it can't be changed unless you reinstall the software. However, changing the way your username appears in headers and footers is simple. Open the **Tools** menu and click **Options**. In the Options dialog box, click the **General** tab and reenter your username.

➤ *Sheet.* This tab lets you control whether or not Excel prints gridlines and column/ row labels. You'll find a collection of checkboxes for changing the things that appear on your printed document. This page also sets up your sheet order when your spreadsheet is too large for the paper.

The Page Setup dialog box also contains a set of print action buttons. The following table describes the function of each of those buttons.

Print action buttons in the Page Setup dialog box

Button	Description
Options	Accesses the dialog box for your own printer. Although this dialog box varies depending on which printer you use, a typical Printer dialog box contains options for print quality, page orientation, and page size.
Print Preview	Shows you a preview of your file before you print. You can also access this feature by selecting the File, Print Preview command. (Print Preview is described in detail later in this chapter.)
Print	Opens the Print dialog box, described later in this chapter.
Cancel	Returns you to the main screen without printing and without recording any changes you made in the Setup box.
OK	Records the changes you made in the Setup box and returns you to the main screen without printing.

If you choose the Options button and Excel displays information for the wrong printer, change it by selecting File, Print. In the Print dialog box, open the Printer drop-down list and select a different printer.

Don't Go Breaking My Page

To access Page Break Preview, click **View** on the Main menu. Select **Page Break Preview**. The screen displays the print area of your worksheet, and the page breaks show up as heavy lines.

Viewing the Page Breaks

Page Break Preview is new for Excel 97. It displays all the areas of the worksheet that are fit to print, and shows you the location of the page breaks. Page breaks can be moved by dragging them with the mouse to their proper location. For more details read on.

Whenever your worksheet is larger than the paper size, Excel automatically sets the page breaks. These are displayed as heavy dashed lines in Page Break View. Page breaks that have been manually set from the Insert menu, Page Break command appear as solid lines.

Here are some useful tips for breaking it easy:

➤ You can move a page break by pointing at it with the mouse and dragging the page break to a new location.

➤ To insert page breaks, click the cell below and to the right of where you want to insert a new break.

➤ To remove page breaks use the right mouse button and click the cell below and to the right of the page break. A shortcut menu will appear onscreen. Click the **Remove Page Break** option from the shortcut menu.

➤ Of course the simplest way to remove page breaks is just to drag them right off your screen.

Look Before You Print

After you've set up your page, use the Print Preview feature to see how it will look before you commit it to paper. To preview a worksheet, click the **Print Preview** button in the Page Setup dialog box or click the **Print Preview** icon.

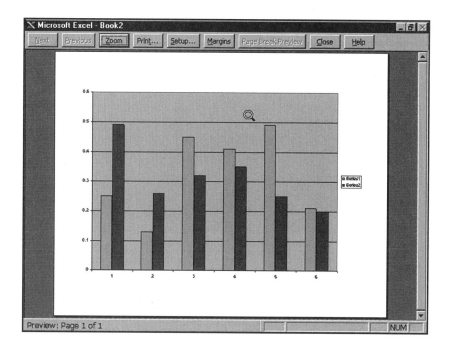

Print Preview shows you exactly how your page will look when printed.

Color or Black and White

If you use a color printer, Excel displays the graphics in the Print Preview screen in color. Otherwise, it displays the preview in black and white.

Across the top of the Print Preview screen, you see a number of buttons. Next and Previous show additional pages of a multi-page document. You can examine smaller areas of the printout in fine detail with the Zoom button. The Print icon sends the current document straight to the printer. Setup returns you to the Page Setup dialog box. Use the Margins button to adjust the margins. Close shuts down the Print Preview screen and returns you to the main screen. Help displays an overhead hologram of the Beatles live, in concert, Shea Stadium, 1965. This option works only if you have the special *Rubber Soul* edition of Excel. You'll learn more about Help in Chapter 4, "Help, Help."

Time to Print

When you're happy with your page as displayed in Print Preview, click the **Print** button. The Print dialog box appears.

35

The Print dialog box.

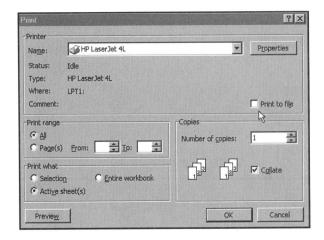

In the Print dialog box, you give Excel all the instructions it needs to print your file. The Printer option lists all the printers you have installed under Windows 95. (If you've installed a fax option with other software, it appears here as an additional printer.) Select the printer to which you want to print, if necessary. The Properties button accesses a dialog box of options for the selected printer.

Print to File

The Print to file check box in the Print dialog box saves your document as a file with a .PRN extension. The theory is that your .PRN file can then be printed from any program. Unfortunately, we've yet to see anyone actually make this work. Excel isn't able to reopen .PRN files for printing. Go figure. The best alternative? If you want to save the text of your worksheet, select File, Save As and choose the Text (Tab delimited)—or *.txt—option in the Save as Type box. Excel saves your text as a .TXT file.

If you want to save a graphic (a chart or a graph), press the Print Screen button on your keyboard to copy your entire screen to the Windows Clipboard. Then open a graphics program such as Windows Paint and press Ctrl+V to paste the graphic. Save your graphic as a .BMP file, and you can easily distribute it to non-Excel users.

Other Print dialog box options let you choose how much of your workbook or worksheet you want to print. You can also indicate how many copies your printer will spit out. Make the appropriate selections and press **OK** to start printing.

If you decide, instead, that you would like to make additional changes to your worksheet, click the Cancel button to return to the main screen.

Free to Choose: Printing an Area

There may be times when you don't want to print all of the cells in a worksheet. Here's how you limit your printout to a few chosen cells.

1. Use your mouse to highlight a rectangular block of cells you want to print. (Start at one corner of the print area, press and hold down the left mouse button, and drag your mouse to the opposite corner.)

2. Open the **File** menu, click **Print Area**, and select **Set Print Area**. You can ensure that the selected area is correct by using Print Preview (see the earlier section "Look Before You Print").

3. When you are satisfied with your preview, click **Print** to print the page or pages in the usual way.

4. To clear your selection, open the **File** menu, choose **Print Area**, and select **Clear Print Area**.

Closing Up Shop

Now it's time to shut it all down. This is a two-step process.

Closing a Workbook

It's déjà vu. Closing a workbook is (not surprisingly) similar to saving a workbook. Excel automatically saves and closes your workbooks when you exit the program. However, if you want to continue working in Excel, you can simply close the current workbook and open another.

To close a workbook, open the **File** menu and choose **Close**. (If that's too slow for you, use your mouse to click the **X** button in the corner of your workbook.) If you haven't made any changes since the last time you saved, the workbook immediately disappears. If you have made changes since your last save, a dialog box appears to ask if you want to save your changes or cancel the close operation. Select **Yes** to have Excel save and close the workbook. Select **No** to have Excel close the workbook without saving the changes. (Make sure you don't need any changes you've made to the file because once you select No, all your unsaved work is gone for good.)

Closing Excel

Ah, the easiest step of all. Click that **X** button in the upper-right corner, and Excel shuts itself down. (You can also choose the **File**, **Exit** command.) If you have workbooks open, Excel closes them one by one and asks you about saving any changes you may have made since the last save. Keep answering questions until Excel completely disappears from your screen.

There. You've done it. Your first Excel session was a complete success.

The Least You Need to Know

This chapter taught you how to name, save, and print an Excel document and how to shut down Excel. These are the things you mustn't forget:

➤ To save a file, choose the **File**, **Save** command.

➤ To save a new workbook or give a new name to an old workbook, choose the **File**, **Save As** command.

➤ Preview your work with the Print Preview feature (select **File**, **Print Preview**) before you print. Print Preview gives you easy access to most of your print options.

➤ To print, choose the **File**, **Print** command.

➤ To print a select group of cells, highlight the group with the mouse and choose the **File**, **Print Area** command.

➤ To close a workbook, select **File**, **Close**.

➤ Nearly all those commands have a corresponding pushbutton icon.

Chapter 4

Help, Help

In This Chapter

➤ Help me if you can

➤ For your assistance, an Assistant

➤ Alternative forms of assistance

➤ Details for Diligent Direction Seekers

Whenever we invited friends out on our brand-new 14-foot yacht we took great pains to mask our sea-faring ignorance. After all, is there any reason to let people who must trust your judgment discover you're ten cents short of a dime when it come to knowing how to operate your own vessel? To maintain the illusion of competence, we concealed laminated 3×5 help cards in strategic areas of our little ship. For instance, the cards on the underside of those large orange things lying on the front seats said, "It's a lifejacket, dummy. Wear it!"

It was a great system until one wild and wet afternoon. The winds kicked up more than expected and our tiny craft began taking on water. While we frantically searched through our collection of help cards, our passenger and ex-buddy decided to take matters into his own hands. He grabbed the flare gun and fired. Fortunately for us, he missed, and the flare shot low over the horizon where it was intercepted by an angry Coast Guard vessel.

Later, from the deck of the Coast Guard ship, we sadly watched as our "Queen Merry" disappeared below the waves. The captain, knowing of our sorry tale, offered his condolences. It was a good idea, he said, to paste helpful guides in strategic locations. Too bad we didn't know where to find the right card at the critical moment. He handed us a card of his own, suggesting we never let it out of our sight. It read, "High water, little boat; fills with water, doesn't float."

Navigating the Sea of Help

Getting help used to mean you'd lean over to a guy at the next desk and ask, "Hey, how do you print from this thing?" Well, welcome to the '90s, where you need help figuring out how to get Help.

It's the artificial intelligence that did it. Artificial intelligence (AI) is an overly optimistic computing term meaning that software is a heck of a lot more complicated than it used to be. In theory, AI means that when you ask for help, the software should be smart enough to see not only what you're doing and where you're doing it, but why you can't figure out how to do it right.

What it means, in reality, is that Microsoft found a way to keep you from calling its technical support line with stupid questions. When 2.3 billion people complained they couldn't figure out how to move the cursor to the end of the line, Microsoft set up Excel 97 with an onscreen, animated Office Assistant to politely say, "Use the Control key, Dummy!"

As is the case with many new programs, Excel's Help function has become so complex that learning how to use it is like learning completely new software. In this chapter, you learn how to manipulate the Excel Help system to find the things you probably would have figured out on your own, given time, interest, and a helpful coworker one desk over.

Excel has many forms of Help. We'll start with the newest Help function, the Office Assistant.

Using the Office Assistant

It's a dog, it's a cat! No. It's Office Assistant! Office Assistant is a great toy—an onscreen animated companion that offers help and advice—but not a cup of coffee. In addition, Office Assistant is a bit of a changeling. It can be more than just a cat or a dog. It may also resemble Albert Einstein, William Shakespeare, a paperclip, or a bouncing ball. Your choice, but pick your Office Assistant with care. Expect your colleagues to conduct a mini-psychoanalysis as they discuss your decision.

The Office Assistant probably appears on your screen even as we speak. On the off chance that it doesn't, you can easily call it up. Click the **Office Assistant** icon—at the far right end of the standard toolbar—or press the **F1** key.

The Office Assistant box appears onscreen. Click anywhere on the Assistant to see the yellow balloon dialog box.

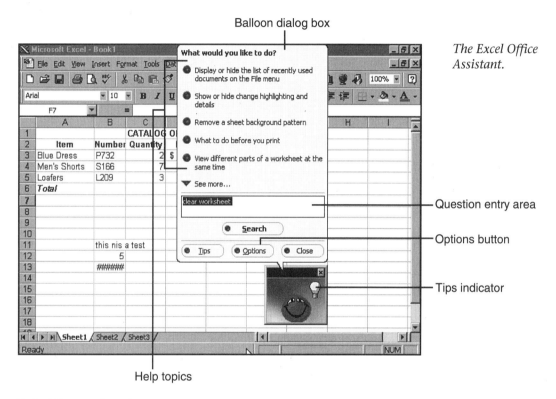

The Excel Office Assistant.

It's Your Option

Before actually employing Office Assistant, take a few minutes to assure that you're getting the kind of help you really want.

Click **Office Assistant**, and then click the **Options** button. The Office Assistant dialog box will appear. Click the **Gallery** tab. Clicking the **Next** button will set you scrolling through Office Assistant's cast of characters.

Click the **Options** tab after you've found an Office Assistant that suits your personality. We prefer tall, athletic brunettes, ourselves.

The Office Assistant dialog box open to the Options tab.

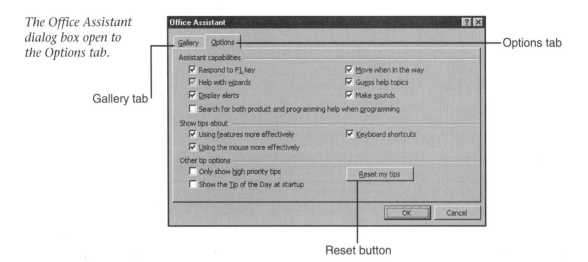

Reset button

Assistant Options

There are six check boxes in the Assistant dialog box:

➤ *Respond to F1 key.* Check and Office Assistant will appear when you press F1. Clear and F1 sends you to the help files—alone.

➤ *Help with Wizards.* Check to call Office Assistant whenever you call on a wizard. Calling wizards will be covered in greater detail in the special Wicca edition, as well as in various other chapters of this book.

➤ *Display Alerts.* Select to enable Office Assistant's epigrammatic messages.

➤ *Move When in the Way.* Check and Office Assistant will nimbly clear a trail for you while you work. Not checking this box is the moral equivalent of placing the coffee machine in the middle of your worksheet.

➤ *Guess Help Topics.* The Jeanne Dixon of check boxes. Check to have Office Assistant predict your next question.

➤ *Make Sounds.* If your coworker's rude noises make you giggle, you'll enjoy this. Check to enable sounds.

Show Tips About

Show tips about features three check boxes: Using features more effectively, Using the mouse more effectively, and Keyboard shortcuts. Unless you'd prefer to become less effective and do things the long way, check all three boxes.

Other Tip Options

These are a matter of personal choice. Frankly, even the authors of this book, who sleep with CD-ROM copies of Office under their pillows, haven't committed every Excel quirk to memory. The Tip options remind us of those valuable hints that time, wine, and song have caused us to forget.

Back to Business

To get the Office Assistant to work, just click it. In moments it will answer your questions, offer helpful suggestions of its own, and scrub toilet bowls—although we haven't quite figured out how to enable that last feature.

In the Question entry area you write English-language sentences and Office Assistant responds appropriately. For best results, phrase your question in the form of an answer. Office Assistant will ask the question, "What would you like to do?" You type **Delete all files.** (Ignore this advice during appearances on "Jeopardy.") Office Assistant will respond by displaying a menu of related topics. Click the topic that best answers your inquiry and you'll be launched into a Microsoft help file.

Using the Help Files

The Help files are generally self-explanatory. Just read 'em. But occasionally you'll run across something unusual.

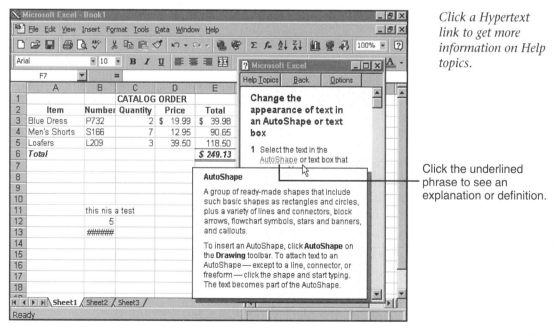

Click a Hypertext link to get more information on Help topics.

Click the underlined phrase to see an explanation or definition.

When viewing a Help file, you may see underlined words and words written in green letters. These words are called *Hypertext links*. "Hypertext link" (*hyperlink* for short) is a techy-sounding word that describes a really cool trick. Click a Hypertext link, and Excel jumps to a related topic or displays a definition of the specified word. As you'll see in Chapter 7, "Excel on the Net," hypertext is also a significant part of the Internet, and in particular, the World Wide Web. The difference is that on the Internet, a hyperlink can send you flying around the entire world for information related to the word you're clicking!

Excel's Hypertext help links also appear as icons or as toolbar buttons with double arrows. Click on any of these devices to get help on related topics.

Another help tool.

Hyperlinked icon —

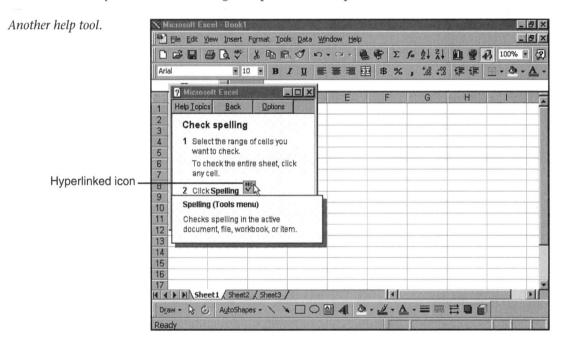

Big Tipper

Tips—helpful suggestions related to the task you're working on—are also an Office Assistant forte. Tips will guide you to program features not normally documented in a book. (We were hoping to keep this book light enough to mail with a 32-cent stamp. If we were to document all of Excel's features, we'd require a Dodge Dakota and several thousand postage stamps.)

It's easy to tell when Office Assistant has a tip to share. A yellow light bulb appears in its box. Click the bulb to see the tip.

Even if the Office Assistant is not on the screen, it can still offer tips. The light bulb appears on the Office Assistant icon. Click the bulb and you'll see the tip.

Other Help Sources

If terminal cuteness has got you down, click **Help** on the main menu one more time. Select the **Contents and Index** option, and a grown-up Help dialog box appears. Click one of these three tabs for a more genteel pathway to the help files.

Contents Tab

You use the Contents tab when you want a general overview of a topic. To use Contents, click the **Contents** tab of the Help Topics dialog box. In the Contents screen, the Help topics are categorized into "books." Select the book that appears to contain the information you need. For example, double-click the book called Working with Charts and Maps for information on adding data to a chart. That book opens to display Help chapters or topics. Continue to select chapters or topics as necessary until you find the help you need.

Index Tab

Use the Index tab when you know the name of the topic you're looking for and want to see specific related subtopics. The Index tab brings up a page that looks a great deal like the index in the back of that printed User's Guide you wish you could find. Help topics are categorized alphabetically and are detailed by subcategories.

Find Tab

The first time you open the Find tab, Excel attempts to index all of its Help files. Let 'er rip, because once the indexing is finished, you have a handy index of every word in the Help files (including all the "the's" and "and's" and "nevermore's").

Find works much like the Index tab. Just start typing a word or phrase in box 1, and watch while box 2 begins narrowing the list. For example, in box 1, type the letters "fun" and pause. In box 2, you'll see Function, function_num and several variations on that theme.

Here's where Find gets fun: Press the **Spacebar** on your keyboard, and type **datab**. The Find feature narrows down your options to all topics containing both "fun" and "datab," the initial letters of the words function and database. In box 3, Excel displays a list of all topics that contain both terms. You can view the list box 3 by clicking any topic in the list and using the arrow keys to scroll up or down through the list. Select the topic that you need help on, and press the **Enter** key on your keyboard to display it.

The Options button in the Find window gives you access to the Find Options dialog box, in which you can change the way Find searches for help topics. The following figure shows the Find Options dialog box.

The Find Options dialog box.

Indicate whether you want Find to search for all the words you type or to expand the search to include any of the words you type. Then tell Find whether to show words that begin with the letters you type, simply contain the letters you type, end with those letters, or exactly match the letters. And, finally, select an option to tell Find when to start searching.

The Files button at the bottom of the dialog box enables you to add or subtract Excel help files from the list of files indexed for the Find feature. Select all to maximize your search capabilities. If you change the number of Help files, you'll need to click the Rebuild button in the main Find window to change the actual index.

When you finish setting the Find options, click **OK** to return to the main Find window. Let Find run the search, and when it finishes, select the topic you need help on.

Find can lead you on wild goose chases, of course, because any given word can be used so many different ways. However, it proves to be a good last resort when you don't know the official jargon for the thing you want to do.

ScreenTips

Excel's Help system provides easily accessible definitions and explanations about virtually any item that appears onscreen. The nice thing about ScreenTips is that you don't have to go into the Help system and wade through a lot of topics to find the information you need. The following list tells you how to find explanations and definitions for certain types of screen elements.

What's This? icon

Standard screen items.

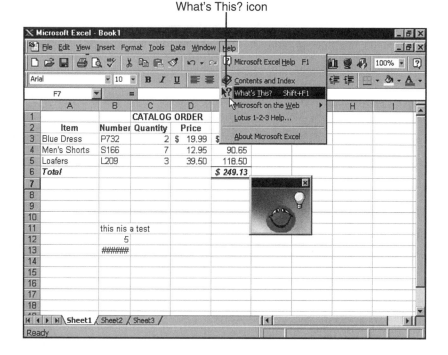

➤ For explanations of items you see onscreen or on a menu, click **What's This** on the Help menu or press **Shift+F1**. A special icon will appear on the screen. Position the icon over any item and click. An explanation of the item appears onscreen in a pop-up window. Press any key or click any place on your screen to make it disappear.

➤ Click the question mark button in the upper-right corner of most dialog boxes, and then click the item in question to see an explanation. Again, press any key or click any place in the dialog box to make the explanation disappear.

➤ For an explanation of a toolbar button, position your pointer over the button, and a definition of that button appears onscreen.

Dialog boxes.

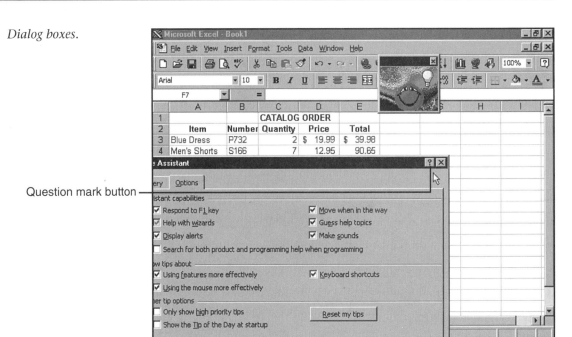

Question mark button ⎯

Toolbars.

A definition appears
onscreen. ⎯

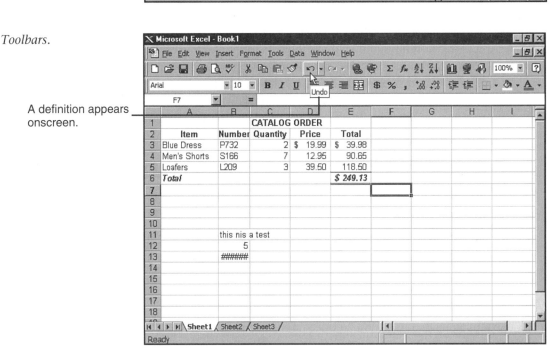

Information About My Computer

Here's dubious help, at best. If your computer hardware or software isn't working properly, your best move is probably to bribe your brother-in-law, the computer geek, with a box of Ding Dongs. However, if you've already expended this month's entire pastry allowance, you might be forced to examine the hardware and software settings yourself. Before you do, you can use the Help system to learn more about your particular computer system.

To see listings of important information about the hardware and software your system uses, open the **Help** menu and select **About Microsoft Excel**. In the dialog box that appears, choose **System Info**. Excel displays critical system information that includes complex data about memory and hardware usage (ugly numbers that might keep you lying awake nights worrying). Remember, you're probably better off not knowing this.

This dialog box does have one thing that might come in handy, though. Excel provides a button that gives you access to a list of Microsoft technical support services.

Check This Out...

Don't Close Help

To move back and forth between the Help file and Excel without closing the Help file, hold down the **Alt** key and press **Tab**. In this way, you can page through all your open applications, including the Help file and Excel.

The Least You Need to Know

If there is such a thing as an ultimate "The Least You Need to Know" list, this is it. Learn to navigate the Help files, become pals with Office Assistant, and you can find out everything you ever wanted to know about Excel but didn't know whom to ask:

➤ F1 is the magic button for Office Assistant, an animated helper buddy for the young at heart.

➤ The Contents and Index command, found on the Help menu, is the more mature—and specific—gateway to Excel's help files.

➤ To get help with screen or menu items, click **What's This?** on the Help menu—or press **Shift+F1**—and then click the screen or menu item in question.

➤ To get help in a dialog box, click the question mark button and then on the item you want to know about.

➤ To get help with toolbar buttons, position your pointer over the button and an explanation appears.

Part 2
Getting to Work

All the fun stuff is hidden in this section. You'll learn to build your worksheet, write all your own formulas, audit for errors, manage multiple documents, make it all pretty, and leap tall buildings in a single bound.

In addition, there's an all-new Internet section. Create World Wide Web-ready documents that'll amaze your friends and be the envy of your colleagues.

Chapter 5

Shake, Copy, and Move: Filling Blocks of Cells

In This Chapter

➤ Fills good!

➤ Pack 'em up, move 'em out

➤ Well filled out

➤ Exciting expansion exhortations

Blocks were invented for the movers and shakers of the world. Working with entire blocks—and not just a single cell—appeals to busy people who are smart enough to walk while chewing gum. They also appeal to mere mortals like the authors, who want only to get a bit of work done between blocks of sleep.

Fill 'Er Up: An Introduction to Filling Blocks

Sure you could type the same word hundreds of times across your spreadsheet. But eventually, you'd get to the point where the word didn't look like a word anymore and you were cross-eyed from trying to read the unreadable. Rest your eyes, because Excel's block-filling functions make repetition a thing of the past. The copy, move, and AutoFill commands automate repetitive tasks and save you hours (okay, maybe minutes) of time.

Let's take a look first at Excel's simplest block functions: copying and moving.

Back to Work

 If you closed up your worksheet in Chapter 3, "Saving and Closing Documents," you can reopen it with the Open icon. A detailed explanation of opening files is found in Chapter 13, "An Open and Shut Case."

If you'd rather start fresh, click the New icon. A brand spankin' new worksheet will appear on a screen near you.

To Move or to Copy: That Is the Question

Just when you thought it was safe to show off your masterpiece spreadsheet, it hits you: Everything would be so much clearer if that column on the left was moved to the right. And you could drag this stuff from up top and place it toward the bottom. And instead of using column B as your master list, maybe you should use D. No problem. Just copy a column...or do you move it?

Excel users tend to lose their hair for two reasons: One is male-pattern baldness; the other is from pulling it out after they move a group of cells they meant to copy. Moving and copying are similar functions in Excel. And because they can wipe out existing information, both are fraught with danger if you perform them without carefully surveying the terrain first.

Oh, What a Drag: The Copy Function

The simplest, safest way to copy cells a short distance on a worksheet is to drag them across the screen with the mouse. To copy a cell or a group of cells, follow these steps:

1. Select the area you want to copy by clicking one corner of the group, holding down the left mouse button, and dragging to the opposite corner. The area becomes highlighted.

Prefer the Keyboard?

If you love your keyboard and hate that injury-inducing mouse, you can select cells without ever leaving home. Use the arrow keys to move the active cell indicator (the black square that shows where you are on the spreadsheet) to any corner of the cell group you want to select. Press and hold the Shift key and continue to use the arrow keys to move the active cell indicator to the opposite corner of the group. Your cell block appears highlighted, and you are free to copy it, move it, or flat out delete it.

2. Position the mouse pointer over the highlighted border of the active cell. The pointer changes to an arrow. Don't land on that tiny block in the lower-right corner, though. That little block does something completely different. Don't ask! (Okay, you can ask. But we won't answer until you get to the AutoFill section, later in this chapter.)

3. Press and hold the **Ctrl** key. A tiny plus sign appears next to the mouse pointer.

4. Press and hold the left mouse button.

5. Drag the cell(s) to the new location. The screen will look like this:

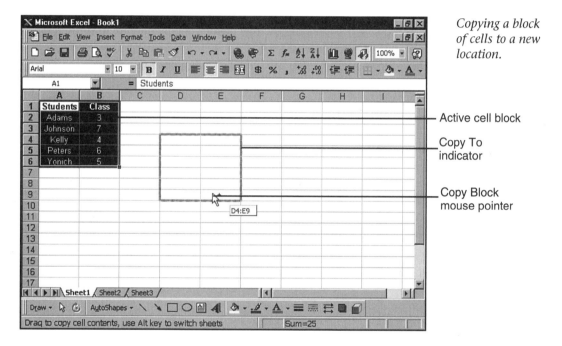

Copying a block of cells to a new location.

— Active cell block

— Copy To indicator

— Copy Block mouse pointer

6. Release the mouse button and the Ctrl key. Excel now displays your data in both the original location and the new location.

Check This Out...

A Word of Caution

If you copy data over cells that already contain data, you lose whatever information was stored there.

Moving Day

The procedure for moving a cell or group of cells is very much the same as that for copying a cell. Follow these steps:

1. Select the area you want to copy by dragging over it with the mouse or by pressing Shift plus the arrow keys.

2. Position the mouse pointer over the highlighted border. The pointer will change to an arrow when it's correctly positioned.

3. Press and hold the left mouse button.

4. Drag the cell(s) to the new location.

5. Release the mouse button. Excel removes the data from its original location and places it in the new location.

Great References

Copying a cell or a group of cells has the obvious consequence of doubling what you had originally. It has some other consequences, as well.

If you simply move a block of text, all *cell references* (addresses that describe the location of another cell) within that block remain the same. For instance, if a cell contains the formula "=A1+B1" before you move it, it still contains the same formula after you move it. (And it no longer appears in its original location.)

If you copy a block, all cell references in the new block become relative, meaning that they change accordingly. For example, if a cell contains a reference to cell A1, and you copy it to a new location one column to the right, the formula in the new location refers to cell B1 (the relative position of the new cell).

The problem, of course, is that you might still want to refer to cell A1. Chapter 9, "Home on the Range," explains how to solve this, and every other reference problem you might ever encounter.

Keyboard Cuts and Pastes

You can also accomplish moving and copying tasks using the Cut, Copy, and Paste commands on the Edit menu. This may be useful if you have spreadsheets the size of tablecloths or if you simply refuse to deal with a mouse.

56

To copy or move using the keyboard, first select the cells you want to work with. To copy, open the **Edit** menu and choose **Copy** (or press **Ctrl+C**). Your original stays in place. To move the selected cells, open the **Edit** menu and choose **Cut** (or press **Ctrl+X**). The box surrounding your selection changes to a moving dotted line.

To paste your cells in the new location, place your cursor in the upper-left corner of the new location. Then do it! Open the **Edit** menu and choose **Paste** (or press **Ctrl+V**), and Excel moves or copies your selection to its new location.

AutoFill

One of the best time-savers you'll find in Excel is the AutoFill function. AutoFill is a sort of glorified Copy command. But AutoFill is better than simple copying because it looks at a series of numbers or words, and—in its own Carmack-the-Magician way—figures out where the series is going.

Suppose you wanted to list the numbers 1 through 50 in a column. You could type each number individually, or you could use AutoFill to do all the grunt work for you.

Boring? Hold on a moment. It gets better. Suppose you're creating a worksheet showing quarterly earnings over a 10-year period, and that your fiscal year starts in May. Instead of entering May 1980, Aug 1980, Nov 1980, *ad nauseam*, you can just tell Excel the first two entries in the series and allow AutoFill to figure out the rest. There. Just like that you can save yourself the effort of typing 40 nearly identical column labels.

Using AutoFill is simple. In the next few sections, we'll walk you through the basic process, show you what sorts of data you can AutoFill, and teach you the rules for AutoFilling.

Quick AutoFill Practice

To start the basic AutoFill process, enter the number 10 in a blank cell. Then move one column to the right and enter the number 20. You have now defined the series: Numbers in increments of 10.

To perform the actual AutoFill, select the two cells you just entered. A dark line appears around the selected cells, and all but the first cell become highlighted. With the cells selected, position your pointer over the *fill handle*, the small black square at the bottom right corner of the selection box (see the following figure). The mouse pointer changes to a black cross.

When you've selected the cells, you're ready to AutoFill.

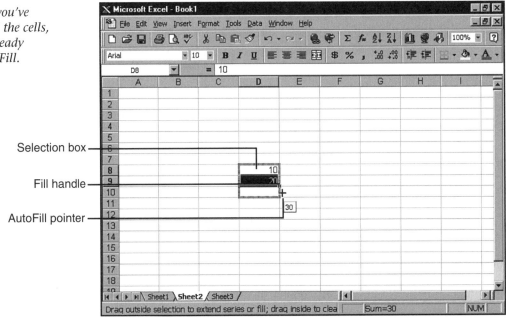

Selection box ——

Fill handle ——

AutoFill pointer ——

One-Cell Show

AutoFill has more than one use. Suppose your "series" is a series of one: You want to repeat the word Total across several columns, for example. Easy enough. Simply select that one cell, and AutoFill as usual. If there is no pattern to follow, AutoFill just copies the cell contents across.

To complete the AutoFill, hold down the left mouse button and drag the right side of the selection box. When you release the mouse button, the newly highlighted cells are AutoFilled with 30, 40, 50, and so on. Well, you did it: your first AutoFill. You can now breathe again and pass out the cigars.

Kinds of Data You Can AutoFill

AutoFill works on the principle that series are logical. This list defines the kinds of series AutoFill recognizes, and the tables show examples of how AutoFill would complete each series.

Numbers

AutoFill recognizes straight consecutive numbers, as well as any series of numbers that change by increments.

If You Type	AutoFill Completes
1, 2	3, 4, 5
5, 10	15, 20, 25
2.1, 2.2	2.3, 2.4, 2.5
12, 6	0, -6, -12

Calendar Entries

AutoFill completes series of times and dates, and can even operate on them as if they were incremental numbers.

If You Type	AutoFill Completes
Monday, Tuesday	Wednesday, Thursday, Friday
Mon, Wed	Fri, Sun, Tue
January, July	January, July, January
Feb, Jun	Oct, Feb, Jun
2 am, 5 am	8:00 am, 11:00 am, 2:00 pm
2:00, 12:00	22:00, 8:00, 18:00
Qtr1, Qtr2	Qtr3, Qtr4, Qtr1
Q1, Q3	Q1, Q3, Q1

Mixed Entries

AutoFill can combine series elements with text and increment or copy each element separately.

If You Type	AutoFill Completes
Quarter2, Quarter4	Quarter2, Quarter4, Quarter2
July 7, July 8	July 9, July 10, July 11
Aug 1, Oct 1	Dec 1, Feb 1, Apr 1
1 Sep 94, 3 Oct 96	05-Nov-98, 07-Dec-00, 09-Jan-02

Rules for AutoFill

If you intend to do a lot of AutoFilling, you should know the ground rules:

➤ *Define the series.* You must define enough elements in your series for Excel to discern the pattern. Two elements are generally sufficient.

AutoOops

What if you didn't intend to AutoFill? After all, the AutoFill function works a great deal like the copy function described above. If you find you AutoFilled when you only wanted to copy, there's an easy fix. Just press and hold the **Ctrl** key and repeat the command. Or easier yet, use the **Undo** command from the **Edit** menu.

➤ *Add and subtract only.* AutoFill isn't smart enough to discern patterns that involve multiplication, division, algebra, trigonometry, or the preferred provider list from your HMO. Nor does it recognize the names of your childhood pets, your genealogy, or your record of traffic violations. If those series are important to you, investigate the "Creating Custom Lists" section later in this chapter.

➤ *AutoFill will guess.* If you input the series 5, 7, and 11, you won't get a list of prime numbers. Instead, you'll get numbers like 13.6666667, which is Excel's best guess at the trend you've started.

➤ *Down or out.* AutoFill works across rows or down columns, but cannot do both at once. You can, however, use a single element in two intersecting AutoFills, as long as you perform the AutoFills separately.

➤ *Cut it out.* If you drag too far, just reselect the cells you originally input and drag back over the offending parts. They'll disappear from the series.

➤ *Back it up.* AutoFill works backward as well. Drag your series up a column or to the left in a row to get AutoFill to work in reverse.

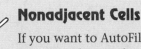

Nonadjacent Cells

If you want to AutoFill cells a few rows or columns away, no problem. Just enter the numbers or words for the series you want and select the beginning of the series as usual. Press **Ctrl** and select the destination location, where the rest of the series will appear. (The destination location, must be on the same row or column as the original.) Then open the **Edit** menu, select **Fill**, and select **Series**. In the Series dialog box, click the **AutoFill** option button and click **OK**. AutoFill completes the series in the destination location.

Creating Custom Lists

Suppose you regularly create spreadsheets that list your company's product names. (If you work in a pastry shop, you might list the doughnuts, the pies, or the cupcake flavors.) You can easily create a custom AutoFill list so that the entire list appears each time you start the series.

There are many kinds of custom lists you might want to include: Your company's geographic regions, employee names, part numbers, the alphabet, work groups, supervisor names, product categories, or product line divisions. Any way you regularly break out your spreadsheets is a candidate for custom lists.

These steps outline the procedure for creating a custom AutoFill list:

1. Create your list in Excel or a word processor, making sure to use hard returns (press the **Enter** key) after each item on the list.

2. Highlight the list. If it's a non-Excel list, press **Ctrl+C** to copy it to the Windows Clipboard.

3. From Excel's Main menu bar, choose **Tools**, **Options**. In the Options dialog box, click the **Custom Lists** tab.

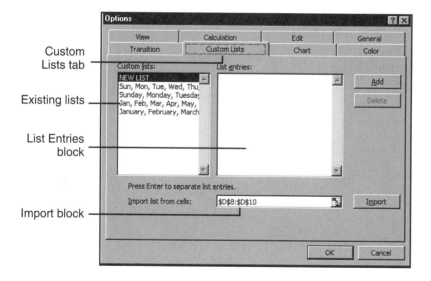

Custom Lists tab

Existing lists

List Entries block

Import block

Use the Custom Lists tab of the Options dialog box to create custom AutoFill lists.

4. Enter the list. Here's how:

If you created an Excel list, the cell references appear in the Import box. Click the **Import** button to display the list in the List Entries box.

61

If you are bringing in a list from some other application, click in the **List Entries** box and press **Ctrl+V** to paste the list you saved to the Clipboard in step 2.

5. Click **OK** to save the custom list and close the dialog box.

Going Through Customs

You can return to the Custom Lists tab at any time and edit or delete the list. To edit a list, highlight it in the Custom Lists box and make your changes in the List Entries box. Deleting is even simpler. Just highlight the unwanted list and click the **Delete** button. Click **OK** to close the dialog box and save your changes.

Now whenever you enter a word from your new list, Autofill is available to complete the list!

Use the Custom list exactly as you would Autofill. Type one of the elements of the list in a cell. With the cell selected, position your pointer over the fill handle and drag the corner an appropriate number of cells.

The Least You Need to Know

This chapter taught you the ins and outs of going back and forth. Here's what you should have copied, good buddy:

➤ Excel lets you quickly fill a lot of cells at once by copying, moving, or AutoFilling.

➤ All block operations require you to first select an existing group of cells (a block).

➤ The simplest way to copy is to hold down the **Ctrl** key plus the left mouse button and drag one side of the block to a new location.

➤ The simplest way to move a block is to drag it to a new location.

➤ The AutoFill function extends a series or a pattern across several rows or columns.

➤ You can make custom AutoFill lists for items you use frequently.

Chapter 6

The Editing Test: Change the Contents of Your Spreadsheet

In This Chapter

➤ Change little things you don't like

➤ Clean up the errors

➤ Wipe out the big things you hate

➤ Four friendly fixes

Have you ever wished you could rewrite history—even a little? Come on, admit it. Wouldn't it have been great to have kicked the ladder out from under Adolph Hitler while he was still a paper hanger, to have sold your white polyester suit the week before the disco craze died, or to have been born the favorite nephew of Donald Trump? In a way that's what editing is all about: Changing the past.

It's not important why you edit: Changes in the original conditions, forgotten formulas, or out-and-out mistakes. (Did you really intend to charge poor Aunt Anna 150 percent interest on that hearing-aid loan?) Fortunately, Excel was designed for mere mortals. After you've spent hours perfecting that spreadsheet, you can still look at it and say, "Naaa." Then you can reach back, rewrite a bit of history, and move on with your backside covered.

Ch-ch-ch-Changes to Cells

One of the fun things about working in spreadsheets is that you can always find a harder way to do anything. When you made a mistake back in the good ol' days, you'd turn your pencil over and erase it. This chapter takes a look at all the entertaining ways computers have found to complicate that task.

Getting Ready to Edit

The first step toward editing your spreadsheet data is to select the cell. If you've had your hand surgically attached to a mouse, select the cell that contains the bad words or numbers by clicking it.

Un-do-delly Do

Excel can boast a multi-level undo feature. What this means is that Ctrl+Z not only undoes your last change, but press Ctrl+Z again and Excel will undo the previous change. And so on, and so on…

If your hands don't get out much and would rather stay at home on the keyboard, use those arrow keys to position the active cell indicator.

Go In for the Kill

Now you're ready to change the contents of a cell, and you have several options to choose from. This is the fun part. Use any of these methods to change the data in a cell:

➤ Easiest of all: Just start typing. Mow right over the darned thing. If your cell contains very complicated or lengthy information, however, you'll want to be more selective. That's why there are more options in this list.

➤ Double-click a cell you want to change, insert the new data, and then delete the stuff you don't like.

➤ Double-click the cell, select all or part of the data in the cell, and then type over it.

➤ Double-click the cell, then press **Backspace** to delete a character to the left of the cursor; press **Delete** to remove a character to the right.

➤ Make your changes in the formula bar, above the column headers. This is the procedure: Select the cell and press **F2**, the edit key. The active cell's contents appear in the formula bar. The blinking cursor in the formula bar indicates where characters you type will appear. Enter your changes.

Blinking cursor at insertion point

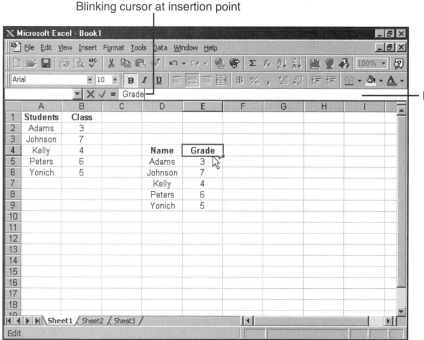

The active cell's contents appear in the formula bar.

Formula bar

Ending It All

Once you've changed the information in your cell(s), your natural tendency is probably to simply hit the Enter key and get on with things. Go with that feeling. Although Excel provides alternatives, they're nothing but trouble.

Check This Out...

Line Up Changes

If you've selected a block of cells that involves more than one column, pressing the Enter key works a little differently. After you change the contents of one cell in the block, pressing the Enter key moves you one cell to the right, where you can make your next change. If you haven't selected a block, or if your block is in a single column, pressing the Enter key always moves you down a row.

See those icons up there in the formula bar? The ones with the red X and the green check mark? Don't touch them! No! Don't do it! Well, okay, if curiosity is killing you, click the red X, and all your changes will disappear. (Of course, if that's what you wanted, you could have just as easily pressed the **Esc** key on your keyboard.) Click the green check mark, and you'll discover a complicated new alternative to the Enter key.

Cleaning Up Words

Spelling: It's the drudge work of all editors. But Excel can handle it. In this section, learn to check your spelling, prevent spelling errors in the first place, and find and replace words that are misspelled throughout your worksheet.

Spell Check

Excel's spell check feature searches your worksheet for spelling errors and typos. To start a spell check, click on the **Spelling** icon on the Standard toolbar. (Alternatively, you can press F7 or open the Tools menu and choose Spelling.) Somehow, some way, the road always leads to the Spelling dialog box shown in the following figure.

The Spelling dialog box.

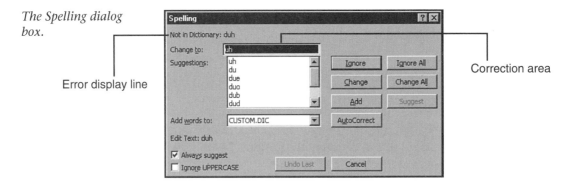

Error display line

Correction area

The first line of the Spelling dialog box shows the misspelled word, and the Change To box displays Excel's best guess at how the word should be spelled. You can select a different spelling suggestion from the Suggestions box, or you can simply type the correction in the Change To box. Then click **Change** to correct this occurrence of the word or click **Change All** to correct the error throughout your document.

If the word is spelled correctly, you may want to add it to your custom dictionary so Excel won't stop on it during future spelling checks. If so, click the **Add** button. If you don't want to add the word to your dictionary but you don't want to change it, click **Ignore** to ignore this occurrence of the word or click **Ignore All** to ignore it throughout the document.

The Spelling dialog box also contains options you can select to control whether the spell checker always suggests changes and whether it ignores uppercase/lowercase errors.

(A check in these boxes indicates that the feature is turned on.) In addition, Excel provides command buttons with which you can undo your last change or close the spell checker altogether.

The last command button, the AutoCorrect button, lets you add a change to your AutoCorrect list. Read on to find out the more complicated details of using AutoCorrect.

AutoCorrect

It's numbers you're good at, right? Then why should you be any good at typing? You don't have to be.

Excel understands. That's why it now includes a feature called AutoCorrection that's designed to make you look like an Olympic-caliber typist. Because AutoCorrect is, well, automatic, you don't have to do anything to make it work. Just type away, and Excel corrects your errors as you work. AutoCorrection automatically fixes your typos and spelling mistakes on-the-fly. Type "adn" followed by a space, for example, and Excel changes it to "and" before you can even type the next keystroke.

To enable the AutoCorrect feature, open the **Tools** menu and select **AutoCorrect**. The AutoCorrect dialog box (shown in the following figure) appears.

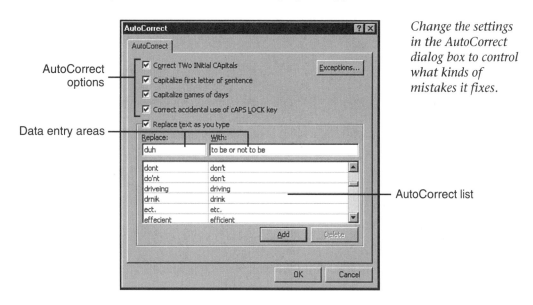

AutoCorrect options

Data entry areas

AutoCorrect list

Change the settings in the AutoCorrect dialog box to control what kinds of mistakes it fixes.

Click the first check box at the top of the dialog box to control whether Excel automatically corrects words with TWo INitial Capitals. You might not want to use this, of course, if you're from Los Angeles and have employees with names like JEnnEfur. Click the

Capitalize Names of Days check box to have Excel correct those errors. And be sure to check the **Replace Text as You Type** box; it turns AutoCorrection on or off. The Exceptions button lets you input abbreviated words that might appear in mid sentence, and add words that have unusual capitalization, such as dBASE. Click **OK** to implement the settings you selected.

AutoCorrection works from a list of common typing and spelling errors. Because the AutoCorrect list starts out short, you will probably amend it from time to time. There are two ways to do this:

➤ *From the Spelling dialog box.* If you find a frequently recurring error, click the **AutoCorrect** button, and Excel adds the change to your AutoCorrect list.

➤ *From the AutoCorrect dialog box.* To add an entry to your AutoCorrect list, type the common error in the Replace text box (for example, type "helo"). Click or press **Tab** to move to the With text box. Input the correct replacement (in this case, "hello"), click the **Add** button, and click **OK** to return to the worksheet. In the future, AutoCorrection will make that correction anytime it occurs.

Really Cool AutoCorrect Tip
AutoCorrect isn't just for typos anymore. Use AutoCorrect as a shorthand tool for completing phrases. For example, instead of typing "First Quarter Earnings" over and over, just tell AutoCorrect to enter that phrase whenever you type 1E.

In a similar way, you can use AutoCorrect to automatically output a long block of text. To do so, create your replacement text block in Excel or a word processor and select the block. Press **Ctrl+C** to copy it to the Windows Clipboard. From Excel's Main menu bar, open the **Tools** menu and choose **AutoCorrect**. The AutoCorrect dialog box appears. In the Replace box, type the shorthand term you want Excel to replace. Then move to the With box and press **Ctrl+V** to paste the text block. Click **OK** to save the addition and close the dialog box. Each time you type your shorthand abbreviation in the future, Excel automatically replaces it with the text block.

Find and Replace

There's nothing more frustrating than not knowing where something is—whether that something is your only set of car keys or that Nobel prize-winning formula. Excel's Find and Replace feature may not be of much help with the car keys, but if you're looking for something on your spreadsheet, it may be just what you need.

To use either Find or Replace, open the **Edit** menu and select **Find**. (If you prefer, you can avoid all this clicking and dragging by pressing **Ctrl+F**.) Either way, the Find dialog box appears.

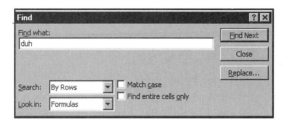

The Find dialog box.

In the Find what text box, type the word or phrase you're looking for. You can enter alphanumeric characters from labels, formulas, dates, times, or values. Click the appropriate check box if you want to limit your search by matching upper- and lowercase letters or by searching for entire cells that match the search text. In a very large spreadsheet, you might also want to limit your task by searching column by column or row by row. If so, select one of the options in the Search drop-down list.

At this point, the Find path and the Replace path diverge. If you want to replace the word or phrase, click the **Replace** button. The Replace with text box appears. Type the replacement text, and then choose whether you want Excel to replace only the first occurrence of the text or every occurrence in the entire spreadsheet. If, on the other hand, you only want to Find something, click the **Find Next** button now.

The Find or Replace function begins. If you chose **Find**, the next highlighted cell you see should be the one you were looking for. If you chose **Replace**, Excel replaces the text automatically.

Clear 'Em Out: Clearing and Deleting

A pop quiz: What's the difference between deleting something and clearing it? Confused? Yeah, you and everybody else. But Excel wants you to learn the distinction. So take a deep breath.

When you *clear* a cell or a range, Excel sweeps out its contents but leaves the actual cell or range in place. When you *delete*, however, it's like taking a pair of scissors to your spreadsheet. Excel actually chops out the cell or range, and the rest of the spreadsheet shifts around to fill in the gaps.

Clearing Cells, Rows, and Columns

Have you ever looked in your closet and wished you could just get rid of everything in it and start over? Although that's not always possible, clearing the contents of a cell, a range, a column, or a row you're unhappy with *is* possible. And Excel makes it easy.

First, select the stuff you don't like. Then take your pick of several different ways to make it disappear:

➤ *The frustration method.* Press **Backspace** to mow right over the text. (This works in a single cell only.)

➤ *The Clear command.* You'll find it on the Edit menu. This method gives you the option of clearing all the contents, or only the formatting commands, the visible contents, the comments or the hyperlinks (discussed in Chapter 7, "Excel on the Net").

➤ *The right mouse button.* When you click on your right mouse button, the Excel Shortcut menu appears. Choose **Clear Contents** from the menu.

➤ *Delete.* Just press the darned **Delete** key. Hey! Why didn't we think of that earlier?

Slash and Burn Deletion Tips

Deleting is lots more fun than clearing. The adventure! The thrills! The—oops!

When you delete cells, you can make fundamental changes to the structure of your worksheet—which makes it all too easy to destroy the whole darned thing. Deleting changes relationships between the elements, and physically moves cells, rows, and columns.

If you're bound and determined to delete anyway, highlight the desired cell, range, column, or row. Open the **Edit** menu and select **Delete**, or press **Alt+E** and then **D**. If you selected a row or column, Excel deletes it immediately. If you selected a range, the Delete dialog box appears, asking whether you want to move the remaining cells up or to the left, or whether you want to eliminate your current row or column altogether.

The Delete dialog box.

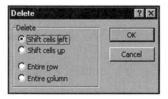

If you are sure you really want to do this, click the appropriate button and press **OK**. There. You probably just destroyed your spreadsheet.

Cool Deletion Tip

Unsure about deleting? Here's a better—safer—way to delete.

First, save your worksheet. Then clear a single cell or a group of cells. STOP! Before you do anything else, see if anything went wrong. Did any errors pop up? Move around your spreadsheet and check for other errors. If you find a mistake, press **Ctrl+Z** now to undo the Clear command. Then re-examine your change.

If everything looks good, go ahead and delete the cells and check immediately to see if the spreadsheet died. If it did, press **Ctrl+Z** immediately to recover.

The Least You Need to Know

This chapter taught you the basics of Excel editing. With an air of nostalgia and a tender tear in our collective eye, let's look back at what we learned:

➤ Changing cells is an unnecessarily complicated process. The quick and dirty way to change the contents of a cell is to place the cursor there and start typing. Delete any extra stuff and press **Enter**. There. You're done.

➤ Spell check is easy. Just press **F7**, and away it goes.

➤ The AutoCorrect feature corrects your typos and misspellings on-the-fly, but you need to add your own entries to the list for it to be really effective.

➤ Clearing and deleting are not the same thing. When you clear a cell, only its contents are removed. When you delete a cell, the entire cell disappears, and the rest of the spreadsheet moves in.

Chapter 7

Excel on the Net

In This Chapter

➤ Get onto the Internet

➤ Exchange and access files on the Web

➤ Make your files worth exchanging

➤ Guidance through the great Internet gate

Once, when one of us was young and foolish, she climbed aboard a charter bus full of other young and foolish people for a multi-day, multi-state journey. After a full day of driving, teenaged bus riders began climbing on the luggage racks and lying in the aisles just to get comfortable. Your friendly author slid her once-svelte body under a bus seat and fell asleep. Lights went out, kids dozed off, and all was well... until she awoke in the middle of the night not knowing where she was, pinned under a bus seat, and in a full-on panic. To this day, being locked in small spaces—Delaware, for example—sends her pulse a' pounding. That's why she's so happy to have the Internet—she can hang out with her neighbors in Southeast Asia without even putting on a robe.

Playing Spider
Virtually every-
thing you'll find in
this chapter about
the Internet and
World Wide Web applies also
to corporate intranets, a sort of
internal Web. If you've got one
in your office, it'll look exactly
like the real Web, and will use
all the same software.

Stepping Out

Hey, Excel! Welcome to the '90s! While the rest of the
world was out travelling the Internet, spreadsheets stayed
curled up at home with a good CD. Never more! Excel is
now Net-savvy, and we spreadsheet users can all come out
and play.

We'll look at each of Excel's Internet functions separately.
This chapter covers only the bare essentials of Internet
life.... A complete discussion would require, well, a book.
A whole book. And then some.

Getting Online

OK, this can be real easy—or really complicated. Let's start with easy: Get an Internet
account, install the software, and click the hyperlink. Got that?

No? Then we'll have to do this the old-fashioned way.

Step One: Get the Internet Account

To get to the Internet and World Wide Web sites, you need an account either through a
direct network connection (read: an employer so big that you've never met your boss's
boss) or through a dial-in Internet service provider, called an ISP.

Shameless Plug
This chapter has
the bare-bones
fundamentals of
Internetting. If
you want to
know more, we recommend (as
you might expect) *The Complete
Idiot's Guide to the Internet, Fourth
Edition.*

If you have a generous employer, or a teenager, you've
probably already completed this step. Otherwise, you'll need
to check a few newspapers, watch a few TV ads, or make a
few phone calls in order to find your ISP. They're multiplying like cockroaches, and can be found every place in the
world—with the exception of certain counties in Wyoming
where they were eaten by rabbits. They all charge about
twenty dollars a month for unlimited—or virtually
unlimited—access, and they all give you the software you
need to get connected. (You have to supply your own
computer, modem, telephone line, office chair, and "I can't
quit playing with this thing" Mountain Dew.)

Install the Software

Having trouble? Harass your new ISP morning, noon, and night until you're online, trouble free. Make him earn his twenty bucks.

Among the pieces of software your ISP will give you is a thing called a Web browser. It's very likely that your Web browser will be called either Netscape Navigator or Microsoft Internet Explorer.

Treat this Web browser gently, for it is the key by which you unlock a thing called the World Wide Web. Hello? You still there? The Web is fun, really. OK, it's mostly advertisements for Ford Escort Ponies and bad Disney movies—but the ads never stopped you from watching *Bewitched*, did they?

Make It So

By keeping Explorer hidden in the background, Excel lets you roam the Internet without ever leaving the program. It does so with a new toolbar, called the Web toolbar, which emulates the commands used most often in Internet Explorer, thereby eliminating the need to leave Excel to use the Net.

Bring up the Web toolbar by clicking this icon. When you do, you'll see the following toolbar appear either mid-screen or as a typical toolbar in the position below the existing toolbars. Here we display the toolbar mid-screen, but you can drag it to a better position with your mouse.

The Web toolbar.

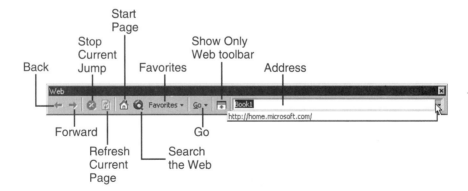

Search Your Engines

Webs—whether World Wide or companywide—are vast. If you know exactly where you want to go, you're fortunate. If you're a regular person, though, you need help. Use a search engine, a free tool that searches a web for any information you want. A fine place for searching the World Wide Web is http://www.msn.com/access/allinone.asp. Go there to access all the most popular Internet search tools. Just enter a word or two in the box, and click the Search button. If your search generates too *many* choices, you'll find instructions for narrowing your search on the related site.

If you've followed along so far, you'll understand immediately what most of these buttons mean:

➤ Back and Forward navigate through Web sites you've already seen.

➤ Stop Current Jump lets you quit when you're tired of waiting for a Web page to load.

➤ Refresh reloads the current Web page.

➤ Search the Web button does just that, going to a predefined Search page.

➤ Favorites remembers your favorite Web sites, as you define them.

➤ The Go button brings up a menu of options for places to visit on the Web.

➤ The Show Only button changes your screen display to hide all the other Excel menus and toolbars.

➤ Most fun of all is the Address button, where you enter all those great Internet addresses—also called *URLs,* or uniform resource locators—that you see in movie credits, presidential debates, and other advertisements.

Tossin' the Ball Around

Entering URLs looks a little tricky, but it's actually quite simple. Ninety-five percent of the Internet addresses you run across in your life will begin with the designation `http://`. Another 4.5 percent will begin with `ftp://`. If you run across the other .5 of a percent, you'll probably be looking at things so obscure they don't really bear learning about.

Naming Conventions

Most Web addresses look something like this: `http://www.`*something*`.ext/`*filename*`.htm`. The www part is obvious. The *something* is generally the name of an organization. And the *ext* tells you what kind of place the site might be. The most common extensions are

`.com`	Commercial site. Cover your wallet.
`.edu`	A university or college.
`.net`	Smaller site using an Internet service provider.
`.gov`	Site affiliated with the U.S. government. Lobby for more public holidays.
`.org`	Means it's some kind of non-profit organization. Churches and diseases get most of these, but politicians like them, too.

As a rule of thumb, the http designations indicate an address for a graphically enhanced, magazine-cover-like World Wide Web page. The ftp designations, on the other hand, indicate ugly, non-graphical, non-viewable files that you nearly always download to your own computer—at which point they might get installed and become quite pretty after all. FTP is actually more significant than it sounds because it's the method by which you will do virtually all of your Net file transfers.

If you've started using the Search tools, you've already begun collecting a list of favorite addresses.

To open up your navigational options, click the **Go** button on the Web toolbar, and select **Open**. The Open Internet Address dialog box opens.

Known Addressee

If you type in Web addresses without the trailing filenames, your software will always try to open up the default home page for that site. This is good, because sometimes you overhear snatches of conversations on buses, and don't catch the file names. Other times, you know only the name of a company, and want to guess at the URL. As long as you know or can guess the first part of the address, you're in!

*The Open Internet
Address dialog box.*

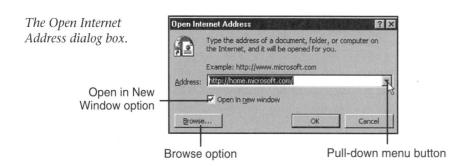

Open in New
Window option

Browse option   Pull-down menu button

Select recently used addresses from the pull-down Address menu. Use the Open in New Window option to start on a clean page. And click the **Browse** button to look for other stored addresses. Click **OK** to go to the site displayed in the address box.

Pretty It Up

Once you start viewing other people's Web pages, the bug will hit. Within 24 hours, you'll be itching to build a page of your own. In this book, we're going to teach you how to build a Web page from Excel—only a slightly more complicated process than it would be to build a simple text-only Web page.

Preparing to Go Home

Before you even get started, talk to your ISP (or, if you're on a company intranet, talk to the people who created it) to find out the address of your soon-to-be *home page*. The home page is like the cover of a magazine. Once readers log into your home page, they can click hyperlinks you create in order to view the "inside" pages.

Write down the home page address. Then ask for the "parameters" for *"FTPing"* (a fancy word for "transfering") your page. Write those down, too. They're kind of complex, so don't even try to memorize them. Finally, ask for some free FTP software so that you'll be able to send your home page file to its new home on your ISP or company server computer. If all else fails, you can download a nice FTP program yourself. We recommend WS_FTP32. You can get it by typing this address into your browser: **ftp://ftp.digital.com/pub/micro/pc/simtelnet/win95/inet/ws_ftp32.zip**. Long address, eh? No more, we promise. Now install the program on your PC, and enter those parameters you wrote down. (Click **Connect**, and in the Session Profile dialog box, click **New**. A blank page will open, and you can enter the parameters there.)

Zip-ideedoodah

Often you'll discover that files arrive with a name ending in .ZIP. These files are compressed, and you need to unzip them to uncompress them, before you can install them. No problem. Use a program called WinZip, from Nico Mak Computing, to unzip your file. You can download the latest version of WinZip from http://www.winzip.com. Try it for free, but if you continue using it, the developer asks you to send him $29.

To use WS_FTP, start up your communications software as usual, then click **Connect** and choose the name of the session profile you just created. You'll find your own computer directory in the left-hand column, and the directory from your ISP's or company's server in the right column. Once you create your home page (coming right up!), you'll simply highlight it and click the right arrow key to copy it to your ISP's computer. If you're able to see these directories, you're ready to start building a Web page. Ready to give it a try? Close up the FTP software and head back to Excel.

Build That Page

Start with something simple. Open a blank worksheet in Excel, and type your name in cell A1. You'll learn about text formatting in Chapter 14, "Customizing the Spreadsheet," so for the time being, keep in mind that everything you color and paint and draw (Chapter 16, "Graphics Workshop") can appear in all its glory on your Web page. Now put a number in cell B1. Then save the file as you learned to do in Chapter 3, "Saving and Closing Documents." This is the beginning of your future Web page.

Skip ahead to Chapter 14 if you want to learn how to pretty up your worksheet. So far, your worksheet looks exactly like any other worksheet you might create. Now it's time to get fancy.

Working on the Chain Gang

The beauty of a Web is that it lets you jump around from one place to another through a series of what are known as *hyperlinks*. You learned a little bit about hyperlinks in Chapter 4, "Help, Help," where they helped you jump around within help files. Clicking a hyperlink from a Web page, or indeed, from anywhere in Excel, can take you to marvelous places.

You can create links that take you (or your reader) from as close as the next worksheet in the workbook on your screen, to as far away as a database on the other side of the planet. In fact, we're going to practice hyperlinking by making a connection in space: the final frontier.

Go to a blank cell in your worksheet. From the Insert menu, select **Hyperlink**. The Insert Hyperlink dialog box appears.

The Insert Hyperlink dialog box.

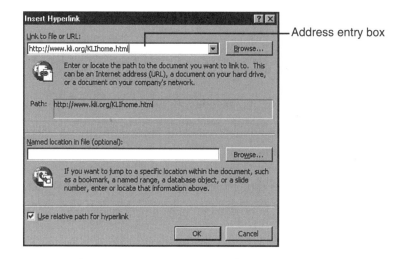

Enter the name of our favorite Web site, the Klingon Language Institute, in the address entry box. The address is `http://www.kli.org/klihome.html`. Click **OK** to save the hyperlink. When you return to your page, the new hyperlink will appear underlined on screen.

The hyperlink appears with an underline.

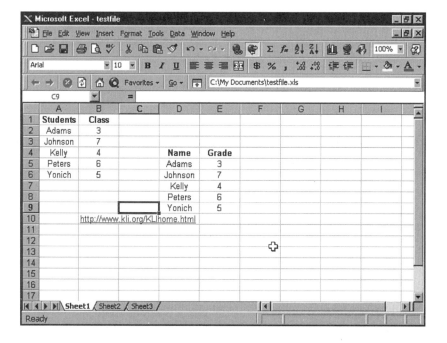

Now you can click the link, and Excel will throw you into the transporter and beam you straight to Klingon-ville.

But wait! It gets better! You can click the Hyperlink icon on your standard toolbar to reopen the Insert Hyperlink command. This time, though, click the **Browse** button and select the name of a file on your own computer or network. Just for fun, make it a word processing file. If your word processor is Microsoft Word or WordPerfect, for example, click a file that ends with .DOC. Click **OK** again, and the link to your file appears in your worksheet. Now you can click the filename, and Excel will open the file *from within your word processor!* You can repeat this trick with graphics files, databases, or virtually any file on your computer, your network, or an entire web.

Whew. Nearly there. Now it's time to prepare your worksheet to become a home page. The steps are simple.

1. First, delete any practice hyperlinks to files on your own computer. You don't want your boss to come snooping around, right? Seriously, unless your machine is accessible from the server where your home page is located, users will only be frustrated if they click the hyperlink. It won't link to anything!

2. Second, save your worksheet in the proper format. Most people assign their main home page the same file name: INDEX.HTM. Don't buck the trend. Using a standard filename simplifies access to your page. To save the worksheet as a properly formatted *HTML* file (the standard format for Web pages), go to the **File** menu and select **Save As HTML**.

When you save, a four-step Internet Assistant Wizard appears.

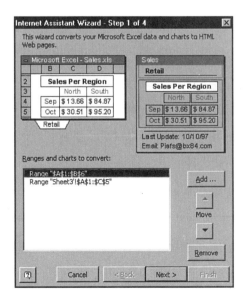

Save as HTML, Step 1.

If you want to save multiple worksheets or sections of worksheets, click the **Add** button and add them to the list. The arrow buttons change the order of the list items. When you've completed your list, click **Next** to go to Step 2.

Save as HTML,
Step 2.

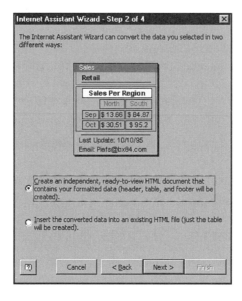

In Step 2 you decide whether to create a new HTML page, or simply add to an existing page. Click **Next** to continue to Step 3.

Save as HTML,
Step 3.

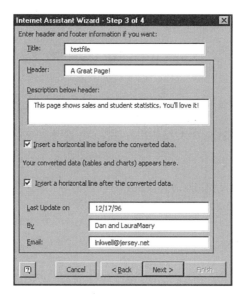

In Step 3, enter some of the text you want to have appear on your completed HTML page. The title will appear in the title bar at the top of the screen. The Header appears in large type at the beginning of the page. The Description below the header can be fairly long, if you'd like. It appears on your page as normal type. Decide which horizontal divider lines you'd like, and enter update and contact information at the bottom. When you're done, click **Next** to continue to Step 4.

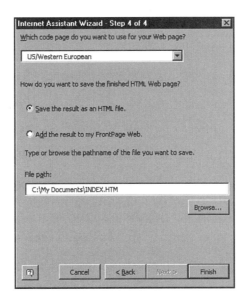

Save as HTML, Step 4.

Users with non–Western-language text will choose a different Code page, but most users should stick with the default US/Western European option. Most users will also want to save the results as an HTML file, rather than saving to FrontPage (a separate software product from Microsoft). We advise changing the filename for your first Web page to INDEX.HTM, because—well, because that's the way these things are done. HOME.HTM is also a nice, default home page name. Subsequent files deserve memorable names as well. When you're done, click the **Finish** button.

Surprisingly, you won't see your new HTML page. Instead, you'll have to open it manually if you want to see how it looks. Click the Web toolbar icon.

In the Address box of the Web Toolbar, enter the path and filename for your HTML page. In our example, the path is `C:\My Documents\index.htm`. Depending on how your software is set up, you'll view your page in either a standard Web browser such as Internet Explorer, or an HTML-enabled word processor, such as the newest version of Microsoft Word.

The new Web page.

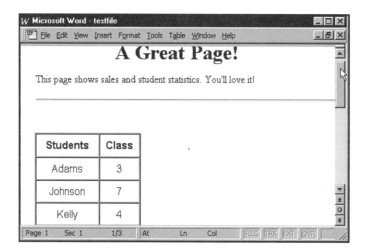

Honk if you're happy with your Web page. If you want to manipulate it a bit—add colors, change data, insert graphics—you can do so from within Excel. From the File menu, select **Open**. The Open dialog box appears in the usual way. At the bottom, where you see the Files of type option, select **All Files**. Select your home page file (INDEX or INDEX.HTM in our example). Format, edit, and manipulate to your heart's content.

The Web page edited in Excel.

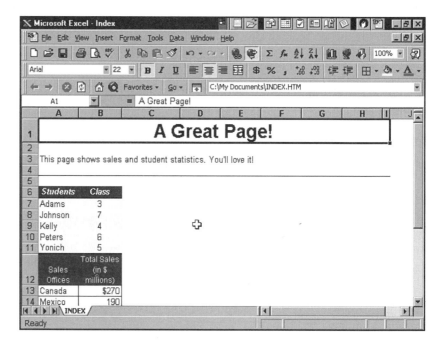

Satisfied? Great! You're almost there!

Finally, *upload* (fancy talk for copy) the page to your server using the FTP procedure we described in the previous section.

That's all there is to it. Now you can browse your new page, continue to amend it, link it to new pages, add pictures, and go crazy!

The Least You Need to Know

If you got through this chapter on Internetting and intranetting with Excel, you know far more than nearly anyone on the planet. Congratulations. Here are the bits you'll want to have tattooed on a piece of anatomy:

➤ Excel's new communications features make Web browsers transparent to the user.

➤ The Web toolbar contains nearly all the commands you've grown to love with your old browser.

➤ HTML tags are best unseen.

AutoPilot: Excel's Automatic Features

As automatically as tears appear in the eyes of an impoverished televangelist, Excel's auto-features can have you moving along to the next channel in no time! Watch as columns add themselves and outlines create themselves. In fact, keep watching as everything you ever wanted happens with almost miraculous regularity.

Shifting to Automatic

Hey, Detroit did it! So isn't it about time the computer industry figured out how to do automatic? Excel's auto features are designed to get you out of the kitchen fast. Top 10 lists, outlines, subtotals, macros—Excel's got 'em all. We start this chapter with an examination of the AutoFilter feature.

AutoFilter

Imagine that the list of employees at your widget company has grown from half a dozen salesfolk to several hundred worker bees. That's one long list on your spreadsheet, and when it comes time to check up on individual performance, you certainly don't want to look through all those names. You're interested only in finding the top and bottom 10 percent. Great news! AutoFilter is the answer to your prayers.

AutoFilter lets you enter criteria for searching and viewing spreadsheet data. Based on your selections, it filters out the details that don't interest you.

Now You See It; Now You Don't

To work through this section on AutoFiltering, you might want to create a small test spreadsheet of your own. You can work with something similar to the spreadsheet you created in Chapter 2, "Getting Started": a couple of columns, one with names and one with numbers. (A dozen or so rows of each will suffice.) Label the top of each column with a name that describes its contents. Or you can label it "Elephants on the March" if you like, because Excel can't read English and won't know the difference. You must put a label at the top of each column, because AutoFilter considers the first entry in a column a non-event.

AutoFilter ignores the first entry in each column.

AutoFilter arrow buttons

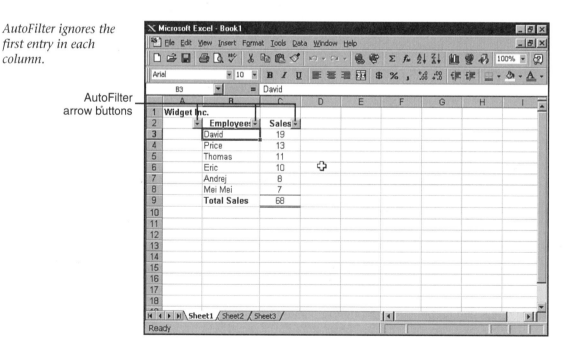

AutoFilter at Work

Click any cell that contains data to make it active. Then open the **Data** menu, choose **Filter**, and click **AutoFilter**. When you begin the AutoFilter, arrow buttons appear at the tops of the columns in your worksheet.

Click the arrow at the top of the column you want to filter. A pick list appears containing all of the values found in the column, an All selection, and Top 10, Custom, Blanks, and Non-Blanks.

We'll start with an easy filter. From the pick list that drops down when you clicked the arrow, select one of the items that originated from your column, an employee name, for instance. AutoFilter can hide all rows in that column that do not contain the selected employee name. Click the arrow button again and select **All**. The filter disappears, and everything returns to normal.

It's a Chameleon
The AutoFilter arrow button changes color when that column is an active filter.

Column values appear in the pick list.

Only the Good Get Viewed

Let's move on to the features that really make AutoFilter special. Click an arrow button at the top of a column containing number values—no names, please. Choose Top 10 from the pick list, and Excel displays the Top 10 AutoFilter dialog box.

89

The Top 10 Auto-Filter dialog box.

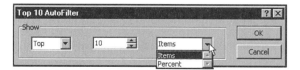

This dialog box contains three controls you use to make your AutoFilter selections. In the first box (on the left), indicate whether you want to filter from the top or the bottom (the highest or the lowest values). In the second box, you can make an adjustment to the number 10. Do you really want to see 10? Or do you need to see the top/bottom 5, 100, or 500 values? The third box enables you to control whether the numbers in the second box represent real numbers or percentages. (For example, do you want to find the top 10 or the top 10 percent?)

When you've made your selections, click **OK**. Excel hides all rows that don't match the selected criteria. To re-expand the column, click the arrow button again and select **All**.

To disable AutoFilter, open the Data menu, select **Filter**, and choose **AutoFilter**. The check mark disappears, and the AutoFilter arrow buttons disappear.

Exactly What You Were Looking For

If you'd like to have an even more precise view of your data (if, for example, you want to see a list of employees who sold more than 217 widgets this month or a list of employee names that start with the letter P), you'll want to investigate the Custom AutoFilter function.

This time around, click the same arrow button and choose **Custom** from the pick list. The Custom AutoFilter dialog box appears with four boxes from which you select the filtering criteria.

Choose customized filter criteria from the Custom AutoFilter dialog box.

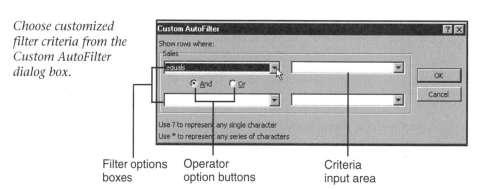

Filter options boxes · Operator option buttons · Criteria input area

Click the down arrow of the first filter options box. Excel displays a list of mathematical operations you can use to indicate the criteria for your filter. Choose from 12 different options for comparing numbers, including "equals," "contains," and "is greater than or equal to." For example, if you were really trying to find which employees had sold more than 217 widgets, you would select "greater than." But it's a free pick, and this is only a demo, so knock yourself out. "Don't ask, don't tell" is not an option.

Next, click the down arrow of the first box on the right (criteria input area). Excel displays a list of the values in the selected column. Pick one (such as 217). Or if you'd prefer, you can enter a number that does not appear in the list. For instance, if you're looking for all items with a value of 100, just enter 100. There is no need to go up and down the list searching for the closest value. Why settle for 101 or 99 when you can have exactly what you want? If you've finished selecting your filter criteria, click OK to start your custom AutoFilter.

If, on the other hand, you want to add another filter criteria, don't click OK. For example, if you want to see not only the top performers but also those at the bottom of the barrel, you need to use the other options in the Custom AutoFilter dialog box.

In the middle of the Custom AutoFilter dialog box are two option buttons, AND and OR, which you use to tell Excel what kind of logic you want to use. Use the AND operator to make each item on the list fit all the criteria. You'll get a small list of possibilities. Use OR to select items that fit any of the criteria. Your list of possibilities is larger. If, for example, you want to see who sold more than 11 widgets and who sold fewer than 9, you enter filter criteria for greater than 11 in the top box, and less than 9 in the bottom box. Then select OR, as shown in this figure. Click **OK**.

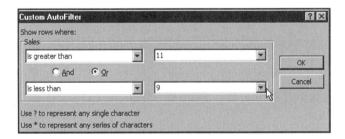

The Custom AutoFilter criteria.

AutoFilter finds all values in that column that are greater than 11 and all that are less than 9, and hides all other rows. The following figure shows the result of such a filter.

Putting a Stop to It

At any time, you can restore the complete list by clicking the **AutoFilter** arrow button in the selected column and selecting **All** from the pick list. To turn off AutoFilter itself, open the **Data** menu, select **Filter**, and select **AutoFilter** to remove the check mark.

The completed custom AutoFilter.

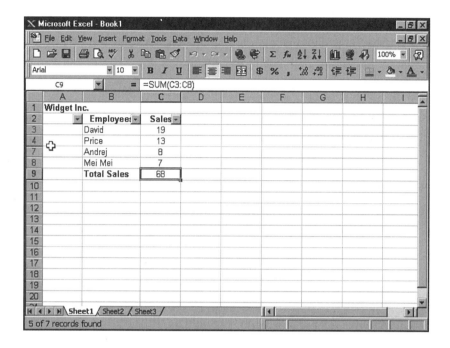

Use Wild Cards in Your Criteria

You can use wild-card characters in the Custom AutoFilter dialog box to broaden your filter criteria. Suppose, for example, you want to filter employee names or towns where your employees live. You could enter a partial word, instead of a number, in the Custom AutoFilter criteria box. Here's how the wild cards work.

The question mark represents any single character in a sequence of characters. For example, you can enter **P?st** to find Post and Past.

The asterisk represents one or more characters in a sequence of characters. For example, you can enter **Che*** to find Cher and Cheralike.

If you really want to find a question mark or asterisk in your string of characters, preface it with the tilde (~) character. For example, enter **Whatthe~?** to find "Whatthe?"

AutoOutline

My, how your widget factory has grown: A list of six employees has grown into a list of 6,000. But you don't need to spend time scrolling through these seemingly endless rows and columns. It's 3 o'clock in the morning, and your eyes are about to pop out of your head now. Put any more caffeine in your system, and you'll be dead three weeks before you can get any sleep. What to do? You use the AutoOutline feature to view employees by department, by job title, or by any other system you've arranged to give you summary statistics.

Getting to the Bottom Line

AutoOutline offers a quick way to jump to the all-important bottom line on your worksheet: the sums, averages, and percentages that "auto" be the final result of all your calculations. Having traveled a mile for that bad pun, you should be ready to begin. How many widgets did everybody sell?

AutoOutline collapses entire sections of data and leaves behind only summary information, taking you right to your bottom line quickly and easily... well, sort of. This feature does have a few requirements of its own.

➤ Your data must be organized into, say, departments or product lines or age, and each category must be subtotaled.

➤ The subtotals for the data in the columns and rows must be located in the same columns and rows as the data. In other words, the sum of the entries in column B must be located at the bottom (or top) of column B. The rule concerning rows is similar: The sum of the entries in row 3 must be at the end (or beginning) of row 3.

➤ Your layout must be consistent from section to section; all subtotals must be located consistently. You can place them at the top or at the bottom, but not top and bottom. (This is also true when you subtotal at the end of rows. Put all your subtotals at either the beginning or the end.)

To automatically outline a worksheet, be certain that all subtotals are located in the same row or column as the data they total. Then click any cell, open the **Data** menu, select **Group and Outline**, and choose **AutoOutline**.

That's it! If your totals and subtotals are located at the bottoms or tops of your columns, the Outline symbols appear to the left of your worksheet. If your totals and subtotals are to the right or left side of row entries, the Outline symbols appear above the worksheet. It is possible to have outline symbols on both the top and left of the worksheet.

AutoOutline view with outline bars in place.

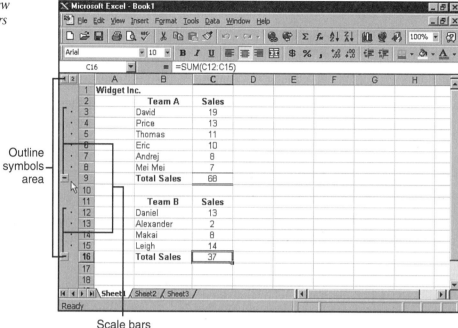

Outline symbols area

Scale bars

The scale bars give you an indication of what will be hidden. In the figure, clicking the first minus-sign icon hides rows 3 through 8, and changes the minus sign to a plus. Click the plus sign, the minus sign, and the number buttons in the outline symbols area to display different views of the worksheet. When you click **1** or the + button in the outline symbols area, Excel displays only the number that you are interested in. The following figure shows the spreadsheet after we clicked the + button to see Total Sales.

To turn off the AutoOutline feature, open the **Data** menu, select **Group and Outline**, and click **Clear Outline**. It's over. Bag the coffee and get some sleep.

AutoSum

At last: an automatic feature that's really automatic! AutoSum couldn't be easier. Select a cell or a block of cells, and the sum of the numbers in that block appears in the AutoSum area on the right side of the Status bar. When you select a different block of cells, AutoSum... guess what?... figures the new sum.

AutoSum does several other tricks, as well. Right-click the AutoSum block, and a shortcut menu appears. You can select **Count** to have AutoSum automatically count the number of filled cells in any given selection. None hides the entire display. Average gives the numerical average of the numbers in a block of cells. Count tells you how many cells you've highlighted. Count Nums counts the cells in a highlighted block that contain numbers only (no text). Max and Min show the maximum and minimum values in a range.

To copy the results of the AutoSum into your worksheet, simply click the **AutoSum** button on the Standard toolbar or press **Alt+=**.

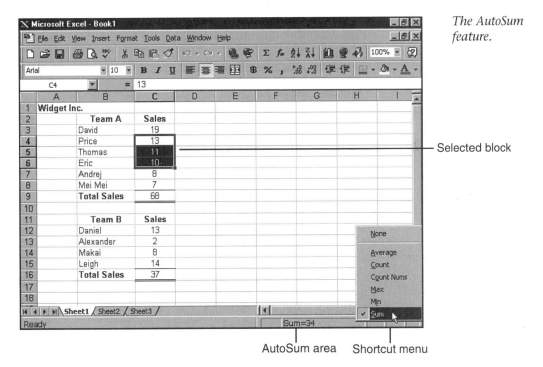

The AutoSum feature.

Selected block

AutoSum area   Shortcut menu

Automate with Macros

The only thing worse than that feeling of *déjà vu* that you get when you perform a task is that feeling of *déjà vu* that you get all over again when you repeat that same time-consuming task time after time. Or did we already say that?

Anyway, macros can fix all that. A macro lets you record a boring, repetitive multiple-keystroke process and reduce it to a single keystroke or menu command. Any task that contains a finger-numbing series of keystrokes or that you do more than five or six times a day is a good candidate for turning into a macro. But because what is mindless repetition to one person is a great Van Damme action flick to another, we won't try to anticipate what combinations of operations make worthwhile macros. We'll just point the way and silently step aside.

Macronucleus

For this lesson in macro creation, start out by clicking a worksheet cell that contains text. Open the **Tools** menu and select **Macro**. In the macro submenu that appears, select **Record New Macro**, and the Record Macro dialog box appears.

The Record Macro dialog box.

From here you can choose a name for your macro and include a description if you want to. The first character of your macro name must be a letter but after that you're fairly free to be as creative as you'd like. You cannot, however, have any spaces in your macro name, and the name cannot contain any tasteless references to the president of the United States.

You might also want to assign a "shortcut" key to run your macro. Place a letter—any letter but not a number or special character—in the Shortcut key box. In our example, we used the lowercase "e." When the time comes to run your macro—and that time is near—you'll type **Ctrl+*the letter*** to make it work. The key combination to run this demo macro would be **Ctrl+e**. If you decided on an uppercase letter, the key combination would become **Ctrl+Shift+*letter***.

Choosing a Shortcut

The shortcut key you choose for your macro will override any Excel shortcut keys while the workbook containing the macro is open.

Creating a shortcut key to run a macro is a neat trick but it's not the law. There's more than one way to get a good macro started, including rerunning the Macro command from the Excel menu.

The Store macro in box offers other options. To make the macro available whenever you use Excel, click the arrow button and choose **Personal Macro Workbook**. To limit use of the macro to the current workbook select **This Workbook**. A third option, Next Workbook will open a new workbook and place the macro there. We'll discuss running the macro in this manner after going through the necessary steps to create one.

Assuming the macro has been given a satisfactory name, assigned a shortcut key, and placed in the workbook of your choice, we can continue. Work through the following steps to create a sample macro that changes the appearance of a selected cell:

1. Click **OK**, and the screen view returns to the normal worksheet, except that a small box featuring two icons appears.

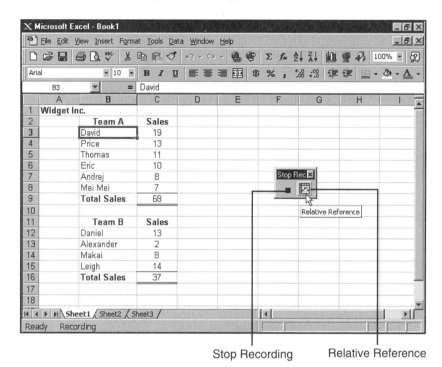

The Stop Record Box.

Stop Recording   Relative Reference

2. To have your macros function in *any* area of the worksheet, click the **Relative Reference** icon. In the default startup mode, macros are recorded with absolute cell references. This means that they will function only in the cells in which you build them. With a relative reference, the macro will function from any cell. Relative reference recording will remain active until you click the **Relative Reference** icon again.

3. Click any worksheet cell containing text.

4. Click the bold icon on the Formatting toolbar.

5. Click the macro **Stop Record** button.

Now go back to the worksheet and try running your macro. Go to any other text cell on your page.

To run via the shortcut key method—we chose **Ctrl+e**—press **Ctrl+***letter*. The text in the cell changes to bold.

97

To run without a shortcut key, choose **Tools** from the main menu. Choose **Macro**. From the macro submenu, choose **Macros**. The Macro dialog box will appear. Select the macro to run and click the **Run** button. The text in the cell changes to bold.

You have successfully completed your first macro. Give yourself a pat on the back (or automate the process by running backwards into a wall).

Other Automatic Excel Functions

Excel has other automatic functions as well, all of which are covered in more detail in other chapters of this book. For more information on one of these features, auto-flip to the following chapters.

AutoComplete. This feature tries to complete words for you as you type. Bothersome, don't you think? The suggestions come from a list of words already entered in the same column. See Chapter 2 for an explanation.

AutoCorrect. This function corrects your errors as you type. (Were these features developed by ex-wives?) Fortunately, you can choose the list of errors you want AutoCorrect to correct. Chapter 6, "The Editing Test: Change the Contents of Your Spreadsheet," explains how.

AutoFormat. Got a range? Change it to a table with AutoFormat. Just select the range, open the **Format** menu, and choose **AutoFormat**. Turn to Chapter 9, "Home on the Range," for more explanation.

AutoShapes. USING ALL CAPS IS ONE WAY OF DRAWING ATTENTION TO YOUR DOCUMENT. Another is the more civilized use of bold graphics. Run the gamut from dignified and tasteful to garish and ostentatious by adding ready-made shapes—lines, stars, arrows, or hearts—to your Excel worksheet. Follow our slings and arrows to Chapter 16, "Graphics Workshop," for more details about this shapely delight.

AutoTemplate. When you begin building worksheets so that novice users can enter data, you need AutoTemplates. You'll find a complete description in Chapter 19, "List Management."

The Least You Need to Know

In this chapter, you learned about Excel's great automatic features. These you must learn by rote:

➤ Use AutoFilter to quickly view the most, the least, or the best matches. AutoFilter works only in columns, and each column must have a label.

➤ AutoOutline telescopes worksheets into a more manageable view. Each section you want to outline must be formatted identically, with subtotals in the same place in each section.

➤ AutoSum subtotals a block of numbers and displays the sum automatically in its own onscreen box. You can also use AutoSum to display averages or to count the items in a group.

➤ Macros simplify repetitive tasks. Start a macro, record your keystrokes, and then play them back when you need to repeat that task.

➤ Excel contains loads of other automatic features, all of which are detailed in related chapters.

Chapter 9

Home on
the Range

In This Chapter

➤ Reference rap

➤ Keep your options open

➤ References

➤ Ranger Rick

➤ Instant Intersection Intelligence

In 1972, American Battleship champion Bobby Fissure defeated Soviet challenger Boris Spatzy in a converted airplane hangar in an inhospitable area of Iceland. Playing before a full house (they had managed to requisition the only working space heater within 100 miles), Fissure brilliantly attacked Spatzy's formations, picking him apart one cell at a time. After hours of icy anguish, the multitudes were finally awakened by the last anguished cry of "You sank my battleship." A thunderous roar filled the arena as a hundred thousand or so Icelanders simultaneously cheered the new champion and plotted ways to relieve him of his space heater.

Imagine how history would have changed if Boris Spatzy had known about ranges. Instead of a lame attack on a single cell, like A3, he could have designated an entire range:

"Boris Number 1"

"What's that?"

"All the cells from A1 to Z99."

"You sank all my battleships!"

But, alas! The poor fellow didn't know the first thing about the power of designating ranges. By the end of this chapter, you will. But first, you need to know some components of ranges.

Excellent References

Every cell on your spreadsheet has a life and an address. No, you can't send them email… not yet, anyway. But you can refer to each cell by its address, and that comes in handy when you need to move around, find your place on the worksheet, or write a formula.

This chapter is a brief introduction to references and ranges, including information you need to know before you start writing formulas in the next chapter. While we're at it, we also examine the all-important Options dialog box.

You learned in earlier chapters that each worksheet cell has a unique address that consists of its column letter and row number. The cell in the third row of the third column is—quite naturally—C3. Excel permits as many as 16,384 rows per worksheet, numbered 1 through 16,384 (what did you expect?).

You're allowed a slightly smaller number of columns: 256. But column heads don't get numbers; they get letters, and that's a bit more problematic. Once you've gone past the 26th letter, Excel begins labeling columns AA, AB, and so on, right up to the 256th column.

If Excel's column-lettering system is too cumbersome, you can set up your spreadsheet to number the columns instead. In that case, cell B3 becomes R3C2 (Row 3, Column 2), and you've got some really ugly references. But for a few people, particularly those who are transferring from other spreadsheet packages, this alternative system is easier to understand.

To initiate the alternative reference format, pull down the **Tools** menu and choose **Options**. In the Options dialog box, click the **General** tab. The first option you see there is for R1C1 Reference Style. The default style is A1. If you want to change it, click the **R1C1** option check box.

In this text, we stick with the A1 reference style.

Other Options Dialog Box Options

While we have this dialog box open, this is probably a good time to explain the other features in the Options dialog box. (This particular dialog box is sort of the Miscellaneous box, and doesn't fit neatly into any particular Excel category. Sort of like a Woody Allen movie.) So we'll continue where we left off, with the General tab.

General Tab

Here's where you change all the obscure options. To wit:

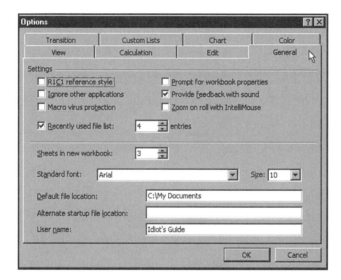

The General tab of the Options dialog box.

➤ In the Settings area, check the **Ignore Other Applications** box to have Microsoft Excel ignore all requests from other applications. Not recommended. It could cause problems if you have embedded objects in your worksheet.

➤ To enable Macro Virus Protection box, click its box. This feature is not as awe-inspiring as you might expect. It neither protects or finds viruses. It does warn you that the worksheet you're about to open contains macros. Macros created by evil people, or by dummies, may contain viruses.

➤ The prompt for Workbook Properties option controls whether Excel displays the Properties dialog box when you save your worksheet. In the Properties dialog box, you can enter identifying information about your worksheet. It's explained in Chapter 12, "Keep It Clean, Keep It Accurate, Keep It Safe."

➤ If you're one of the godspoken who have been blessed with an IntelliMouse, click the Zoom on Roll with IntelliMouse box to zoom in a manner that no man has ever zoomed before.

➤ Check the **Recently Used File List** box to have Excel display as many as the last nine files you had open in the File menu. This makes it easy to reopen any of the last few files you were using.

➤ At the bottom of the Options dialog box are several data entry areas. There you define the number of worksheets in your workbook, the standard typeface (font) and type size you want to use, the default and alternate locations of your files (which you enter in the format Drive letter:\Folder\Subfolder), and your username.

Edit Tab

These features enable you to edit your worksheets. For the most part, your best bet is to turn them all on.

The Edit tab.

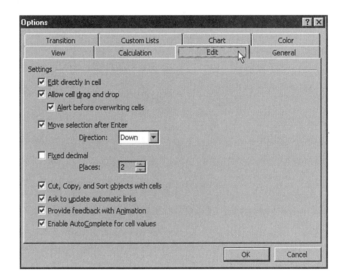

You use the Edit tab settings to control whether you can edit (make changes) directly in a cell or drag-and-drop the contents of your cell with your mouse when you copy or move. You can tell Excel which direction you want to move when you press the **Enter** key after entering information in a cell.

➤ Use the Fixed Decimal setting to set the number of decimal places in your numbers (usually two). If you select Fixed Decimal and enter the digits 1 2 3 into a cell, for example, Excel records 1.23. When this feature is selected, you can override it by manually entering the decimal.

➤ This tab also contains an option for copying objects (pictures, notes, maps, and so on) along with the contents of a cell. Another fun Excel trick you can implement is to animate your insertions and deletions (for example, slow them down so you can watch the progress). This is also the section where you choose to use the

AutoComplete feature to automatically fill in cell values. (See Chapter 2, "Getting Started," for more about AutoComplete.)

Calculation Tab

Generally, when you enter a formula, Excel calculates the result immediately. If you work in very large spreadsheets, you might find yourself spending a lot of time waiting for Excel to calculate. Use the Manual option (instead of the default Automatic option) to turn off the automatic calculations so you can control when Excel calculates the formulas.

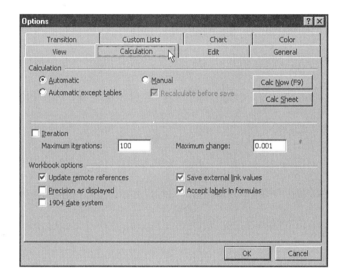

The Calculation tab.

Normally you want Excel to calculate all its formulas just one time. Very rarely, though, you might want it to calculate all its formulas several times. Iterations repeat a calculation a designated number of times (in case you want to calculate 1/3 of 1/3 of 1/3, and so on for 10 repetitions, for example). You might also use this feature if you want to see a calculation whose results depend on the results of another calculation.

➤ The Workbook options are obscure, and you probably want to check only **Update Remote References**, **Accept Label Names**, and **Save External Link Values** in this section. Update Remote References lets you *link* (connect) a cell on your worksheet to a cell on some other worksheet. Label names give you more flexibility in writing formulas (see Chapter 10, "The Winning Formula") and Save External Link Values remembers the value of links made to data in programs other than Excel (see Chapter 20, "Retrieving and Consolidating Data").

➤ The Precision as Displayed option changes Excel so that it calculates based only on the figures you see on the worksheet. If a number has been rounded for display

105

purposes, Excel normally calculates based on the real number instead of the rounded number that appears; this feature changes that. The 1904 Date System is almost never used. It calculates all Excel dates with serial numbers that begin in the year 1904, instead of in 1900 (the default).

Transition Tab

Here's help for users who are moving in from other spreadsheets. If you're still playing with Lotus 1-2-3 or Quattro Pro, raise your hand.

The Transition tab.

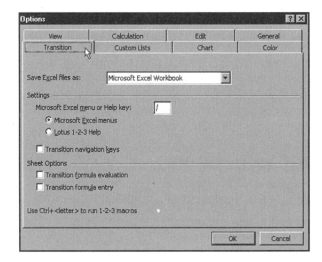

➤ In the Saves Excel Files As: dialog box, select the format you want your files saved in. Microsoft Excel Workbook is a popular choice. This is your default selection. For those special occasions when you might want to save a single workbook in another format, use the **Save As** selection from the File menu.

➤ The infamous slash (/) key should be familiar to all 1-2-3 users. In the Settings area, choose the Help files and menus you want to use and turn on the Transition Navigation Keys if you want the home key to move you back to cell A1. If you want to maintain your old formula habits, check the appropriate options in the Sheet Options area.

Those Other Tabs

The options on the View tab enable you to decide how cluttered your worksheet will be. The default leaves most, but not all, items visible. In the Objects area, you'll probably want to choose **Show All**, which makes all your pictures and maps and graphics visible as you work. Turn the other Show and Window Options features off or on individually.

In the Comments area, clicking on **Comments & Indicator** will display any cell comments (see Chapter 12) plus the indicator—a small red triangle in the upper-right corner of the cell—to be displayed. We recommend clicking the **Comment Indicator Only** option. We're neat freaks. This option will place the indicator-triangle in the cell but the comment won't be displayed unless you point to the cell.

The Color tab contains options you can use to change the colors for your worksheet, charts, and lines. The Chart tab options are available only when you have a chart displayed. (See Chapter 17, "Top of the Charts," for an explanation of these features.) And the options on the Custom Lists tab deal with the AutoFill feature, which was explained in Chapter 5, "Shake, Copy, and Move: Filling Blocks of Cells."

More on References

We return now to our discussion of references. References can be categorized in a couple of different ways: as absolute or relative, and as internal, external, or remote.

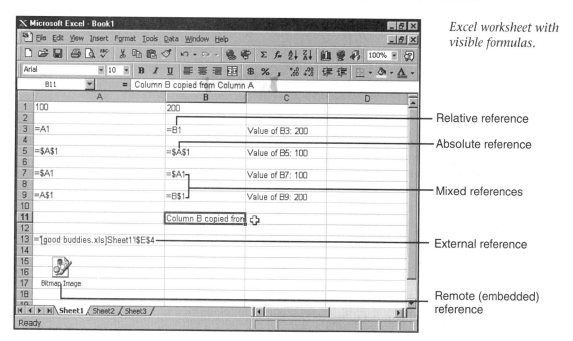

Excel worksheet with visible formulas.

Absolute Versus Relative

In the next chapter, you'll see that instead of calculating formulas like 2 + 2, it's more useful to calculate cell A7 + cell A8. This way of calculating lets you change the contents of cells A7 and A8, without having to rewrite the formula. When we talk about numbers like 2 and 3, we're using *values*. When we talk about cells A7 and A8, we're using *references*.

When you create an entire column of formulas and use Excel's Copy or AutoFill features to fill them in automatically, you run into some interesting problems. What if, for example, your original formula contains a reference to cell A7, and you copy that formula down a row? Should the copied formula continue to refer to cell A7, or should it now refer to a new cell one row below cell A7?

Most references are *relative*, which means that they refer to a relative location (such as "the three cells immediately above this cell"). For example, when you copy a reference to cell A1 to a location one column to the right, the reference changes to B1, which reflects the amount of the relative change. The default copy status is Relative.

Absolute references, on the other hand, always refer to the same cell (such as cell C3) no matter where they are copied to. You make a reference absolute by including dollar signs ($) in the reference, like this: C3. (When you refer to a cell by clicking it, instead of actually typing it in, you can make it absolute by pressing F4 before you enter the next keystroke.)

Mixed references combine absolute and relative (such as $C4 or C$4). You use mixed references when you want a group of calculations to refer to multiple rows in the same column or multiple columns in the same row, but not both.

Internal Versus External Versus Remote

There are some other twists to the story of cell references. It's easy to see where a cell reference like A3 comes from. Sometimes, though, you want to refer to information that's not found on your current worksheet.

Most references are *internal*, that is, they refer to other cells on the same worksheet. To include an internal reference in a formula (a mathematical equation), you can type in the cell reference manually, or you can simply click the cell you want to reference. A simple formula with an internal reference might look like this:

    =A1+6

The equal sign starts the formula, A1 is a relative reference to cell A1, the + is an operator, and the 6 is the next factor (element) in the formula. Chapter 10 explains formula writing in more detail, so all you need to learn now is that A1, in this example, is the moral equivalent of a number, and that worksheet formulas use the Reverse Polish notation of old Hewlett-Packard calculators, where every entry must be preceded by an operator.

An *external* reference refers to cells in another worksheet or even an entirely different workbook. To use an external reference to another workbook in a formula, open both workbooks. (This step is not necessary if your external reference is only to another worksheet in your same workbook.) Start entering the formula, and when you're ready to add the external reference, select the other worksheet from the Window menu or use the worksheet tabs at the bottom of your screen to open it. Click the cell you want to reference. Then continue the formula with the next operator and switch back to the original worksheet when necessary. A formula with an external reference might look like this:

='[budget.xls]Sheet1'!E5+6

The equal sign starts the formula. The apostrophes signify the location of the worksheet. The portion in square brackets is the name of the second workbook, Sheet1 is the name of the worksheet, and the exclamation point (!) separates the worksheet name from the cell reference. The E5 is an absolute reference to cell E5, the + is an operator, and the 6 is the next factor in the formula.

Check This Out...

Go Outside!

Your formulas can include multiple references. And Excel doesn't even mind if you mix and match internal, external, remote, relative, absolute, and mixed references.

You're limited only by the total number of characters in your formula and the amount of memory in your computer. Remember, though, that exceedingly complex references are difficult to trace and increase the risk of a software crash.

The *remote* reference is highly advanced and has limited use. A remote reference imports data from another application altogether. A formula containing a remote reference might look like this:

=RISKCALC|SMITH.INS!1995+6

The equal sign starts the formula. RISKCALC is the name of an application that supports Object Linking and Embedding (OLE). The pipe character (|) pipes in the document name (SMITH.INS), and the exclamation point separates the document reference from the cell reference (1995). The + is an operator, and the 6 is the next factor in the formula.

Linking and embedding are complicated ways of copying information from other applications. A generally easier (and safer) alternative is to do what you need to do in the other application, and then simply copy and paste the results into your Excel worksheet.

Range Roving

A *range* is a specific group of cells. Ranges most often comprise a group of cells in the same column or row, or in a rectangular block encompassing multiple rows or columns. It is possible, however, to have a range of noncontiguous cells (cells that are not adjacent to one another).

The normal syntax for a range is A1:A10, which means the range includes all the cells in the first 10 rows of column A. Like cell references, range references can be relative, absolute, or mixed. Fortunately, you can assign an English-language name to a range so you don't have to figure out later what you meant when you said BA64:GC72. You might, for example, name a range Oct Expenses, 90 Thru 95 Taxes, Taco Bell, or Yamaha.

You use ranges in a number of ways:

In formulas. If you want to add up a column of numbers, use a range so you don't have to enter =A1+A2+A3+A4+A5... .

To move around. When worksheets and workbooks start getting huge, it helps to give different areas different names. Excel's range-naming command enables you to quickly go to a specific area of your worksheet.

In macros. Simplify macro writing by using range names instead of selecting ranges on-the-fly. See Chapter 8, "AutoPilot: Excel's Automatic Features," to learn how to use Excel macros.

Creating a Range

Here's the process for creating and naming a simple range:

1. Select the range by highlighting a block of cells (as described in Chapter 7, "Excel on the Net"). If you intend to use the range in formulas and calculations, make sure the range you select contains only numeric values, and no labels. (Labels don't affect most of your calculations, but they do affect your spreadsheet housekeeping.)

2. Click in the **Name Box** at the left end of the Formula bar, and type the name of the new range. The name can contain no spaces. Excel adds the new name to the Reference List; you can recall it by clicking the **Name Box** down arrow and choosing the name from the list.

   Alternatively, you can select the range, open the **Insert** menu, and choose **Name and Define**. In the Define Name dialog box, type the new range name, click **Add**, and click **OK**.

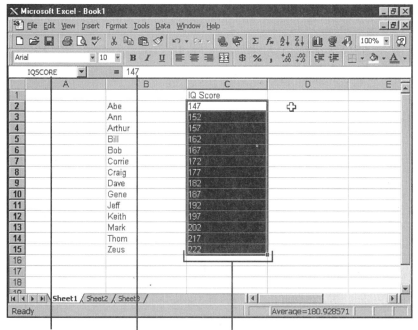

Naming an Excel range.

Name box   New range name   Selected range

Selecting Nonadjacent Cells

You can create a range that contains not only multiple cells, but also multiple blocks of cells. To do so, select the first block (click the corner cell and drag to the cell at the opposite corner), press and hold down the **Ctrl** key, and select the next block. You can add as many blocks as you want using this method. Then name the new range, as described earlier in this chapter.

Keep Your Head Up

If you want to use existing labels that are at the top of a column or the end of a row to name a range, you don't even have to type in the name. Just select the cells that contain the headings, open the **Insert** menu, choose **Name**, and select **Create**. The Create Names dialog box appears, asking where you want the names to come from. Each column or row label becomes a separate range.

Look, Ma! No Hands! The AutoFormat Function

Never downplay the importance of style when making any kind of presentation. (After all, what would Robin Hood have been but another thief in the forest if he hadn't slipped on those kelly green pantyhose?) When you've got nice, neat ranges, rows, and columns, it's time to add some… Pizzazz!

There's no Pizzazz command exactly, but AutoFormat comes pretty close. AutoFormat can invigorate your ranges by adding color and depth. It can help you get rid of that tired old—uh—worksheet look.

The Look That Says You

Before you start AutoFormat, you must select the range of cells you want to dress up. Then open the **Format** menu and select **AutoFormat**. The AutoFormat dialog box appears.

The AutoFormat dialog box with options selected.

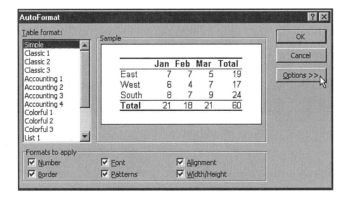

Use the scroll bar in the Table Format list box to select a format. In the Sample area, Excel displays a sample of what you can expect to see. Click the **Options** button to open the Formats to Apply section of the dialog box. This section contains options you can use to customize the look of your display. Again, you can view the effects of each option in the Sample area, so experiment a little. Click **OK** when you've settled on a look that you like.

Back to the Past

To clear the effects of AutoFormat, go through the same steps again: Select a range of cells, open the **Format** menu, and click **AutoFormat**. In the AutoFormat dialog box, select **None** from the Table Format list and click **OK**. The cells revert to their dull, drab, uninspired, unformatted selves. To undo AutoFormatting, use the **Undo** command from the Edit menu.

The Least You Need to Know

➤ References describe the location of a cell or a group of cells.

➤ References take the form A1, where A is the column and 1 is the row number.

➤ Relative references change when they're copied. Absolute references, which contain a dollar sign in their address, don't change.

➤ The Options dialog box (select **Tools**, **Options**) is the place for modifying the way Excel operates. If you don't know where else to go to make a change, try the Options dialog box.

➤ A range can be a block of cells or multiple blocks of cells. If you want to remember later what data the range contains, you can name the range.

➤ When it's time to pretty up a range of cells, choose **AutoFormat** from the Format menu.

Chapter 10

The Winning Formula

In This Chapter

➤ Form-ula feed

➤ Work it out

➤ Stop problems dead

➤ Juggling a jumble of formula junk

Oktoberfest in Munich is about drinking, eating, drinking, merrymaking...and drinking. The most significant part of Oktoberfest is, of course, the beer. And the second-most-significant part would have to be what goes in the beer.

Brewers compete side-by-side for the accolades of Germans and beer-guzzling tourists. Staying within the strict guidelines of German brewing law, they still find room for individuality. Brewing beer is an art, they say, and brewers guard their formulas with care.

Fortunately, you don't have to travel to Munich to brew up a few formulas of your own. Get the spreadsheet formula right, and you'll find yourself with all the right numbers in all the right places—and with the aftertaste of success. Choose the wrong formulas, and you'll face an illogical maze of values—a messy brew that will leave you in a stupor, unable to tell what's happening, and suffering a sure-fire spreadsheet hangover.

Brewing instructions follow.

Formula for Success

Formulas. They're the heart and soul of spreadsheets; without them, you might as well use a pocket calculator, a tablet of paper, and a pencil with a good eraser. Formulas give Excel's worksheets the power to compare, select, calculate, iterate, manipulate, and eliminate the data you put into its grimy little hands.

What Is a Formula?

A *formula* is a mathematical computation involving multiple factors: values, references, names, operators, and functions. To qualify as a formula, the equation has to return new information from the data you enter. In Excel, all formulas begin with an equal sign (=).

Some Definitions

Before we get too far into this discussion, let's establish a few definitions. We'll do these alphabetically, shall we?

Formula jargon

Term	Definition
Address	The location of a cell or a group of cells. Takes the form B3, where B is the second column, and 3 is the third row. You can also call it a reference.
Argument	The part of the equation that's not an operator. How's that for a bum definition? Okay, it includes constants, functions, names, cell references, and values.
Constant	A number or text that you type directly into the formula (as opposed to something like a cell reference, which tells Excel where to find its own numbers or text).
Equation	You learned this in the third grade, right? Something equals something else. In Excel, however, you don't know what it equals until you hit the Enter key. You might also call this a formula.
Factor	An element of a formula; can be a value, reference, name, operator, or function. Yeah, you're right: that's the same thing as an argument.
Formula	A mathematical computation involving multiple factors and resulting in a new value. Pretty much the same thing as an equation.
Function	A built-in formula. (See Chapter 11, "Fully Functional.")

Term	Definition
Label	Text—not numbers. Okay, maybe numbers and text together. For our purposes, labels are the words at the top of a column or the left end of a row that describe the contents of the column or row.
Name	The English-language name that identifies a particular range. (French and Spanish names work, too. But no Chinese names unless you know how to Romanize them, like this: Hau Bu Hau?)
Operator	The mathematical symbols that tell Excel how to calculate a formula. The operators include Add (+), Subtract (-), Divide (/), Multiply (*), Percents (%), Exponents (^), and Equivalencies (equal [=], not equal [<>], greater than [>], and less than [<]).
Range	A cell or a block of cells identified by a name or an address. (See Chapter 9, "Home on the Range," for more information on ranges.)
Reference	The name or address of a cell or range. (See Chapter 9 for more information on references.)
Result	The answer you get after Excel calculates your formula.
Syntax	The rules about where to put the parentheses, commas, asterisks, and operators within a formula.
Value	Numbers—not text.

Working Through Formulas

Now that you can talk the talk, let's walk through a simple formula. In this example, we'll add up a column of numbers.

On a blank worksheet, enter the numbers 1, 2, and 3 in the first three rows of column A. Draw a line through cell A4 to indicate the end of the data.

Check This Out...

The Bottom Line

If you have a column of numbers you need to total, and you want to draw a line in the cell above the total, select the cell and type a backslash and a hyphen (\ -). Excel fills the cell with dashes, creating an underline that expands and contracts automatically when you change the width of the column.

In the same way, you can use any character to fill a given cell. If you want a line of asterisks, for example, just type *.

Your formula can contain numbers or references (addresses that tell the formula where to find the numbers). For our sample formula, we want to add the numbers 1, 2, and 3 (the data in column A). Instead of typing the formula =1+2+3, we'll tell Excel to go find those numbers itself.

Adding cell references to a formula.

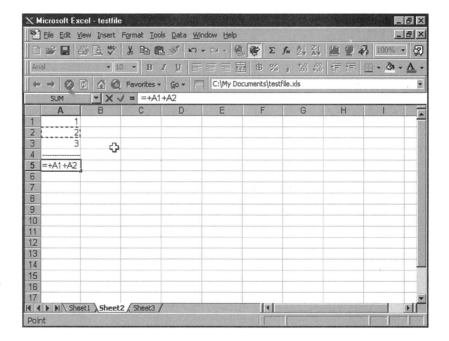

Go to cell A5 to begin writing your formula. Enter an equal sign (=) or a plus sign (+) to let Excel know you're starting the formula. To tell Excel what three numbers you want to add, move to cell A1. (A moving line around the current cell indicates where you are.) Press + to enter the reference. Your formula now reads =A1+. Move up to cell A2 and press + again, and then move back up to cell A3. This is the last entry in your formula, but don't enter anything else yet. Instead, read on for more useful information.

The Formula Bar

Before we continue, take a look up north at the Formula bar (the line above the column headers). There you see a duplicate of the formula you're entering in your active cell. Later, you can edit your formula in the Formula bar by adding to the formula or deleting parts of it. Characters you type will be inserted at the location of the blinking cursor in either the Formula bar or the active cell. Use the I-beam-shaped mouse pointer to click the spot in the Formula bar where you want the cursor to appear. Once you have a cursor, you can press **Backspace** to remove the character to the left of the cursor or **Delete** to remove the character to the right.

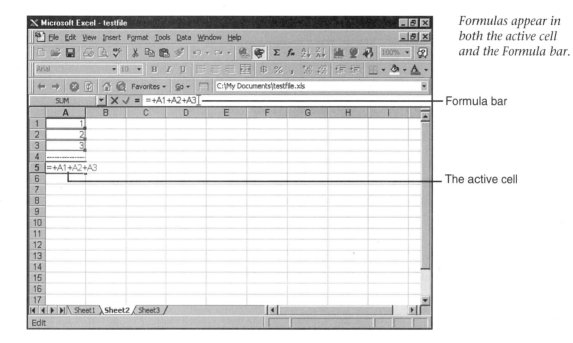

Formulas appear in both the active cell and the Formula bar.

Formula bar

The active cell

Let's complete the formula now. Instead of pressing + again (which will confuse Excel to death), press the **Enter** key to tell Excel you've finished. Your formula disappears, and in its place you find your result: 6. You can click in cell A5 at any time, and the formula reappears in the Formula bar, while the result remains unchanged.

Now What?

Now that you've entered your first formula, it's time to see the power of Excel. If no formula did more than this sample did, well... you'd be better off doing your math in your head. But, suppose that instead of the numbers 1, 2, and 3, you wanted to figure the total of all your annual income, the total of all your annual expenses, and the rate of tax on the difference.

In that case, you'd find yourself writing a formula that looked more like =(A1 - A2)*A3. Or, if you named your cells, your formula would be =(INCOME - EXPENSES)*TAXRATE. Then you could subtract your TAXDUE from your GROSS to find your NET, and suddenly, things get much more interesting.

Imposing a Syntax

Pity poor Mr. Hartman. While teaching high school algebra he had to do daily battle with the plaintive whining of "Why do I need to learn this stuff? What good is it in real life?"

Mr. Hartman, if you're reading this, you can relax now. All the rules of precedence and order and logic finally make sense. Too bad you couldn't demonstrate a spreadsheet in 1977!

Remember these basic principles when you enter formulas:

➤ *Formulas have order.* In Excel, formulas begin with an equal sign (=). If you cannot afford an equal sign, one will be appointed for you when you enter a plus sign (+) at the beginning of your formula.

➤ *Operators have order.* Multiplication (*) and division (/) take precedence over addition (+) and subtraction (-). In addition to those four basic operators, there are other operators that control the order in which a calculation is performed. We've included a handy table in this section to remind you of the order of operations. The table shows you the order of operators, listed in order of precedence. (For example, arguments in parentheses are calculated before negative arguments.)

➤ *Calculations are performed logically.* When operators are equal, Excel calculates left to right.

➤ *Ranges can operate like single cells.* In Excel, the address A1 is as valid as the number 6, which is as valid as the range name "DOGFOOD."

Priority order of operators

Operator	Symbol
Parenthetical calculations	( )
Negative numbers	-
Percentages	%
Exponents	^
Multiplication and division	*, /
Addition and subtraction	+, -
Equivalencies	=, <>, >, <, >=, <=

Following the priority order of operators, consider these formulas and their results.

Formula	Returns
= - 2+4*3	10
= - (2+4*3)	- 14
= - (2+4)*3	- 18
=(- 2+4)*3	6

=1*(- 2+4*3)	10
=(- 2+4*3	Error

Note that, unlike what you learned in your high school algebra class, you cannot use a number followed immediately by parentheses as a substitute for the multiplication symbol. Every argument in an Excel formula requires an operator.

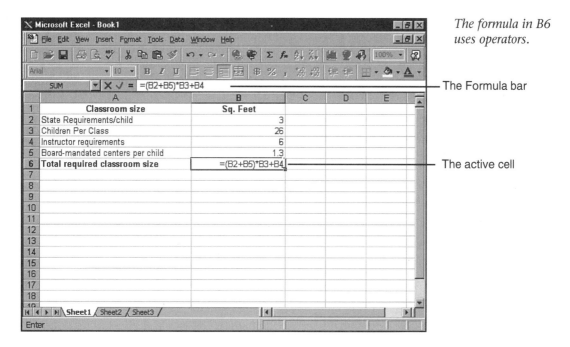

The formula in B6 uses operators.

The Formula bar

The active cell

Changing the Contents

Even after you create a formula, you have the freedom to change the referenced cells at will. Excel cheerfully accommodates your fickleness and recalculates the formula with every change. So you can edit to your heart's content (Chapter 6, "The Editing Test: Change the Contents of Your Spreadsheet," explains how) and witness the true power of spreadsheets as Excel changes factors and updates results. And you never again have to retype the formula.

A Cell by Any Other Name

Okay, you're probably wondering what the excitement over Excel is all about. So what if Excel gives you the ability to add 1+2 and A1+A2? You could probably do that on your own. Right? But it gets better than that. If you name your cells and ranges, you can also add DOG+CAT and RUSH+HILLARY. (Try that without Excel!)

The simplest way to use the naming power of Excel is to first input your data into the spreadsheet. In our last example, we tried to determine the number of square feet required for a school building project. We listed several factors along with the corresponding numbers.

Now we'll illustrate the same procedure using range names. Our ranges here are small—only a single cell, but as you learned when you named ranges in Chapter 9, a range can be any size.

In the formula shown in the following figure, we used the rather long labels in column A to name each corresponding cell in column B. To name each range, we went to the Insert menu and used the Name, Create command. We could have assigned short names (State, Kids, Teacher, Centers) instead, but this way we didn't have to type anything in twice. (Call us lazy.)

A formula using named cell or ranges.

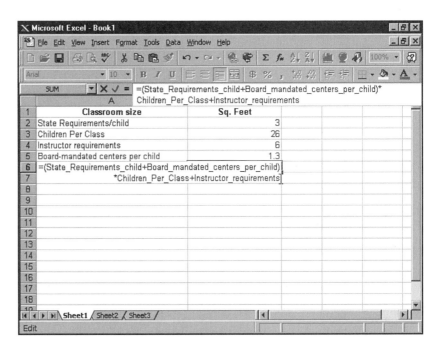

Later, as we created the formula, the new names appeared in the formula in place of the original cell addresses. Naming ranges and cells before you enter them into formulas makes it much easier to remember six years from now what you intended to do with that formula if you can see a descriptive name instead of a cell or range reference.

The Nesting Instinct

Remember the example formulas we used earlier to show the order of operators? Those formulas indicate the importance of parenthetical arguments. A formula is a routine, and parenthetical formulas within the larger formula are called subroutines. By "nesting" subroutines (such as 2+4) within a larger formula, you give Excel even more power.

The rule is that you can have subroutine within subroutine within subroutine, but you must be precisely accurate with your parentheses. If you misplace or neglect even one, your entire formula will be either incorrect or incomplete. Hope for the latter, because Excel displays a warning message when you don't have an equal number of opening and closing parentheses. If you've just put the parentheses in the wrong place, you get no warning, and you probably won't know.

You can nest subroutines up to seven layers deep. Here's an example of nesting:

=1+(2*(3+(4*(5+(6*(7+8))))))

Notice that each opening parenthesis has a corresponding closing parenthesis. This formula returns the result 767 by calculating from the interior parentheses first. Excel calculates the formula in this order: 7 plus 8, multiplied by 6, plus 5, times 4, plus 3, multiplied by 2, and add 1.

Preventing Formula Problems

Preventing formula problems may sound like an impossible task—and maybe it is—but that doesn't mean you have to give up the fight. Here are a few things to look for that might help you along. But don't fret if none of these solutions solve your problem; there are some great problem-solving tools up ahead in Chapter 12, "Keep It Clean, Keep It Accurate, Keep It Safe." However, the suggestions in the following sections could help keep those formula problems from ever appearing.

Circular References

A circular reference can be thought of as the spreadsheet rendition of the classic chicken-and-egg problem. A circular reference occurs when a formula refers to itself, either directly or indirectly.

Anytime you create a circular reference, Excel alerts you by displaying a warning message. And then it lets you continue on your merry way. Unless it was your intention to create a circular reference, you should rewrite your formula to break the circle.

A circular reference.

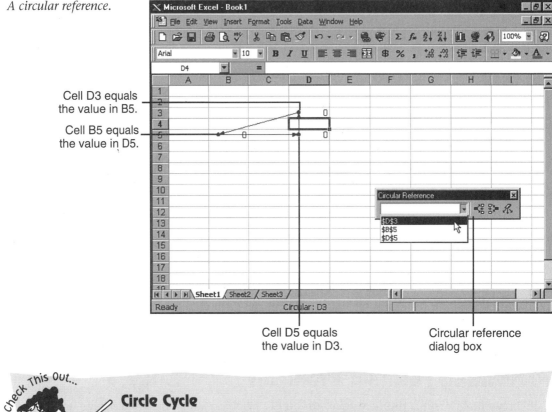

Cell D3 equals the value in B5.

Cell B5 equals the value in D5.

Cell D5 equals the value in D3.

Circular reference dialog box

Circle Cycle

Not all circular references are accidental. However, if you want to try using them, there are a few things you should know.

Excel cannot use normal calculations to solve formulas with circular references. Therefore, Excel stops recalculating the value of the cell after 100 iterations or anytime the value in the cell changes by less than .001. To change these defaults, open the **Tools** menu and select **Options**. In the Options dialog box, click the **Calculation** tab. Then select the **Iteration** check box and modify the default values as desired for Maximum Iterations and Maximum Change.

Unexpected Error Messages

Error messages are ever-looming possibilities. You can enter all the right values and punch all the right keys, and still there is a chance you'll end up with some unexpected results. No, we're not just talking about the negative numbers that sometimes appear when balancing a checkbook—although they are often unexpected. We're talking about results like #####, and #NUM!, and other cryptic error messages. The following table shows a few of those unexpected error messages, most of which are left over from a time when computers had 48KB of memory and when a portable PC was one you could fit it in the back of your truck.

Excel error messages

Error Message	Description
#####	This indicates that the results of your calculations are too large to fit in the cell. Although it might be annoying, it's not exactly an error. The correct answer is in the cell, Excel is just unable (or unwilling) to display it on your screen in the space allotted. All you have to do to correct this is make your column wide enough to accommodate the answer. (See Chapter 14, "Customizing the Spreadsheet," for instructions.)
#DIV/0!	You get #DIV/0! when you attempt to divide by 0. It couldn't be done when we were in school (we have the test scores to prove it), and it can't be done now. The only solution is to track down the formula in which you are attempting to divide by 0, and correct it. One last vital hint: Excel interprets empty cells as 0.
#N/A	This is not an error. In fact, it isn't even a message from Excel. This is just a note that you write to yourself when you don't have a real value to enter. If the value for a cell is not available, enter #N/A. If you leave the cell blank, Excel interprets its value as 0. If you enter text into the cell, you'll get another type of error (#VALUE!).
#NAME?	The #NAME? error value indicates that you have used a name Excel doesn't recognize. Maybe you entered a typo, or maybe you meant to enter it that way. Either way, you need to correct your formula to include only those references that Excel recognizes. And don't despair over a simple spelling error; you might still become vice-president one day.
#NUM!	#NUM! indicates that the cell contains a number too large to handle. Unlike ####, which represents a value that's just too large to display, #NUM! tells you that the value is beyond the bounds of what Excel can deal with. Try to re-create the formula to produce an acceptable lower representation of the number.

continues

Excel error messages **Continued**

Error Message	Description
#REF!	The #REF! error occurs when your formula references cells that are no longer valid (such as cells you have deleted, but which are still referred to in formulas). This error also appears in any cell that refers to a cell with the #REF! value. All references to cells that have been deleted must be changed to valid cells.
#VALUE!	This message appears if you try to use the wrong type of value in your formula (if you attempt to add text to numbers, for instance). Check the referenced cells and confirm that all cells are formatted as required by the function and formula.

The Least You Need to Know

In this chapter, you learned how to write and repair a formula. If you've mastered these points, you've mastered Excel:

➤ Formulas are the power spot for Excel. Learn how to use them, and you've learned the most important part of spreadsheeting.

➤ Formulas contain operators and arguments. The operators are the math symbols you learned in elementary school. The arguments are everything else. All Excel formulas begin with an equal sign (=).

➤ An argument can take the form of a number, a range name, a cell reference, or a function. Functions are explained in the next chapter.

➤ Careful planning prevents problems with your formulas.

Chapter 11

Fully Functional

In This Chapter

➤ Function fun

➤ The function whiz

➤ Key function keepsakes

We had two pizzas delivered today. After all, we couldn't take the time to grate the cheese and slice the mushrooms ourselves when we had so much work to do. That's why our kids love us: Toss 'em a pizza and a video, and let 'em party. We're on auto-function!

Functional Family

At last! The fun part of Excel: functions. Functions are built-in formulas that enable you to automatically total, convert, calculate, and manipulate all the values on your spreadsheet.

Excel has more than 300 functions at its beck and call. Among those are functions with particular appeal to engineers, statisticians, accountants, and mathematicians. But a large number of the functions are immediately useful to just about anybody who has to deal with numbers. We detail some of the most useful functions in this chapter. If you need to learn about any of the others, flip to Appendix B, "The Function Guide."

Before we demonstrate how functions work, let's examine some of the leading lights in the world of Excel functions.

Getting to Know You

Nobody, but nobody, can remember all of Excel's functions. To make it easier, though, Excel has grouped them into these categories:

Financial. This group contains more than 50 functions for tracking loans and investments. Use these functions to calculate principal and interest, yield, depreciation, time periods, and present and future values.

Date & Time. Excel can show the time and date, of course. That's no big deal. But Excel can also tell you the number of workdays between dates, the number of minutes that have elapsed since your birth, and the day of the week of any particular date (and that's just the beginning). Groovy, don't you think?

Math & Trigonometry. A grind?! No, this stuff might actually make math fun. Use these functions to calculate all kinds of logarithms; round off numbers; generate random numbers; and find square roots, tangents, sines, and cosines. Heck, you can even generate Roman numerals.

Statistical. These functions are really obscure: Weibull and Poisson distributions and even a Pearson product moment correlation. But wait! There's useful stuff here, too. You'll find all kinds of averages, trends, and rankings, as well as probabilities, bell curves, and standard deviations.

Lookup & Reference. These functions can look up information in a table for you and give you information about where a certain reference is located on the spreadsheet. Unfortunately, they can't find your car keys. That's a feature in the next upgrade of Excel.

Database & List Management. You can use a database from outside of Excel or a database from within Excel (any table you can assign a name to), and then use these functions to count the elements that meet your standards, add them up, or filter them.

Text. Most of the Text functions operate like the word-processing features of Excel. Use them to find or search, replace, and adjust the capitalization of your text. The other Text functions are useful mostly to software programmers.

Logical. Put on your Vulcan ears. You can use logical functions to create if/then statements with all the best Boolean statements: AND, OR, NOT, and TRUE/FALSE.

Information. Most of these functions check a cell to see whether or not it IS something (an even number, logical, blank, or whatever). These functions test the cell and tell you "Yep, the thing you're looking for is there," or "Nope, it's not."

Engineering. Check your pocket protector. A few of the 40-some engineering functions in Excel do simple things (such as finding the square root of a number and multiplying it by Pi), and there are a couple of comparison functions. All the rest of the functions are high-end engineering functions that normal people (those of us who hate polyester) can't even pronounce.

Form Follows Function

Now that you know the categories, it's time to examine a few of the most useful functions. The following table outlines the most common functions, their categories, usage, and syntax. (We explain syntax in the section "The Wages of Syntax," later in this chapter.) If you don't find the function you're looking for here, look in Appendix B, which lists all of the Excel functions. For even more help, press **F1** from 'most anywhere on the worksheet, and look for the Help topic "Worksheet Functions Listed by Category." You can also find help under each of the category heads, as listed previously.

Excel's most useful functions

Category	Function	Task	Syntax
Financial	DB	Finds depreciation of an asset for a specified period using fixed-declining balance method	DB(cost, salvage, life, period, month)
Financial	EFFECT	Finds effective annual interest rate	EFFECT(nominal_rate, npery)
Financial	PMT	Finds periodic payment for an annuity	PMT(rate, nper, pv, fv, type)
Financial	YIELD	Finds yield on a security that pays periodic interest	YIELD(settlement, maturity, rate, pr, redemption, frequency, basis)
Date & Time	NETWORKDAYS	Finds number of whole workdays between two dates	NETWORKDAYS (start_date, end_date, holidays)
Date & Time	TODAY	Finds serial number of today's date	TODAY( )

continues

Excel's most useful functions Continued

Category	Function	Task	Syntax
Math & Trig	INT	Rounds a number down to nearest integer	INT(number)
Math & Trig	PI	Finds value of Pi	PI( )
Math & Trig	RAND	Finds a random number between 0 and 1	RAND( )
Math & Trig	ROMAN	Changes an Arabic numeral to Roman, as text	ROMAN(number, form)
Math & Trig	ROUND	Rounds a number to a specified number of digits	ROUND(number, num_digits)
Math & Trig	SQRT	Finds a positive square root	SQRT(number)
Math & Trig	SUM	Adds up arguments	SUM(number1, number2, ...)
Statistics number2,	AVERAGE	Finds average of arguments	AVERAGE (number1, ...)
Statistics	PERCENTILE	Finds k-th percentile of values in a range	PERCENTILE(array, k)
Lookup & Reference	VLOOKUP	Searches first column of an array and moves across to find related data	VLOOKUP(lookup_value, table_array, col_index_num, range_lookup)
Database	DGET	Extracts from a database a single record that matches specified criteria	DGET(database, field, criteria)
Database	DSUM	Adds numbers in field column of records in database that match criteria	DSUM(database, field, criteria)

130

Category	Function	Task	Syntax
Text	REPLACE	Replaces characters in text	REPLACE(old_text, start_num, num_chars, new_text)
Text	TRIM	Removes all space from text except for single spaces between words	TRIM(text)
Logical	IF	Performs logical test	IF(logical_test, value_if_true, value_if_false)
Information	CELL	Finds information about formatting location, or contents of a cell	CELL(info_type, reference)
Engineering	GESTEP	Tests whether a number is greater than a threshold value	GESTEP(number, step)

Now we'll prepare to make a function work. First, the rules.

The Wages of Syntax

Every Excel function has certain syntax, or formatting, requirements. To use functions in formulas, you begin with the usual equal sign, add the name of the function, and add some parenthetical arguments.

The arguments are pieces of information that the function uses to perform its duty. For example, if you use the SUM function, your argument will be a list of numbers (or, more likely, a range) that you want the function to add together. Some arguments are required; others are optional. The syntax for the SUM function, for example, is

SUM(number1,number2,...)

This means that to enter a formula using SUM, you enter **SUM** (the name of the function), no space, and immediately follow that with the arguments, which are separated by commas. The argument number1 represents the first number to be added, and number2 is the second. You can continue adding numbers to the series if you want. In this particular function, the second and following "numbers" are optional. You can SUM a single number (we can't imagine why you'd want to do this, but you could) or multiple numbers, or you can insert a whole range in place of number1. Then you can do the same thing with number2, if you want to.

Let's return to the spreadsheet we started in the last chapter and use the SUM function to total that column of three numbers. This time, however, we'll work in a neighboring column, just to compare. Enter the numbers **1**, **2**, and **3** in the first three rows of column C. Draw an underline in cell C4. Then watch what happens when you use a function.

The SUM function at work.

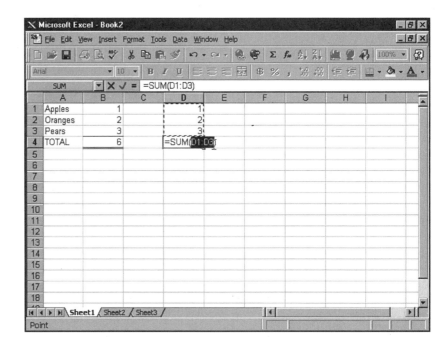

A Manual Tour

We'll continue with functions by walking you through the manual process. This is a little complicated, but once you've done it, you'll understand how functions work, and you'll be able to use the automatic functions more efficiently.

Follow these steps to manually insert a function (in this case, the SUM function):

1. Select cell C5 to make it the active cell. Enter an equal sign (=) to notify Excel that you intend to begin a formula.

2. Type **SUM**, immediately followed by an opening parenthesis. You've started the function. (The word "sum" can be in any combination of upper- and lowercase letters.)

3. Enter your argument. For our example, you need to enter the range of numbers from **C1** to **C3**. You can do this in either of two ways:

Simply enter **C1:C3** and be done with it.

Move your active cell indicator to cell C1 (a moving line surrounds cell C1 when you get there) to indicate that it's the beginning of your range. Enter a colon (or a period, if you want) to separate the first cell from the last cell. Then move your cursor to the end of the range, cell C3. This method seems more complicated at first blush, but if your ranges become immense, it comes in handy.

4. Finish the formula by typing a closing parenthesis. Your formula should look like this:

=SUM(C1:C3)

5. Press **Enter**, and Excel calculates the formula. Once again, the formula disappears, and the cell shows the result: 6. You've now manually entered a function.

The AutoSum Button

As a reward for your hard work, you can now learn the easiest way of all for finding the total of a column or a row: Excel's AutoSum toolbar button.

To automatically total a list of numbers, enter your data in the usual way. (In this case, enter the numbers 1, 2, and 3 in the first three rows of column E and draw an underline if you want.) Then move your active cell to the bottom of the numbers (cell E5, in this case).

It's time now to get automatic: click the **AutoSum** button, press **Enter**, and watch the result magically appear. The AutoSum button works at the end (not the beginning) of any line of numbers. If your active cell is in the middle of several numbers, the AutoSum button totals the column up to that point: above or to the left of the active cell.

Now that you've seen how easy automatic functions can be, let's move on to something called the Function Palette to see how you can perform other functions automatically.

The Paste Function

You could memorize all of Excel's many functions—we were going to, but chose a life instead—or you could invoke the all-powerful Paste Function icon. OK, maybe it's not all-powerful. In fact, it can't do anything you couldn't do for yourself. Don't sell Paste Function short, though, unless you're one of those people—like an angry spouse—who has never forgotten anything in their lives.

A Cheat Switch by Any Other Name

The simplest way to invoke the Paste Function is by clicking on the icon.

 Paste Function performs its magic on the active cell. To see how it works, select a blank cell now. Then click the **Paste Function** icon on the Standard toolbar.

A dialog box called Paste Function appears. Sure it's cheating. But your third grade teacher has retired now, so go ahead.

The Paste Function dialog box.

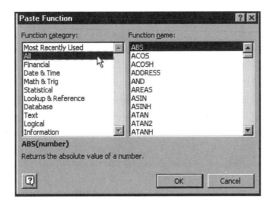

In the Function Category list, you select the function that best represents the nature of your task. If you are unsure which to choose, select All. If you've done this before, you could select the Most Recently Used option instead. Then select a function from the Function Name list.

Functional Help

As you scroll slowly through the list in the Function Name box, a brief description of each function appears in the area above the command buttons. If you need further information on using one of the functions, click the Help button in the Function Paste dialog box. Office Assistant will immediately rush to your aid and show you a detailed explanation of the function currently highlighted.

Once you select a function, Excel displays the correct syntax, or formatting, for the function directly below the Function Category list. Required arguments appear in bold type; optional arguments appear in regular type.

Having chosen the function, you need to start adding arguments. Click the **OK** button to move on to that step.

Pastiche by Paste

Continuing on, another dialog box appears, a box unique to each function.

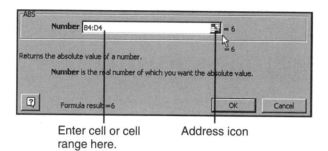

Enter cell or cell
range here.

Address icon

*The Function Paste
dialog box–Second
Step.*

This box contains one or more blank text boxes for your arguments. Enter the address of the argument. If you don't know the address, click the address icon to return to a full worksheet view. The dialog box is minimized and you can select whatever cells are appropriate for the function. To return to the dialog box click the return button at the far right of the pop-up address bar.

For now, enter a cell reference, a range name, or a constant number in the first box. If you need to enter information in another box, click the appropriate box or press Tab to move to it. When you finish entering information, click **Finish**, and your work is done.

The Least You Need to Know

This chapter taught you the basics of using Excel functions (the built-in formulas that give Excel its power). Here's what you need to remember:

➤ Functions are built-in formulas. Excel has more than 300 of them.

➤ You can enter functions manually if you stick to the correct formula syntax conventions.

➤ The arguments in a function can refer to specific numbers, other cells, or even whole ranges.

➤ You can enter many, but not all, functions with the help of Excel's Paste Function.

Chapter 12

Keep It Clean, Keep It Accurate, Keep It Safe

In This Chapter

➤ Ya oughta audit

➤ Vacuum that worksheet

➤ Leave a lasting luster on lovely worksheets

Audit! It's an ugly word, ain't it? Sends your skin crawling and your heart racing. Those awful men from the tax bureau are panting at your door like hell-sired pit bulls... no, stop! That's not the kind of auditing we're doing here. This is light, breezy, fun stuff! (Oh, and we're just joking about the "pit bull" part. You hear that, Mr. Taxman? Just JOKING!)

You're Being Audited

No, not by the Internal Revenue Service—at least not yet. The only auditing going on here is the kind you can accomplish within an Excel workbook. So sit back and relax. That knock on the door is not the IRS. They use certified mail—or so we're told!

When something goes wrong in your worksheet (you get an error message, a circular reference, or an unexpected result, for example), you've got to pull out the auditing tools to get it back to rights. This section explains how to use Excel's auditing tools to repair those mistakes.

Visual Auditing

We feel a little silly saying this (call it overblown maternal instincts), but it's mandatory:

Make sure you visually scan your worksheet for obvious errors before you start pulling out the big auditing guns.

There, we said it. Now let's move on.

The Auditing Process

Anyone who's ever tried to put together a family tree knows it's not hard to find the names of ancestors; the problem is determining which branch to go chasing down. Where do those royal progenitors fit in? Are they ancestors or anecdotes? Do you include dad's extended siblings, great-grandpa's plural wives, or grandma's first boyfriend who looked an awful lot like her first child?

Auditing is a system that traces the genealogy of your spreadsheet problems. It shows you, visually, where all the cells that feed into your formula come from. Just as you might with a family tree, you can follow the graphical auditing lines to see the source of your mistake. Unlike your pedigree chart, though, with Excel you can correct mistakes and get on with your work.

Auditing has its own unique language. Before we go much further, you'll need to know these words:

➤ *Auditing toolbar.* A group of tools you can use to simplify the auditing process.

➤ *Dependent.* Any cell that descends from another cell. The dependent is the offspring of the original cell, and earns the parent a big tax deduction each April.

➤ *Direct Dependent.* Any cell that descends in whole or in part from the active cell. This is the child of the original cell.

➤ *Indirect Dependent.* The grandchild of another cell. It descends from a direct dependent.

➤ *Precedent.* The first ancestors of a formula. The parenting cells. There are two types: direct and indirect.

➤ *Direct Precedent.* The first ancestral line of the formula in the active cell (the daddy cell).

➤ *Indirect Precedent.* The entire ancestral line of the formula in the active cell (the grandpa and great-grandpa cells).

Now that that's clear as tax code, let's start auditing!

138

The Auditing Toolbar

Using Excel's audit commands, you can trace the stuff that leads into your formula (the precedents) and the stuff that comes out of your formula (the dependents). You can also trace errors, attach comments, and display all the available status information about a cell.

All of Excel's audit features are accessible from the Auditing toolbar or via the Auditing command on the Tools menu. For this section, we'll work from the toolbar. To view the Auditing toolbar, go to the **Tools** menu and select **Auditing**. A submenu appears. Click **Show Auditing Toolbar**.

Add It

Sometimes an Excel component doesn't appear the first time you try to use it. If that happens when you try to audit, you'll need to install the component. Reinsert your original software disk, and click Set up. Enter information as requested by the set-up program, and when the Setup screen appears, choose a **Custom** installation. From there you can—and should—add every conceivable Excel component.

Here's what you'll see:

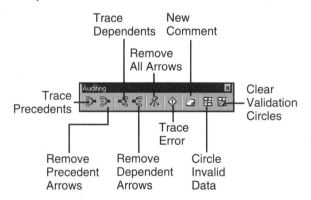

The Auditing toolbar contains all the tools you need to audit your worksheets.

Let's examine each of the auditing elements individually.

Tracing Precedents and Dependents

Tracing relationships has never been easier. First, open the **Tools** menu and select **Options**. Click the **View** tab. Select the **Show All** option button and clear the **Hide All** option button. You're ready to begin.

Click the cell that's giving you problems to make it active. To start off, you'll want to view all the formulas and data that feed into the problem cell. To do so, click the **Trace Precedents** icon. Excel displays a blue arrow connecting the problem cell to its direct precedents. You can follow the blue line to find out how the problem formula or value was created.

No problems? Then click the **Trace Precedents** icon again, and Excel points out any indirect precedents.

Excel displays arrows to point out direct and indirect precedents.

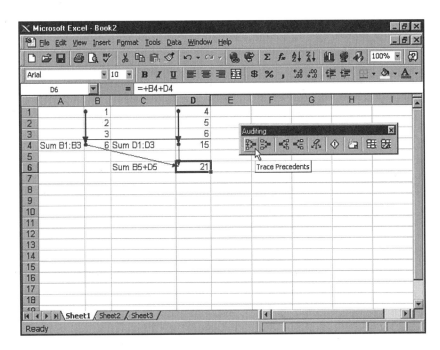

The original direct precedent lines stay visible, and they are joined by additional indirect precedent lines. Follow these lines to see whether you can track down the problem. To clear the worksheet of all arrows, click the **Remove Precedent Arrows** icon.

Sometimes you may want to work in reverse. You've got a piece of information, and you want to know where it's being used. In this case, you'll use the Trace Dependents icon. The procedure is identical. Click the information in question to make it active, and then click the **Trace Dependents** icon on the Auditing toolbar. Excel shows the direct dependents with blue arrows leading out of the active cell.

Dependents and precedents are very similar functions, and can be intermixed on the same screen.

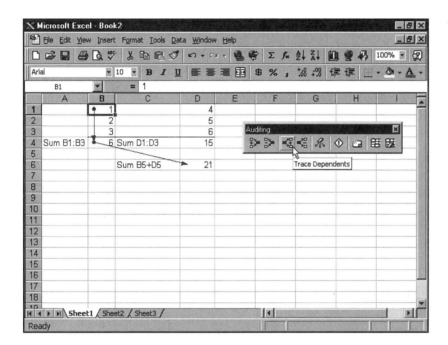

Use the Trace Dependents icon to see which cells' contents depend on the value in the selected cell.

Phase in the Tracers

There's a popular—but errant—belief that Captain Kirk was in the habit of ordering his troops to "Set your tracers on stun." He's being misquoted. Captain Kirk never had the power of the Trace Error icon at his command.

On those rare occasions when an error message appears in a cell in place of a legitimate value, activate the cell and click the **Trace Error** icon. Excel highlights all of the precedents of the troubled cell with blue and red arrows. A red arrow indicates the source of the error condition; blue arrows highlight the remainder of the precedent.

Other Useful Auditing Icons

Now seems like as good a time as any to go through the remaining icons on the Auditing toolbar.

➤ *Remove All Arrows*. What's in a name? In this case, everything. Click this icon, and all the tracer arrows disappear.

➤ *Circle Invalid Data.* Excel lets you place restrictions on the values contained in cells. It may be a great feature for template builders and Excel vets, but it's beyond the scope of this chapter. Still, if curiosity makes you itch, open the Data menu and click Validation.

➤ *Trace Error.* When an unexpected error value appears in a cell (for example: #DIV/0), select the errant cell and click the **Trace Error** icon. An arrow will point to the source of the error.

➤ *New Comment.* This allows you to add a comment to the cell, which will appear whenever someone points to the cell. It also records your name, so don't be too rude. You'll learn more about that process in the section "Attach Comments to Cells" later in this chapter.

Good Housekeeping

Now that you've learned how to clean up your worksheet messes, it's time to learn how to stop them before they start. Using a spreadsheet productively starts with planning—take it from us. We've spent hours and hours looking for lost yellow sticky notes and puzzling out scribbled messages like: "Work in LT's insur. figure."

If you're producing a spreadsheet of any size, take a moment and plan, at the very least, how you want to label all your columns and rows, and what information belongs in separate ranges and tables. Resist the urge to jump right in. Good planning prevents circular references, error messages, and incomprehensible formulas, and saves hours of time.

The following sections outline the things we wish someone had told us before we wasted those hours.

Save, Save, Save

Sure, who doesn't know this? And yet...whether it's a natural disaster that knocks the power out all across the city, or Naturalizers that knock the power cord out of the wall, you're still going to wish you'd saved more often.

Fortunately, you can have Excel save your work automatically with just the flip of a switch, and you even get to tell it how often to save. To do so, open the **Tools** menu and select the **AutoSave** command. The AutoSave dialog box appears.

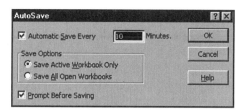

The AutoSave dialog box.

Can't Find It?

If the AutoSave command is not on the Tools menu, you must install the AutoSave add-in. Add-ins are programs that perform highly specialized tasks. When you first install Excel (see Appendix A, "Installation and Technical Support"), you see several options for choosing which add-ins you want to have available. Other add-ins will be available as separately purchased software, or as *shareware* (software you download from places like the Internet. Visit http://www.shareware.com to see what's available).

Here's how to install AutoSave, or any other Excel add-in. Go to the **Tools** menu and click **Add-Ins**. The Add-Ins dialog box appears, with a list of available add-ins. Click any item on the list, and you'll see an explanation of that add-in at the bottom of the dialog box. Click any item in the list to select it, and then click **OK** to add it. You can back out of the dialog box with the Cancel button.

In the AutoSave dialog box, check the **Automatic Save Every** check box. In the Minutes box, set the time interval at which you want Excel to save your workbooks. Make other selections as desired. Then click the **OK** button, and prepare to be saved.

Back Up

You need to do more than save your work. You also need to back it up on floppy disks, another computer, or a tape backup. At the very least, you'll want to keep a backup of your files on the same hard disk as your original files—just in case. You keep backups because things burn, things crash, things get stolen, things get corrupted, and things (like files and minds) get changed.

In the favored backup system, you keep your files on a series of floppy disks that you rotate in and out of your building. This is the "In Case of Fire" or "In Case I Get Fired" scenario. (We understand there are some who advocate keeping one copy of your work on a space shuttle. That's the "In Case of Nuclear War" scenario, and we don't recommend it.)

143

In any event, most modern software, including Excel, has a backup feature that enables you to save not only what you're presently working on, but the previous edition of that file as well. When you turn on Excel's automatic Backup feature, it saves a copy of your file, "CATFOOD," for example, under the name "Backup of CATFOOD."

Name That File

The filenames you see in Excel's Open dialog box aren't exactly identical to their actual DOS-level filenames—unless you've disabled the option that hides part of the name. Go to Windows Explorer (found on the Windows 95 Start Menu), and open the **View** menu. Choose options, and the Options dialog box will appear. Remove the check mark from the box labeled Hide MS-DOS File Extensions. Once you've made the change, you'll see the actual filenames as FILENAME.XLS for the original file and FILENAME.XLK for the backup file.

To recover your work after a power failure or a close encounter with a clumsy child, you must have already enabled the Backup feature. In addition, you must have saved a document more than once for Backup to have a back up of it. (The first time you save, there's nothing to back up.) What that means is, if you haven't done so already, you should turn on the Backup feature now and leave it on. If you wait until you need it, you will have waited too long.

To enable the Backup feature, open the **File** menu and choose **Save As**. Select **Options** and click the **Always create backup** check box. Then click **OK** and click **Save**. Easy enough!

If you ever experience a power failure, you'll find that recovery is just as simple. Click the **Open** icon to access the Open dialog box, and in the Files of type box, choose **Backup Files (*.XLK, *.BAK)**. Look through the folders to find your missing document, select it, and click **Open**.

Use Sequential Filenames

Choose a system for naming your files, and use filenaming conventions that reflect the sequence of versions.

We've found it useful to name each worksheet with a recognizable English name, followed by a number that indicates its stage of revision. Each time you open your worksheet for another shot at building it, give it a new revision number. That way, if something goes terribly wrong, you can fall back to the previous version.

Long Versus Short Filenames

Keep in mind that although Excel for Windows 95 accepts long filenames, previous versions don't. If you're exchanging data with people who are stuck back in Windows 3.1-ville, you should stick with good old DOS filenames: eight alphanumeric characters, followed by a period, followed by Excel's .XLS extension (which it adds on its own). Let it go at that.

Keep Your Hard Drive Cleaned Off

We know this is a frustrating piece of advice, but unless you've got a lot of RAM (at least 16MB, and more if you can get it), Windows 95 requires acres of disk space to run efficiently. (We've found that anything less than 100MB of free space sets Excel and all other applications to crawling.)

Spreadsheet Advisor

All the hints in this section are specific to spreadsheets, and some apply only to Excel. Follow the advice to see your productivity soar.

Work in Byte-sized Pieces

Set one part of your spreadsheet in motion before you add in new parts. If you have planned thoroughly, this step is easy. If you ignored our incessant nagging, you may find yourself trying to juggle all the bits of the spreadsheet at the same time. Remember that it's easier to back up one step than to start all over when nothing comes out right.

Know As You Go

There is no need to pull out a calculator to check your work as you build your worksheet. Use Excel's AutoSum feature instead. The AutoSum area is on the right side of the Status bar at the bottom of your Excel screen. You'll find an explanation in Chapter 8, "AutoPilot: Excel's Automatic Features."

Use the Undo Command

Excel enables you to correct mistakes you enter in your formulas or cancel a formula altogether if necessary. To cancel an error before you actually enter it (for example, while the formula itself—and not its result—still appears in the Formula bar and the cell), press the **Esc** key or click the **Cancel** button in a dialog box or on the Formula bar.

 If you actually enter a formula and then realize you made a mistake, you can undo the change. To do so, simply click the **Undo** icon on the Standard toolbar immediately, and Excel reverses the previous change. If you prefer keeping your hands on the keyboard, use the Ctrl+Z key combination instead.

Undo to the nth Degree

If your mistake occurred several keystrokes ago, don't panic. The new version of Excel can undo your last command, and then the command prior to that, and so on, and so on. Just keep hitting that Undo key.

Understand Toolbars

We've covered each toolbar in detail as we've come to it, but we'll recap that information here because understanding Excel toolbars from top to bottom can really boost your productivity.

A toolbar is simply a collection of task-related icons that represent common commands. By nature, toolbars simplify your work.

Hide-away

If the Windows 95 taskbar gets in your way, you can keep it hidden until the times you require it. To do so, click Windows 95's Start button and select Settings and Taskbar to access the Taskbar Properties dialog box. Click the Taskbar Options tab, and select Always on top and Auto hide. Then close the box. Until you give Windows further notice, the taskbar remains hidden. It appears again whenever you drag your mouse pointer to its location and call it up.

Excel has a built-in collection of more than a dozen toolbars. To see the list, open the View menu and choose Toolbars. Then, to display any given toolbar, click the check box on the toolbar's name. It's not a complete list, though. A few miscellaneous toolbars are brought up from other menus.

You can move a toolbar out of harm's way by "docking" it at the edge of Excel. To dock a toolbar, click its Title bar and drag it off the worksheet. When toolbars are floating, you can resize them by dragging any side; you cannot resize a docked toolbar.

To make a toolbar "float" again, click the vertical lines at the far left of the docked bar and drag it to its new location.

In addition, you can change any toolbar or create new toolbars by adding, deleting, and rearranging icons. You'll learn how to customize your toolbars in Chapter 14, "Customizing the Spreadsheet."

Attach Comments to Cells

In older spreadsheets, attaching a comment to a cell was a complicated process that was rarely carried out and was almost always regretted. Not so, anymore. Attaching comments is easy in Excel for Windows 95, and it enables you to leave a "paper trail" for others who may use your worksheet and—believe it or not—for yourself. (Just try to remember six weeks later why you used a particular cell reference in your formula or where you got the data for a certain range of numbers.)

To attach a comment to a cell in an Excel worksheet, click the **New Comment** icon on the Auditing toolbar. (Alternatively, you can open the Insert menu and select Comment.) The Cell Comment dialog box appears.

Type your comment in the Text area

The cell comment dialog box.

By default, Excel automatically attaches your comment to the active cell. When you finish entering your selections, click **OK**. Excel displays a small red triangle in the upper right corner of the cell to indicate that a comment is attached to the cell. Anytime you move your cursor over a cell with a comment attached, a pop-up box displays your comment on-screen.

To edit or remove comments open the **View** menu, and click **Comments**. The Reviewing toolbar appears.

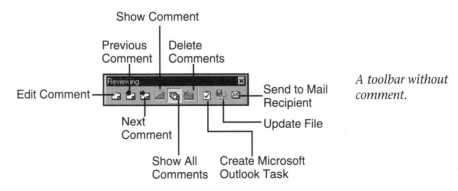

Show Comment

Previous Comment   Delete Comments

Edit Comment

A toolbar without comment.

Send to Mail Recipient

Update File

Next Comment

Show All Comments   Create Microsoft Outlook Task

To remove comments from a cell, select it and click the **Delete Comments** icon.

Editing is just as easy. Select the cell and then click the **Edit Comment** icon. The comments dialog box will appear so that you can make your changes.

Previous Comment and Next Comment will have you going in circles accessing the comments on your worksheet. The Show Comments and Show All Comments icons display comments in the active cell and all comments respectively.

Create Microsoft Outlook Task, Update File, and Send to Mail Recipient tie into other Microsoft applications.

If you want to skip the Reviewing toolbar, a faster way to edit or delete a comment is to just right-click the commented cell. A menu appears, from which you can choose **Edit** comment or Delete comment.

Fill in Workbook Properties

Workbook Properties give you tracking information about any worksheet. Excel fills in some of the properties automatically. If you manually fill in the rest, you have a good record of who has worked on a file, what the file contains, and how it's connected to other information on your computer.

To access Workbook Properties, open the **File** menu and choose **Properties**. The Properties dialog box appears.

Track the use of each worksheet using the Properties dialog box.

Property tabs

Summary input areas

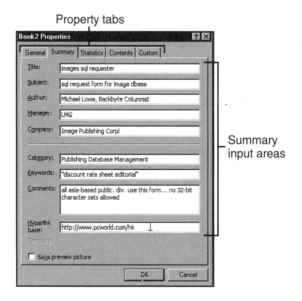

You enter most of your tracking information on the Summary tab of the Properties dialog box. The General tab describes file creation information; the Statistics tab tracks editing time; the Contents tab tells you how the entire workbook is structured, in outline form; and the Custom tab enables you to pick from a long list of other categories you might want to track. To see those categories, click the **Name** down arrow.

When you finish viewing the Workbook Properties dialog box, click **Cancel**.

Protect Cells

Okay, maybe you're no longer a complete idiot about spreadsheets, but one day you're going to do something completely idiotic to a spreadsheet. At that point, you will wish you'd remembered cell protection.

Cell protection is a process by which you can keep other people's grimy hands off your work. More significantly, it keeps your own grimy hands (and your own errant formulas and macros) from destroying existing parts of your worksheet.

When your spreadsheet starts getting cumbersome (as in, larger than the screen), it's probably time to consider locking it up. With Excel, you can lock up the entire spreadsheet, and then selectively unlock the cells or areas where you want to enter data, edit existing cells, or continue building the spreadsheet.

The Protection Theory

If you grew up with older non-Excel spreadsheets, you might find Excel's protection features disappointing. On those old kludge-y programs, you had no trouble locking and unlocking cells all over the spreadsheet. However, Excel works a bit differently. You can protect cells in two ways: by hiding them or by locking them. And instead of choosing a handful of cells and locking them up (as you did in other spreadsheets), Excel requires that you first unlock some cells, and then protect the rest of the worksheet.

Unfortunately, Excel provides no visual indicator to tell you whether or not a particular cell is locked. The only way to find out is by trial and error: Enter information in a cell, and if it's locked, Excel displays an error message.

Check This Out...

Finders Keepers

If you're locking and unlocking cells, consider highlighting the locked cells using the **Fill Color** icon on the Formatting toolbar.

The Practice

To protect an entire worksheet, open the **Tools** menu, select **Protection**, and choose **Protect Sheet** from the submenu that appears. To unprotect a worksheet, repeat those steps but choose **Unprotect Sheet** from the submenu that appears.

Check This Out...

Do Not Pass(word) Go

That Password option in the Protect Sheet dialog box looks mighty tempting, doesn't it? We advise that you pass it by. Do not enter anything in that Password box. Why? Once you've assigned a password, you're under a lifelong obligation to not forget it. You cannot, under any circumstances, talk Microsoft into removing it for you. And if you forget the password, the worksheet is as good as gone forever. You cannot access it through any other source.

The Locking Thing

To keep a few cells unlocked so you can continue to enter information in them, you must first remove protection from the worksheet. To do so, follow these steps:

1. Open the **Tools** menu and select **Unprotect**.

2. Select the cells you want to keep unlocked. You can select multiple ranges by dragging over the first one, pressing and holding the **Ctrl** key, and dragging over any others. Repeat this process as often as necessary, until all your ranges are selected.

3. To actually mark the cells as unlocked, open the **Format** menu and select **Cells** (or press **Ctrl+1**). The Format Cells dialog box appears.

4. Choose the **Protection** tab.

5. Click the **Locked** box to remove the check mark, and then click **OK**. Your cells are unlocked.

Of course, everything else is also unlocked right now, so you have to lock the worksheet again. Open the **Tools** menu, select **Protection**, and choose **Protect Sheet** again. Excel locks all but your chosen cells.

That's it.

The Hiding Place

Sometimes you have confidential information on an otherwise great spreadsheet. You'd love to show off your spreadsheet to, say, your boss, but you don't particularly want her to see the part where you calculate your spouse's annual income.

You can hide and unhide cells in much the same way you locked and unlocked cells. First, make sure the worksheet is not protected by selecting **Tools**, **Protection**, **Unprotect Sheet**. Select the cells that contain the information you want to hide. Then open the **Format** menu and select **Cells** (or press **Ctrl+1**), and click the **Protection** tab of the Format Cells dialog box. On the Protection tab, check the **Hidden** option, and click **OK** to save your setup. Protect the worksheet again, and you're all set. These features toggle on and off like light switches, so you can retrace your steps to undo them.

The Least You Need to Know

In this chapter, you learned how to keep your spreadsheets neat and tidy. Keep these points in mind, and you'll never have a problem:

➤ Excel's audit functions can help you find errors quickly.

➤ You can access all auditing functions from the Auditing toolbar.

➤ Plan, plan, plan. It prevents auditing, auditing, auditing.

➤ Save and back up your files regularly, and follow other basic housekeeping hints to keep your Excel files safe and clean.

➤ With Excel, you can attach comments to any cell.

➤ Careful handling and labeling of your worksheets can save you hours of trouble later on.

Chapter 13

An Open and Shut Case

In This Chapter

➤ Search and rescue

➤ Open wide

➤ Protect and serve

➤ Memorable milestones

It's always a debate: Do we drive through and let the kids drip ice cream on our fine Corinthian leather-like seats, or do we let 'em loose on the good people of Taco Bell, who, really, have done nothing to us? Usually the seat considerations win out. So we open the doors, kids spill out all over the parking lot, a few disappear immediately to the bathroom, and the youngest wisely picks a table of her own. In the end, we add an extra 18 minutes to our visit searching for kids, loading them back into the car, and protecting the youngest from a carload of older brothers and their pilfered packets of taco sauce.

In this chapter, we describe ways to keep track of files on your disk, open them up again, and protect your new creations from the cold, cruel world. Hot sauce is not included.

In Search Of: Searching for Documents

It's not true, what they say. You actually can teach an old dog new tricks. Excel 97 has taken that old trick of loading up existing files, and thrown in a few extra complications to help you out when you can't remember where on the company network you left your salary calculation.

Tools for Prying Open Files

Opening a file is relatively simple—providing you have a good idea where it's located. If you've made it to this point in the book, you've been managing to do that quite nicely. To provide a neat opening for this segment (and also so that you can't say we never told you anything), here's a quick overview.

To open a file in Excel, select the **File** menu and choose **Open**. The Open dialog box appears. Because we haven't been bouncing around in different folders, anything that you've saved should appear in the display area of the Open dialog box. Select the file you want to open and click the **Open** button, or just double-click the filename.

You use this process to open any file you've saved to your current folder. Unfortunately, the file you want is rarely in the current folder. On our PCs, for example, we have an average of more than 3,000 files in more than 100 directories—er, sorry. A slip of the pen. In Windows 95, directories are called folders.

The Name Game

If you've used earlier versions of Excel, don't get confused by the new names you find in Windows 95. Those familiar DOS directories haven't changed one iota. They simply have a new name: Folders.

In any event, what this means is that several times a year we are left scratching our heads, trying to remember exactly where we stuffed the workbook we created last April for Auntie Jo's taxes. What seemed to be a totally logical filing system just a year ago has now disappeared forever in some deep recess of the gray matter lolling about within our skulls.

Search Tools: A-Digging We Will Go

When you can't find a file, it's time to call out the search team. Excel provides a number of mechanisms for locating lost files.

To search for a file without the help of Leonard Nimoy, select **Open** from the File menu. Once again, the Open dialog box appears on your screen (see the following figure).

The Look in box at the top of the dialog box contains the name of the current folder, and the display area contains the names of the files and folders in the current folder. If what you're looking for isn't there, it's time to go hunting. Use any of the following methods to change to a different folder:

➤ Click the down arrow of the Look in box, and Excel displays all available drives. Select the drive you want to search, and its folders appear in the display area. Double-click the icon for the folder in which you want to conduct your search.

➤ Click the **Up One Level** button. The Look in box changes to a folder one level higher than the current folder.

➤ Click the **Look in Favorites** button, and shortcuts to folders you have designated as favorites appear in the display area of the Open dialog box. Select from this elite list of folders to conduct your file search.

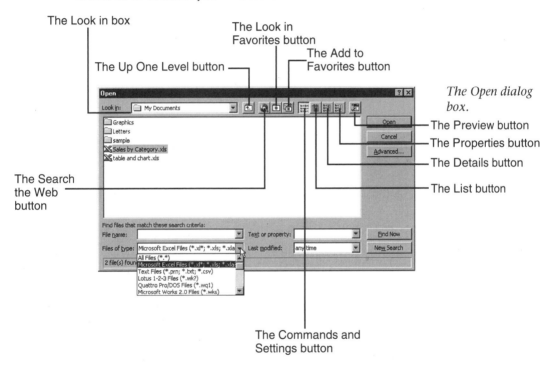

The Open dialog box.

The Look in box

The Look in Favorites button

The Up One Level button

The Add to Favorites button

The Preview button

The Properties button

The Details button

The Search the Web button

The List button

The Commands and Settings button

Add It Up

To add a folder to the Favorites list, select a folder from the display area and click the **Add to Favorites** button. Excel creates a shortcut to the selected folder, which will appear whenever you select the Look in Favorites button.

Once you've selected the folder you want to search, think about the file(s) you want to search for. Use the four boxes at the bottom of the dialog box—Filename, Files of type, Text or property, and Last modified—to enter look-up criteria to narrow your file search.

Another World

Still no file? There's always the slow and agonizing method. Click the **Commands and Settings** button in the Open dialog box and select **Search Subfolders** from the pop-up menu. This command tells Excel to search through every subfolder in the system from the point listed in the Look in box. The actual speed of this search depends on the size and speed of your system. We found the required search time acceptable and, as an added bonus, just about right for a peanut butter and jelly sandwich.

To show all the files in their proper folders, select the **Details** button. Click the **Commands and Setting** button and select **Group** files by folder from the pop-up menu.

Advanced Search

Should you decide that you need to further fine-tune your search criteria, select the **Advanced** button from the Open dialog box. The Advanced Find dialog box (shown in the following figure) appears. Use this box to narrow down the files that match your search. The Find files that match these criteria box lists the types of files you might choose from. The Define more criteria box lets you define the scope of your search. For instance, in the Property box you might select the **Contents** option. In the Condition box select **Includes**, and type a value, such as **Total**, in the Value box. Choose the folder and drive names in the Look in: box, and check the **Search subfolders** options. When you click the **Find Now** button, Excel will return all files that contain the value Total.

The Advanced Find dialog box.

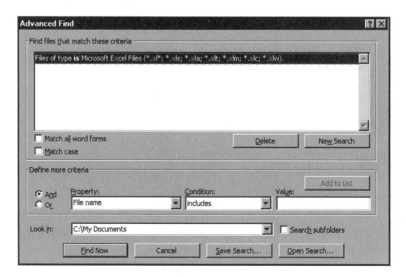

In addition to further refining your search criteria, you can also save your search settings for future use. To do so, select the **Save Search** button to access the Save Search dialog box. Enter a descriptive name for your search and click **OK**.

To call up the saved search criteria in the future, select the **Commands and Settings** button from the Open dialog box. Then select **Saved Searches** from the pop-up menu, and choose the desired search criteria from the displayed menu.

Sneak Views and Previews

Before we continue, let's look at a few other features the Open dialog box has to offer: previews of your files and file sorting.

Excel lets you take a peek at a file, which can be helpful if you think you've found the file you're looking for, but you want to preview it to make sure. To catch a glimpse of what the file will look like before you actually load it up, select the file and click the **Preview** button.

Excel also controls how the filenames are displayed in the display area of the Open dialog box. Use the following methods to control the file display:

➤ To sort files, click the **Commands and Settings** button and select **Sorting**. Then choose whether you want Excel to sort files by Name, Size, Type, or Date.

➤ To view file size, type, and date modified, select the **Details** button.

➤ To view file properties and statistics, click the **Properties** button. Chapter 12, "Keep It Clean, Keep It Accurate, Keep It Safe," explains the workbook properties feature.

The Shortcut Menu

From the Open dialog box, you can now click the right mouse button to access various "shortcut" menus that contain file management options.

Setting Properties

You can lock, archive, or hide all the files in the current folder. To do so, right-click in the middle of the file display and select **Properties** from the shortcut menu. In the dialog box that appears, click the appropriate check boxes to lock, archive, or hide the files in the current folder.

There are three shortcut menus, and which one you get depends on where in the Open dialog box you click your right mouse button. Here are your choices:

➤ Right-click in the middle of the file display area to access the shortcut menu shown here. This menu contains four options: Explore (which opens the Windows Explorer utility), Sharing (which accesses a dialog box showing the attributes of your current folder or file), Send To (which copies the highlighted file or folder to a different disk drive, Briefcase, or fax or mail recipient), and Properties (which accesses a dialog box showing the attributes of your current folder or file). Yes, the second and fourth items are identical. Consider it one of the great unsolved mysteries of the universe.

Shortcut menu 1.

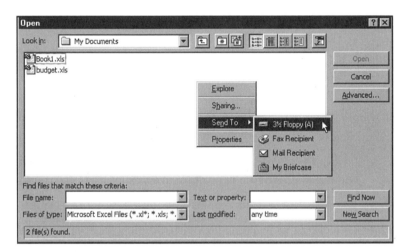

➤ Right-click a filename. The resulting shortcut menu (shown in the following figure) has the same Send To and Properties options, as well as options for creating a shortcut to open the file, opening the file, opening the file as a read-only file (meaning that it can't be changed), and printing the file. Other options let you cut, copy, delete, or rename the file.

➤ Right-click a folder. The following figure shows the third shortcut menu, which contains all the options from the first menu, an option for opening the folder, and options for cutting, copying, deleting, and renaming the folder.

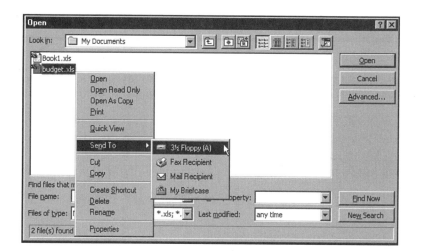

Shortcut menu 2.

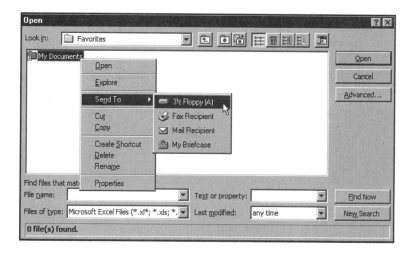

Shortcut menu 3.

Recently Used; Good as New

You'll find people in this world who will tell you that opening documents in Excel is terribly complicated. But the folks who would like you to believe this are the kind who try to impress their dates with plaid trousers and pocket protectors. Do not believe them. Your social status depends on it.

You visited the Open dialog box in the beginning of this chapter, but don't think that's the only way to get to your file. You also have the ultra-easy Recently Used list.

Each time you create or open a file in Excel, the program keeps a little record of your visit. No, it's not a form of corporate espionage. Excel is just trying to make your life easier by giving you quick access to the documents you've been using lately.

In the last segment of Excel's File menu is a list of the files you've used most recently. (Go ahead. Pull down the **File** menu, and you'll see how very honest we are.) To reopen one of these files, double-click its name.

Opening File Imports and Conversions in Excel

Excel works best on its own files, but if you work with other people or other applications, you'll find that you need to share information from time to time. That's where file imports and conversions come into play. Excel uses something called import filters (which you set up when you first install the program) to call up files from other applications. You can call up spreadsheets from other manufacturers, as well as text files, some word processing files, and lots of database files.

Here is the procedure for importing information from other non-database applications (such as word processors, other spreadsheets, and financial packages), text files, and other Microsoft Office applications. What we don't tell you here is how to import from database applications. We explain that complex process in Part 4, "Like a Database," of this book. For now, here's the simple stuff:

➤ To import files from other applications, pull down the **Files** menu and select **Open**. In the Open dialog box, click the **Files of type** box at the bottom of the screen and choose the file type for the file you are importing from the menu. Select your file and click the **Open** button.

➤ To import a *text file* (a rare gem that contains nothing but straight text; no formatting, no commands, nothing! And it can be read by virtually any piece of software in the free world), open the file through the Open dialog box as though it were a regular Excel file, and a Text Import Wizard appears to guide you through the import process.

➤ To import files from a Microsoft Office application, just open the file. When Excel recognizes the format, it performs the conversion.

Use a Wizard

The File Conversion Wizard changes the format of multiple files in one step.

Off to See a Wizard

For those rare occasions when you have more than one file to convert, consider the File Conversion Wizard. This little wizard is able to perform batch conversions of your old files—provided they're all of the same type.

This is the procedure: First, move all the files you want to convert into the same folder. (Windows Explorer, found from your Windows 95 Start menu, is the tool of choice for moving files around.) Go back to Excel, and from the Tools menu select **Wizard**. Click **File Conversion**. The File Conversion Wizard dialog box will appear on your screen in the usual way, without the fiery special effects—unless you're trying to get back to Kansas.

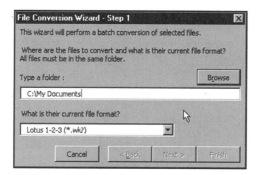

File Conversion Wizard dialog box.

Click the folder containing the files to convert. Select the file type from the types available in the What is their current file format? box. Click the **Next** button. Onscreen instructions will ask you a few significant questions, and then the File Conversion Wizard will handle all of the really tough stuff.

Workbook Protection

Because spreadsheet work often deals with finances and proprietary information, it tends to be confidential. For that reason, Excel gives you a number of ways to protect your confidential information from prying eyes.

In the last chapter, you learned how to protect individual cells from change. In this chapter, you learn how to protect the structure of the entire workbook, protect the windows from change, and require a password for access.

Structural Safety

Excel lets you protect the structure of the workbook so that nobody can hide or unhide certain worksheets, move them, rename them, delete them, or insert others.

But there's more worth protecting. Excel has a good head for figures: Each time you open a workbook, it remembers where you left off previously. Your windows retain their position and size, the most recently used page, and even the position of the active cell. You can protect these aspects of a window to prevent other users (or passers-by) from hiding, unhiding, resizing, opening, or closing the window.

Keep It Safe

To protect the structure or the windows of a workbook from unwanted changes, open the **Tools** menu, choose **Protection**, and choose **Protect Workbook**. The Protect Workbook dialog box appears (see the following figure). Select **Structure**, **Windows**, or both. Click **OK**, and your workbook's structure and windows are safe.

The Protect Work-book dialog box.

Although password protection for the entire workbook is done elsewhere (which we cover later in this chapter), you can enter a password here to protect the structure and windows from being changed. Type a password and click **OK**. Then retype the password to confirm it. *Note:* Don't rely too heavily on this feature. Savvy computer users can get past it.

To remove protection, open the **Tools** menu, select **Protection**, and select **Unprotect Workbook**. If you assigned a password when you protected the workbook's structure or windows, you have to re-enter the password to unprotect.

Keep It Hidden

Whether your worksheets contain confidential information or just too much information, there will be times when you'll want to hide part of your work.

Excel makes it easy for you to temporarily hide your workbooks and worksheets to prevent unwanted changes or to cut down on the number of items in your view. The hidden sheets remain open, and all workbooks and worksheets remain available so that they can be referenced from other documents.

Here's how to hide and unhide workbooks and worksheets:

➤ To hide a workbook, open it and select **Hide** from the Window menu. Easy enough.

➤ To unhide the workbook, go to the Window menu and select **Unhide.** Easier yet.

➤ To hide a worksheet, first open the worksheet. Then open the **Format** menu, choose **Sheet**, and choose **Hide**. Just like that, it's gone. You can run, but you cannot hide a worksheet if it's the only one in your workbook.

➤ Unhide the worksheet by choosing **Format**, **Sheet**, **Unhide**. The Unhide dialog box appears, listing your hidden sheets. Choose the one you want to retrieve, click **OK**, and you've got it back.

Learn to Share

Networked users have the option of sharing files as they work, without wreaking havoc on the files.

The procedure is simple. With a file open, pull down the **Tools** menu and click **Share Workbook**. The Share Workbook dialog box appears (see the following figure). This dialog box has two tabs: Editing and Advanced.

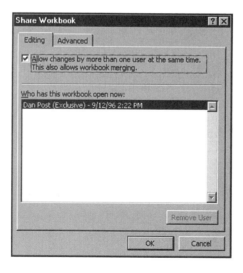

The Share Workbook dialog box.

On the Editing tab, click the **Allow Changes by More Than One** check box and click **OK**. This turns on the feature that lets you share your files with other users on your network.

When multiple users are working on the same workbook, there's bound to be a time when they make dissimilar changes at the same time. Maybe you're planning a trip to Six Flags over Someplace Close, for example, while your spouse is adjusting the workbook to budget a trip to Brazil. The differences, you will have noticed, cause conflicts.

Re-enter the Share Workbook dialog box and click the **Advanced** tab.

The Share Workbook Advanced tab.

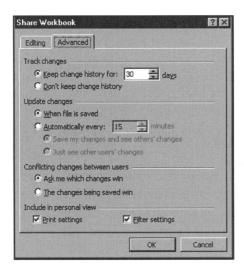

Under the Conflicting changes between users section, there are two radio buttons: Ask me which changes win, and The changes being saved win. Take your choice, and be prepared to defend it to your spouse. If The changes being saved win, there's no telling where you'll be spending your vacation. Choose **Ask me which changes win**, and decide over and over again who wears the pants in the family.

What's the Password?

The final form of workbook protection is passwords. Excel's password protection allows you to save your workbook with complete password protection (so that only you can get back in) or with write protection (so that other people can read your worksheet, but can't make any changes). Excel also lets you assign "read-only recommended" protection, which other users can roundly ignore.

When a document is merely write-protected (as opposed to password-protected), anyone who wants to make changes can simply save the workbook under another name. We imagine there's a reason you'd want to do this. Isn't there?

Forgotten Passwords

Hey, you! Yeah, you, the guy standing in Wal-Mart reading this book because he forgot his password: Sorry, no. You can't retrieve it. Nohow, no way, no calls to Microsoft, no crocodile tears on the Internet, no pleas for help to American Express. It's gone. Forever. We're sorry.

But this is a great book anyway. So buy it, and read great tips like these:

If you're using a password, write it down someplace safe. Place it in your wallet, sleep with it at night. Or safest of all: You could print out hard copies of your document formulas as backup in case you lose your password. To view the formulas for printing, open the **Tools** menu, select **Options**, and click the **View** tab of the Options dialog box. Select **Formulas** in the Windows Options section, and then click **OK**. All your formulas are visible, and you can print them as a permanent record.

In Excel, you assign a password during the file-saving routine. Whether or not you've already saved your file, open the **File** menu and choose **Save As**. Click **Options**, and in the File Sharing area of the Save Options dialog box, choose your level of password protection:

➤ Protection Password keeps Communist spies out of your entire workbook.

➤ Write Reservation Password keeps those spies from writing Communist propaganda in your workbook.

➤ Read-Only Recommended asks them nicely not to write Communist propaganda in your workbook.

Click **OK** and click **Save** to return to your document.

Before you can change or delete a password, you must first prove that you're not a Communist spy yourself by opening the workbook with the password. Once you open the workbook, though, anyone—ANYONE—can change or delete the password. That means you won't want to leave it open while you're visiting the, um, loo—especially if there are Communist spies wandering around your office.

To change the password, open the **File** menu, choose **Save As**, and click **Options** again. Click the hidden password and either delete it or write over it. Then save as before.

The Least You Need to Know

In this chapter, you learned how to search for, open, convert, and protect your files. These are the parts you need to remember:

➤ Excel has a number of complex options for searching for files. But it's still better, and faster, to keep your files in folders with obvious names, and skip the lengthy search process.

➤ Opening Excel files is easy. Just pull down the **File** menu, select **Open**, and click the filename in the Open dialog box.

➤ Importing foreign files to Excel is possible. To import a single file, choose the file type from your list of import filters in the Open dialog box. To import several files of the same type, use the File Conversion Wizard.

➤ Protect your files. Hide them or use passwords to maintain confidentiality.

Chapter 14

Customizing the Spreadsheet

In This Chapter

➤ Back in your cell

➤ Paging Mr. Formats

➤ Excel-erate your screen

➤ Necessary notes for novices

There was a time when the human race was quite content to work with handwritten ledgers and carbon-copied interoffice memos.

Computers have changed all that. Now a memo can't be official unless it's printed in three colors and has a cover sheet, a logo, double bars between the header and body, and at least four different typefaces.

And your spreadsheet? It's gotta have tables, colors, italics!

And you wondered why computers hadn't helped your productivity.

Customs Clearance

There's a bit of artist in all of us. Excel caters to your need to make things look good by giving you all sorts of options for changing the appearance of individual cells and ranges, entire worksheets, and even Excel itself. This chapter tells you how.

Changing Small Things

We start off by describing ways to change the appearance of individual cells or ranges: the fonts, colors, borders, and other formatting features.

Freedom of Choice

You can change the format—the appearance—of cells in several different ways. Throughout this discussion, we instruct you to use the formatting toolbar. Feel free, though, to use any of these alternatives:

➤ Open the **Format** menu and select the **Cells** command to access the Format Cells dialog box, which contains a few options (number, alignment, font, border, patterns, and protection) that you cannot change from the Formatting Toolbar. We discuss cell protection in Chapter 12, "Keep It Clean, Keep It Accurate, Keep It Safe," and we cover borders, patterns, and cell alignment later in this section.

➤ Right-click a cell and choose the **Format Cells** option from the shortcut menu that appears.

➤ Press **Ctrl+1**; that's a shortcut that takes you directly to the Format Cells dialog box.

The Font

The words and letters you type into an Excel spreadsheet have different typefaces, or fonts, that change their basic appearance. You can choose your fonts to fit your own style. The following figure shows you some of the fonts and special effects available in Excel.

Excel uses a default font as the standard typeface for your worksheets. You can change that default font for all of your worksheets, or you can change the font for an individual worksheet, cell, or range. You'll learn later in this chapter how to change the default font. In the meantime, if you'd like to change the font for just some of the cells on your worksheet, follow along here.

Begin by selecting the cells or blocks of text within cells that you want to change. Then pull down the **Font** box on the formatting toolbar and select a new font. While the cells are still selected, choose your new font size using the Font Size box. You can pick from the drop-down list or enter your own number.

Alternatively, you can choose different fonts, sizes, and effects from the Format Cells dialog box, explained at the end of the next section.

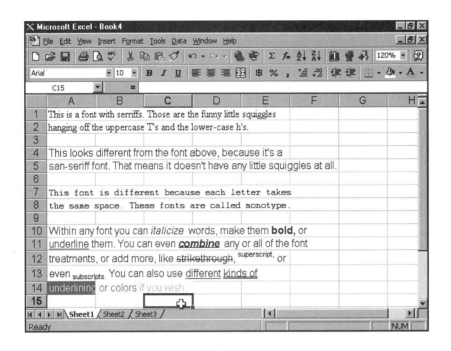

Fonts and special effects change the appearance of text.

Font box   Font Size box

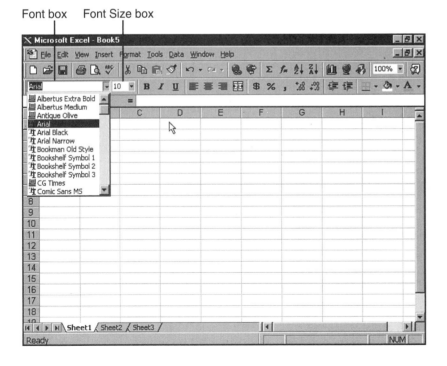

Change the font for individual cells from the formatting toolbar.

Special Effects

You can add special effects to your text with bold, italic, and underlines. Select your text, and then click any of these icons on the formatting toolbar. You can combine them for different effects.

B   Bold

I   Italic

U   Underline

When you move the cursor over any of these icons, a 3D button appears. When the icon's effect is turned on, the icon appears pushed in. To remove special effects, just reselect the text, and click again on the special effects icon. Excel removes the formatting from your text, and the icon no longer appears to be pushed in.

Check This Out...

Key Changes

You can also use key combinations to toggle any of the special effects:

➤ **Ctrl+B** changes the Bold setting

➤ **Ctrl+I** changes the Italic setting

➤ **Ctrl+U** changes the Underline setting

There are other special effects available in Excel, but you have to dig a little deeper to get to them.

Select the text you want to change, and then go to the Format menu and select **Cells**. The Format Cells dialog box appears. Click the **Font** tab to see the options shown in the following figure.

From this tab, you can change the font, font style (bold, italic, or combination), the font size, the underline settings, cell colors (see the following), and other special effects (strike-through, superscript, and subscript). Selecting the Normal Font check box returns all selections to the default, and the Preview window shows you how your changes will appear onscreen. Click **OK** to return to the main Excel screen.

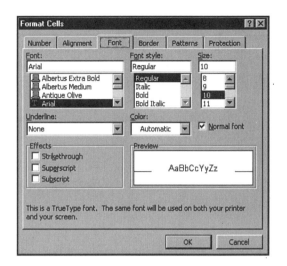

The Font tab of the Format Cells dialog box.

Change Cell Colors

You can easily change colors… twice! Excel allows you to change the color of both the text and the actual cell. Just follow these steps:

1. As usual, select the cell or cells you want to change. You can select noncontiguous areas by holding down the **Ctrl** key as you select additional areas.

2. To change the color of the text, click the down arrow of the Font Color button on the formatting toolbar. From the palette of colors that appears, select the color you want.

3. To change the background color of the cells, click the down arrow of the Color button on the formatting toolbar. Again, select a color from the color palette. The cell changes accordingly.

Color Bind

If you're dissatisfied with the color options in your color palette, you can change 'em! Open the **Tools** menu, select **Options**, and click the **Color** tab in the Options dialog box. Click any color and then on the **Modify…** button. The Colors dialog box will appear. Choose your colors from the available colors or click the **Custom** tab and create your own shade of pale.

Borders and Patterns

Borders and patterns give you more special effects by allowing you to highlight and outline cells to make them really stand out. To add a border or pattern, select the cells you want to highlight. As always, you can choose noncontiguous areas by holding down the **Ctrl** key and selecting additional areas with your mouse. When you've selected all the areas you want to highlight, click the down arrow on the Borders icon on the formatting toolbar. A small box appears with 12 borders you can choose from (see the following figure).

Select a border for your cells.

Border choices

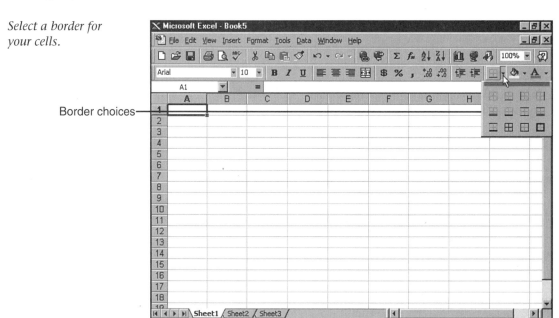

Alternatively, you can open the **Format** menu and choose **Cells**. Choose your border (including color, line style, and placement) from the Border tab, and choose your cell pattern (including its color) from the Patterns tab. When you finish setting options, click **OK**.

Cell Alignment

You can apply simple cell alignment using the four alignment icons on the formatting toolbar. Just select your cells and click the appropriate icon to align the text within the cells. The following figure shows the alignment buttons on the formatting toolbar.

You can choose from other alignment options as well. Open the **Format** menu, choose **Cells**, and click the **Alignment** tab of the Format Cells dialog box.

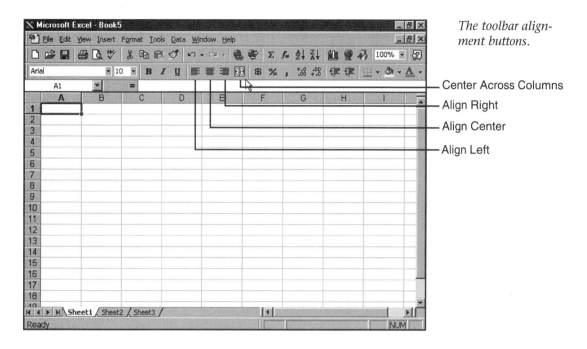

*The toolbar align-
ment buttons.*

Center Across Columns

Align Right

Align Center

Align Left

Text alignment boxes enable you to align your text both horizontally and vertically. Most selections, such as Left, Center, and Right are self-explanatory. In the horizontal alignment box, the General setting aligns text to the left, numbers to the right, and errors and logical values in the center.

An Orientation box enables you to adjust the orientation of text in one-degree increments in the selected cells. The Wrap text check box forces text to wrap within the cell instead of bleeding across blank cells as it usually does. The Shrink to fit check box will automatically adjust the font size to fit in the cell.

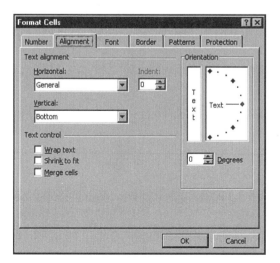

*Text alignment
options.*

173

Number Formatting

In Chapter 2, "Getting Started," you learned how to format numbers using the options on the Number tab of the Format Cells dialog box. You can also format numbers using the five number-formatting icons on the formatting toolbar (shown in the following figure).

The number formatting icons.

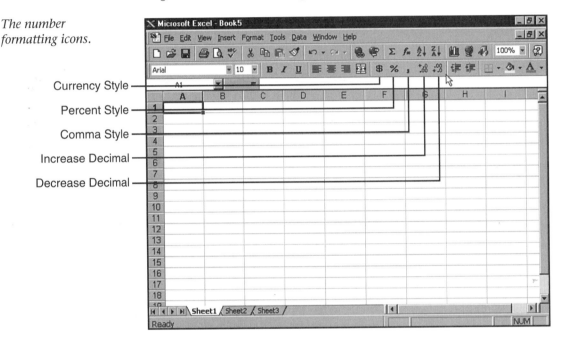

To use the toolbar icons, select the cells containing the numbers you want to format, and then click the icon that contains the desired style.

➤ Currency Style places a dollar sign (or any other currency symbol you used in your original Windows setup) in front of each number in the selected area, and changes the number to two decimal places.

➤ Percent Style changes to an even percentage without decimal places.

➤ Comma Style places a comma to the left of every third number (counting from the right, of course), and changes to two decimal places.

➤ The Increase and Decrease Decimal buttons change the number of decimal places in the selected range. Each time you click the button, the decimal place increases or decreases by one place.

The Format Painter

You can copy all styles, including cell and text colors, from one range to another with the Format Painter icon on the Standard toolbar.

174

First select the text that contains the formatting you want to copy. Then click the **Format Painter** icon and select the text to which you want to copy the format. The format changes automatically.

When One Size Doesn't Fit All

Sometimes you'll find that a single column or row is too large or too small. For example, if a column is too narrow for Excel to display a cell's value, Excel simply displays the error message #### in that cell. You can easily resize the column to fit the text.

To adjust column width, move your mouse pointer to the row of grayed-in column headers. Move the mouse slowly to the right, and the pointer changes to the two-arrow beam (see the following figure). Click and drag the two-arrow beam to adjust the column width wider or narrower as necessary.

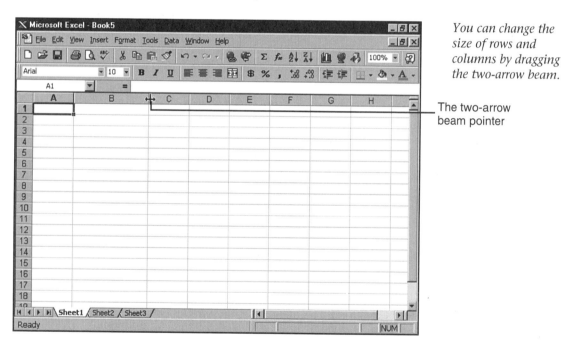

You can change the size of rows and columns by dragging the two-arrow beam.

The two-arrow beam pointer

To adjust the row height, position the pointer to the far left in the grayed-in row header area. Move the pointer to the bottom border of the row you want to change. When the pointer changes to a two-arrow beam, click and drag to adjust the row height.

You can also change the size of a group of rows or columns. First, select the group by clicking and dragging across any number of headers. Then move to the edge of the group until the pointer changes to a two-arrow beam. Drag the group as before until it reaches the desired size. All cells in the group become the same height or width.

175

Do It Yourself

You can tell Excel to figure out its own column width and row height settings with the AutoFit feature. Just select your columns or rows by clicking on the appropriate headers. Then go to the **Format** menu and choose **Column** or **Row**. Select the **AutoFit** option, and your columns or rows adjust themselves perfectly to accommodate the widest or tallest text in each column or row. If your aim is really accurate, you could, instead, double-click the thin line between column or row headers to AutoFit the text.

Changing Larger Things

Most of the changes you make in Excel will affect only individual cells. But there are a few changes you can make universally.

Default Font

Earlier, we showed you how to change the font for a text selection. You can also permanently change the font for both the row/column headers and the worksheet text. To do so, open the **Tools** menu and select **Options**. In the Options dialog box, click the **General** tab to access the options shown in the following figure.

The General tab of the Options dialog box.

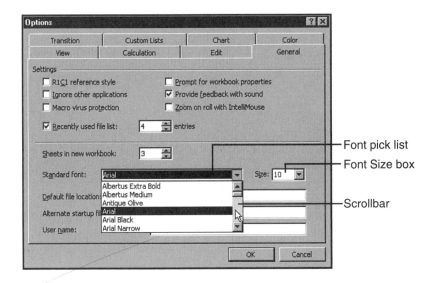

For now, click the **Standard Font** down arrow to display the list of available fonts. Move up and down the list as necessary to find other fonts, and when you find the one you want, select it. Choose the font size from the font Size box. You can enter a specific size, or you can select the down arrow and choose a size from the list that appears. Click **OK**, and Excel tells you that you must restart your computer for the new default (standard) font to take effect.

Other Options dialog box options are described in Chapter 9, "Home on the Range."

Column/Row Size Throughout

You learned earlier in this chapter how to change the width of an individual column or a group of columns, and how to change the height of a row or group of rows. You can also change the standard size of all columns and rows in the entire worksheet.

This is the process:

1. Select all the worksheets for which you want to change the row or column size. (Select the first worksheet, hold down the **Ctrl** key, and click the tabs of additional worksheets.)

2. Click the **Select All** button (the unlabeled block at the intersection of the column and row headers). Excel highlights the entire worksheet.

3. Open the **Format** menu, select **Column** or **Row**, and choose **Height** or **Width**. A dialog box appears. Enter the size of the new height or width. (The height number is measured in points; the width is the average number of characters of the standard font.)

Page Formatting

When it comes time to print your shiny new document, you'll want to set up proper page adjustments: margins, page orientation, page order, and headers and footers. You make all of these adjustments from the same place: the Page Setup dialog box. To access this dialog box, open the **File** menu and select **Page Setup**.

The Page Setup dialog box has four tabs. Although we discussed most of the Page Setup options in Chapter 3, "Saving and Closing Documents," here's a recap to save you the effort of turning a few pages.

Page. Choose your page orientation (vertical or horizontal), page scaling (how much worksheet do you want to cram onto a page?), paper size, print quality (a higher number of dots per inch is a higher quality printout), and the first page number.

From any page, you can also call up the Print, Print Preview, and printer Options screens, all of which are thoroughly explained in Chapter 3.

Margins. Specify how far from the edges you want worksheet and header/footer information to be printed. Choose also whether you want your worksheet to be centered vertically or horizontally on the page.

Header/Footer. Choose from the built-in list of headers and footers, or create your own.

Sheet. This tab lists elements and asks whether or not you want them printed. You can also control your page printing order from this tab.

Changing Excel's Appearance

You change documents for other people. You change Excel for yourself. In this section, you'll learn to customize your own copy of Excel, so that your work environment is friendly, fun, and—depending on the color scheme you pick—safe.

Making It Pretty

Most of your basic screen appearance is determined by your Windows Control Panel settings. The following table shows which Control Panel setting changes each of the aspects of your Excel screen settings.

Changing Excel's appearance

This Control Panel Setting...	Affects This Excel Screen Element
3D Objects	Color of column/row headers, toolbars, scrollbars
Active Title Bar Color	Title bar color
Active Title Bar Fonts	Title bar fonts
Menu Color	Menu color
Menu Fonts	Menu fonts
Window Color	Workspace, Formula bar, View sizer colors

To access the Windows 95 Control Panel, click the **Start** button on your taskbar, select **Settings**, and select **Control Panel**. Select the **Display** option from Control Panel, and click the **Appearance** tab to change your font and color settings.

Hide and Go Seek: Displaying Screen Elements

In Chapter 1, "10-Minute Guide to Excel," you learned that the basic Excel screen contains such elements as bars, objects, grids, tabs. You can choose to display or hide most of these elements by using the Options dialog box.

Open the **Tools** menu and select **Options** to access the Options dialog box. Click the **View** tab to see a list of the elements you can change (shown in the following figure). Excel provides a check box for each element you can turn on and off.

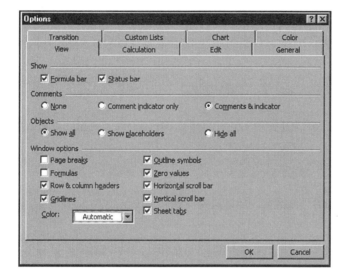

The View tab of the Options dialog box.

➤ In the Show area, use the **Formulas** and **Status Bar** radio buttons to turn the Formula bar and the Status bar on and off.

➤ In the Comments area, the None radio button will hide all cell comments and indicators. The Comment Indicator Only radio button determines whether or not a small red triangle appears when you attach a comment to a cell (see Chapter 12). The Comments & Indicator button will cause the indicator and comment to be displayed on your worksheet.

➤ The Objects options determine how objects such as imported pictures and Excel charts are displayed. You can show them in full, simply mark their location, or hide them altogether.

➤ In the Window Options area, you can turn on Page breaks to prevent printing problems down the road. The Formulas radio button changes the display of data in cells that contain formulas; when the Formulas button is selected, Excel displays the actual formulas instead of their results. This is useful if you need to print out your formulas.

➤ The Gridlines check box sets grids for each cell in your work area. You can pick a color or let Excel assign a color automatically.

➤ The other check boxes in this area (Row & column Headers, Outline symbols, Zero values, Horizontal scrollbar, Vertical scrollbar, and Sheet tabs) turn the display of each of these items on or off.

Zoom In

There's still one more factor for changing your Excel display: the Zoom feature. Zoom determines how much of the worksheet you see onscreen at any given time. To use Zoom, open the **View** menu and select **Zoom**. Excel displays the Zoom dialog box (shown in the following figure).

Use the Zoom dialog box to adjust the scope of your view.

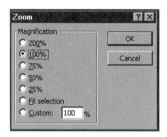

Choose a percentage from the list or pick **Fit Selection** to have Excel fit the selected range on the screen. If your selected range is as small as a single cell, the entire cell fills the screen. You can also select your own view percentage from the Custom box.

 Alternatively, you can adjust the Zoom percentage from the Zoom Control box on the Standard toolbar.

When viewing multiple documents (see Chapter 15, "Managing in Multiples"), you can size each window individually and zoom each window independently. Simply open the **Window** menu and choose **Arrange**. In the Arrange Windows dialog box, choose how you want the multiple windows arranged: Tiled, Horizontal, Vertical, or Cascade. Check the **Windows of Active Workbook** box to view more than one worksheet at a time. Then, to zoom each window individually, use the Zoom feature for each active window in turn.

New Ways of Viewing Documents

Excel permits you to view your documents in a variety of ways. Each of the screen elements previously described is part of the view, as are the Zoom factor and the window size. Once you've determined which elements are best for your active worksheet, you can save them as a "view." Then you can change any or all of those elements and save them again as a new view.

To save a custom view, set up your worksheet display the way you like it. Resize the window, open several windows and tile them, hide the objects, change the font, or do anything else you want. When you're satisfied with the view, open the **View** menu and select **Custom Views**. The Custom Views dialog box appears.

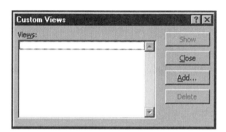

The Custom Views dialog box.

The Views list contains the names of any existing views. Click the **Add** button to add your new view under a new name. The Add View dialog box (shown in the following figure) appears. Add the view name, choose whether to include print settings and hidden rows and columns, and click **OK** to return to the main screen. Excel saves your view selections, and you can return to them at any time.

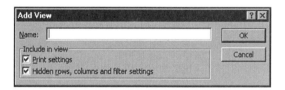

The Add View dialog box.

You can change your view—every element if you want—and repeat the process if you want to save that view also.

When you want to recall an old view, go back to the Custom Views dialog box, choose the desired view from the Views list, and click the **Show** button.

The Least You Need to Know

This chapter showed you how to make changes in the way things look on your Excel spreadsheet. Don't forget:

➤ You can change the appearance of cells, ranges, worksheets, and all of Excel.

➤ You can make most cell formatting changes from the formatting toolbar.

➤ To make more obscure formatting changes, access the **Format Cells** dialog box.

➤ Open the **File** menu and select **Page Setup** to access the Page Setup dialog box, which contains options for most page formatting changes.

➤ The Windows 95 Control Panel contains controls for many of Excel's appearance settings.

Managing in Multiples

Ever listen to a child whine? He acts almost as if his problems were somehow... significant.

"Hey, kid!" you want to holler. "Do I care about your broken gummy worm when I've got a mortgage payment to make and two guys are trying to break into my Ford Escort Pony?! No, I think I do NOT!"

Welcome to Workbooks

In this chapter, Excel makes you grow up. We advance from working in a single worksheet to working with entire workbooks and even multiple workbooks. This chapter focuses on two subjects: moving around in multiple work areas and linking those multiple work areas.

The Workbook Metaphor

Until a few years ago, every worksheet was an independent unit, with no obvious connection to any other worksheet. That made it tough for people who wanted to, for example, produce a separate report for each department in a division, have the results of each department feed into the divisional report, and have the divisional reports feed into a companywide report.

Excel provides workbooks to simplify all that. Because you can have many worksheets in a single workbook, you can have backups for backups for backups. And you can keep all the information related to a single topic in the same workbook. No chasing around the hard disk to find a lost payroll calculation. Of course, if you really liked the old system....

Workbooks also let you put your graphic reports—charts, graphs, and tables—on worksheets separate from those containing the underlying calculations. And that simplifies all your reporting and printing work.

How They're Built

By default, a workbook usually contains three worksheets. Excel displays the worksheet numbers on tabs near the bottom of your screen. These tabs make it easy for you to link one worksheet to any other worksheet using references in your formulas.

In the following section, we explain how to work with multiple worksheets. Later in this chapter, we'll show you how to work with multiple workbooks.

Managing Worksheets

By working with multiple worksheets, you can break your work down into logical segments. That's a good thing, because it keeps you from creating overwhelming worksheets that are larger than O.J.'s financial problems. The following sections outline a few methods you can use to successfully juggle multiple worksheets.

What was that old joke about the word assume? (It wasn't a great joke, but it helped us remember how to spell the word.) Anyway, instead of assuming that worksheet tabs are visible at the bottom (black patent-leather shoes won't help here), you may have to make those worksheet tabs come and go.

To have Excel display the worksheet tabs, open the **Tools** menu and select **Options**. In the Options dialog box, click the **View** tab. Then click the **Sheet Tabs** check box at the bottom of the Window Options section, and click **OK**.

Assign Worksheet Names

Direct from the manufacturer to you, Excel worksheets arrive with clever names like Sheet1 and Sheet2. You can let Excel go on like this for 255 worksheets, or you can give your worksheets names filled with meaning and personality. For us, names such as AmEx, Visa, MasterCard, and Repossessed immediately spring to mind. The names you choose should be appropriate for your worksheet.

To name or rename a worksheet, double-click the tab for the desired worksheet. The current name—most likely Sheet1—will be highlighted. Type in the new name for your worksheet and press the **Enter** key.

Double Trouble?

If double-clicking has got you down, you can just as easily change the name of your tab by clicking on it just once with the right mouse button. Select **Rename** from the shortcut menu that appears, and Excel highlights the worksheet name, ready for edit.

Ain't it nice to have choices?

Switch to Another Sheet

There isn't much point in coming up with brilliant names for worksheets if you can't choose from among them. You learned in an earlier chapter that you can select a worksheet by clicking on the numbered worksheet tab. But naming the worksheets may have added a few wrinkles you didn't have to contend with before.

When you first opened your workbook, the worksheet names were short, and all the tabs were clearly visible near the bottom of your screen. That has all changed now. With longer worksheet names like "Bill's Bank Accounts" and "Nixon's Enemies List," you'll be lucky to see more than two of the tabs at a time.

If the tab you are looking for is not readily visible, do one of two things:

➤ Use the tab scrolling buttons (shown in the following figure) to display the tabs. When you see the tab you want, stop and click it.

➤ Right-click the tab scrolling button, and a list of all the worksheet names appears. Select the one you want from that list.

Change the Number of Visible Tabs

Another thing that might prove helpful is to expand the area where the tabs are displayed. Don't worry; that's easy to do. Simply click the tab split bar and drag it back and forth as necessary. To return the bar to its original position, double-click it.

Scroll through the tabs as necessary to find the one you want.

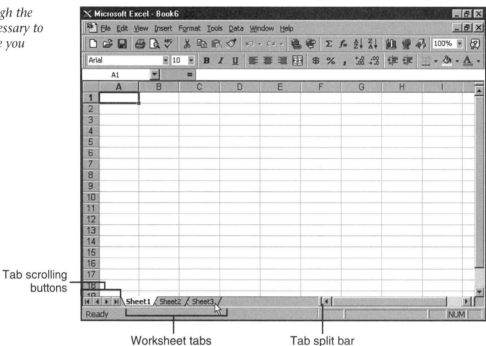

Tab scrolling buttons

Worksheet tabs   Tab split bar

Create Multiple Views

If you're going to take the time to create all of those wonderful worksheets, it's probably safe to assume you'll want to have a few of them on the screen simultaneously from time to time. To view two or more worksheets at a time, open the **Window** menu and choose **New Window**. In the new window, select the tab of the worksheet you want to view. (Don't panic if you can't see the window you had open before. We'll get to that in due time.) Repeat this process until every worksheet you want to view is listed under the **Window** menu. If you open multiple pages in the same workbook, the filenames will be followed by a colon and number. The number describes nothing but the order in which the worksheets were opened.

To arrange the worksheets so you can view them all simultaneously, open the **Window** menu and select **Arrange**. The Arrange Windows dialog box appears, with a few choices

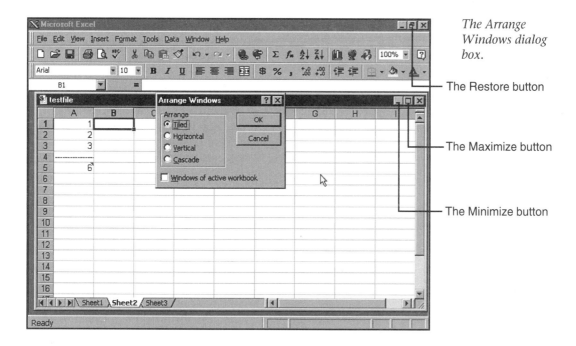

The Arrange Windows dialog box.

The Restore button

The Maximize button

The Minimize button

as to how the multiple screens are laid out. This is a personal matter; we'll close our eyes while you choose.

Near the bottom of the Arrange Windows dialog box is the Windows of Active Workbook check box. Click the box to remove the check. (We'll use it later; for now, it just muddies the water.)

You can restore worksheets to full size by clicking on the **Maximize** button (the second button in the upper right corner of the active Title bar). Click the **Restore** button to revert to the multi-worksheet view.

Adding, Moving, and Copying Sheets

Now that you're into this multiple worksheet stuff, the default number of worksheets just won't do. You want one more—at least. Okay. It's your workbook. You can add, move, or copy worksheets at your discretion.

➤ *Adding worksheets.* The first step in adding a worksheet is to mark where you want it to appear. Click the worksheet to the left of which you want to add a worksheet; that worksheet becomes active. Excel automatically inserts new worksheets to the left of the active worksheet. Try to insert it in the right place, even though you can move it later if necessary.

➤ *Moving worksheets.* If you don't like the order of your worksheets, you can move any worksheet by clicking on its tab and dragging it across the row of tabs to where you want it. A small arrow above the tab indicates where it's going to drop.

➤ *Copying worksheets.* To copy a single worksheet, click the tab of the desired worksheet. Then press and hold the **Ctrl** key while you drag the worksheet across the row of tabs to where you want to insert it. (If you release the mouse button before you release the Ctrl key, Excel inserts a copy of the original.)

➤ *Moving or copying multiple worksheets.* This is a two-step process: First, you select the worksheets and gather them into a group, and then you move or copy the group as a single entity.

To select two or more adjacent worksheets, click the tab of the first worksheet in the group and hold down the **Shift** key. Then click the tab of the last worksheet in the series and move or copy the group as you would an individual worksheet. As you drag across the row of tabs, the mouse pointer changes form to look like a series of pages, which indicates that you are using multiple worksheets.

To select two or more nonadjacent worksheets, click the tab of the first worksheet, press and hold the **Ctrl** key, and click the tabs of the other worksheets you want to include in the group. Then move or copy the group as you would an individual worksheet. The multi-page mouse pointer appears as you drag across the row of tabs. Excel places all of the selected worksheets to the left of the indicator arrow.

Referencing in Multiples

Now that you're using multiple worksheets, you probably want to start writing formulas and functions that cross worksheet boundaries. We're here to help.

To enter a reference to another worksheet in a formula or function, you'll usually just click your pointer on the actual cell you want to reference. The cell reference appears in your formula with a complicated syntax that looks like this: worksheet!cells. If you'd rather enter it manually, you can enter the worksheet name followed by an exclamation point (!) to separate it from the cell references that follow. For example, to calculate the sum of cells A1 through A3 on Sheet8, you'd use the SUM function and enter =SUM(Sheet8!A1:A3). (See Chapter 9, "Home on the Range," for more information on cell references.)

Managing Workbooks

You may be wondering why you should bother with multiple workbooks if you're allowed to have more than 250 worksheets in a workbook. That's a fair question, and if this were the Kung Fu version of this book, we might say something like, "For as the tree grows tall, Grasshopper, the roots wander wide." Then we would leave you to wonder what on earth we were talking about. But we're not like that (at least, not intentionally), so we'll offer an explanation.

The mind generally thinks more clearly when the clutter is compartmentalized. By separating the individual components of, say, a spreadsheet-based accounting system, you can formalize your plan of attack. (There's also the benefit of being able to choose which things you share and which things you keep to yourself.)

Switching Between Workbooks

When working with related workbooks, you'll probably want to view two or more simultaneously. No problem whatsoever.

Open your workbooks by selecting the **File**, **Open** command. Then, to view more than one workbook at a time, open the **Window** menu and select **Arrange**. The Arrange Windows dialog box appears. You can have Excel tile the workbooks (where the resulting patterns are vaguely reminiscent of a bathroom floor), arrange them in vertical or horizontal rows, or cascade them in a virtual waterfall of stacked windows. Choose the window arrangement you want, activate the **Windows of active workbook** check box, and click **OK** to have Excel display all open workbooks.

Restore button to revert to the multi-worksheet view.

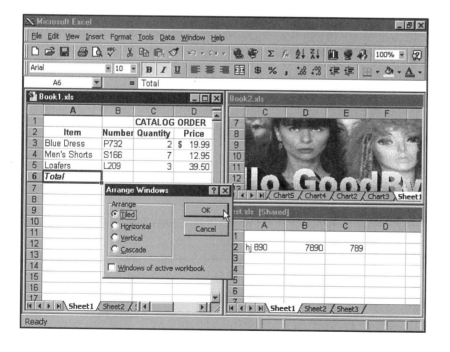

Choose an arrangement for multiple windows in the Arrange Windows dialog box.

Shifty Stuff

To quickly shift from one workbook to the next without using the menus, just use the **Ctrl+F6** key combination. You'll move through all open workbooks, one at a time. They do not need to be visible on the screen to perform this operation.

Referencing in Multiples Part II: Workbooks

As it does with worksheets, Excel provides an orderly method for sharing formulas between workbooks.

To enter a reference to another workbook in a formula or function, it helps to have both workbooks open to their respective worksheets. Begin entering the formula, and when it's time to enter the cell reference from the other workbook, just click it and continue typing your function. (If they're not both visible on the screen simultaneously, press **Ctrl+F6** to toggle to the second workbook.) The reference will appear with the workbook name in square brackets like this: [and]. Yes, you've seen it all before—almost. To calculate the sum of, say, cells A1 through A3 on Sheet8 of a workbook called My Budget and have the answer appear in cell A1 of Sheet1 in workbook My Checking Account, enter =SUM([My Budget.XLS]Sheet8!A1:A3) in cell A1 of Sheet1 of workbook My Checking Account.XLS.

Linking

You link workbooks for the same reason you might link your fence to your neighbor's fence: It would be a waste of resources to run two fences side by side along a common property line. The same is true with workbooks: It would be wasteful and would invite errors to have the same information entered in several areas.

For those times when you want to share data between one or more workbooks, you link. Linking is better than copying because when you change the source cells in one document, Excel automatically updates the same cells in the second document. Think you could get your neighbor to be that cooperative?

You need two components to link workbooks: a source workbook and a destination workbook.

Now you've got two ways to create links.

➤ Use a hyperlink. You learned in Chapter 7, "Excel on the Net," how to use hyperlinks. Because hyperlinks are so easy to use, we recommend hyperlinking wherever possible. Just click the **Insert Hyperlink** icon wherever you want to insert a jump between any two pieces of information. With Hyperlinks, you can link cells to other cells in any worksheet or workbook, or you can link in any other kind of file, including graphics, word processing, audio, and databases.

➤ When you prefer to have the data update itself automatically, you'll use a different kind of link. The technology is called OLE, which refers to object linking and embedding. Here's how it works.

1. To create an OLE link between workbooks, select the active cell group from the source workbook and click the **Copy** icon.

2. Select the area on the destination workbook where you want to place the selected cells.

3. Open the **Edit** menu and select **Paste Special**, and the Paste Special dialog box appears.

The Paste Special dialog box.

4. Click the **Paste Link** button. That's all you need to do. Now you'll see changes in your source worksheet update automatically in your destination worksheet.

Changing Links

Unfortunately, we're not always happy with our first choices, and neither (we suspect) are you. To change the source workbook, select the linked cells from the destination workbook, open the **Edit** menu, and choose **Links**. The Links dialog box appears.

From the dialog box, select the **Change Source** button, and a dialog box similar to the Open dialog box appears. Select the new source workbook and click **OK**.

The Links dialog box.

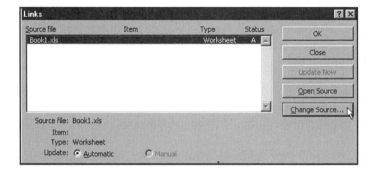

One final note before closing. If you are going to save your source workbooks in directories other than those that contain your destination workbooks, you must save your source workbooks first. If you don't, you could destroy your links.

The Least You Need to Know

Seeing double yet? You don't have to remember everything everything. Just keep these important points in mind.

➤ Multiple worksheets simplify complicated spreadsheeting tasks.

➤ You can name your worksheets in much the same way that you name cells and ranges.

➤ You can reference formulas from one worksheet in a second worksheet so that the first feeds into the next.

➤ You can simultaneously view multiple worksheets or multiple workbooks.

➤ Linking workbooks makes it possible to change a formula in one and have it automatically update in the other.

Part 3
Charts, Graphs, Maps, and Other Things

At last! A break from all those numbers!

In this section, you'll learn to build and change charts, graphs, and maps. Flower children from the '60s will appreciate all the available shapes and colors. Create your own magical mystery charts. In fact, we wrote this whole section wearing bell-bottom trousers and love beads.

Chapter 16

Graphics Workshop

In This Chapter

➤ Graphic reminder

➤ Pulling 'em in

➤ Draw the line

➤ Twist and shout

➤ Perfectly polished prettying-up

Orange crates. Bad posters taped to the wall. Brick-and-board bookshelves. Air mattress.

Yeah, we've done the "I'm single, I'm in college, and I don't care!" school of decorating. Nowadays, though, we prefer glass in our picture frames, counter-sunk screws in our bookshelves, and actual drawers for our undies.

Is it too much to expect the same level of panache from a spreadsheet? We think not.

Welcome to Graphics

As anyone who has ever viewed *Baywatch* knows, there's a lot to be said for visual aids. The right visuals can direct interest where you want it directed.

This section of the book focuses on various sorts of visuals for Excel. These are the features that spice up your worksheets and divert the attention of your audience from the hard cold numbers of your worksheet. Chapter 17, "Top of the Charts," looks at charts, and Chapter 18, "Mapping Your Future," explains maps. In this chapter, though, we introduce graphics as a whole, and tell you how to create, import, and manipulate your own.

If you're lucky, you might end up with graphics that are better looking than the life-guards on… naaaahhhh….

Types and Shadows

Excel allows you to attach graphic objects to your worksheets and workbooks. You can attach existing graphics you've imported from other places or pictures you've drawn yourself, and you can manipulate either kind of graphic. With Excel tools like AutoShapes, Organization Chart, and WordArt, you can create charts, tables, and maps, all of which are described in other chapters.

Your imported graphics can take the form of photographs, drawings, clip art, symbols, charts, and software screen shots. Once you've imported or drawn your graphic, you can use Excel's drawing features to manipulate them. Let's start by learning to import.

Importing Existing Graphics

You don't have to be a Leonardo, Michelangelo, or any of the other Ninja Turtles to place great-looking graphics in your document. There are literally thousands of stock photos and graphic images available from other software packages (including Microsoft's ClipArt collection), online services, electronic bulletin boards, and CD-ROMs located in the "we didn't know where else to put them" rack at local discount stores. Use a classic shot of the Eiffel Tower or use your desktop scanner to copy in that group photo of your kids on vacation.

You can import any of the bitmapped Microsoft ClipArt Gallery images that are included with Excel. In addition, Excel allows you to import other bitmapped (.BMP) files, popular Internet graphics formats (.JPG and .GIF), tagged image format (.TIF) files, PC Paintbrush (.PCX) files, WordPerfect Graphics (.WPG) files, and several other types of graphic files into your documents.

To import a favorite graphic from an outside source, open the **Insert** menu and select **Picture**. Click **From File** if the graphic is on disk. The Insert Picture dialog box—star-tlingly similar to the Open dialog box described in earlier chapters—appears on your screen (see the following figure).

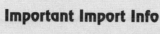

Important Import Info

Although Excel can import several types of graphics files, you must already have installed the proper graphic import filter or converter, usually as part of your original software installation. If you are unable to import a file that's in an acceptable format, run Setup again to install the necessary filters. You can import the following graphics file types into Excel:

.BMP	Bitmapped image
.CDR	CorelDRAW!
.CGM	Computer Graphics Metafile
.DRW	Micrographix Designer/Draw
.EPS	Encapsulated PostScript
.GIF	Graphic Image Format
.HPGL	HP Graphics Language
.JPEG or .JPG	Online compressed graphics format
.PIC	Lotus 1-2-3 graphic
.PCT	Macintosh PICT filter
.PCX	PC Paintbrush
.TIF or .TIFF	Tagged Image Format
.WPG	WordPerfect Graphics

Search for an image in this dialog box just as you would search for any file (refer to Chapter 13, "An Open and Shut Case," for search techniques). You can preview some images in the Picture dialog box before you load them. Click the **Preview** button, and then scroll through your graphics images. The viewable images will appear in the Preview window.

Click the **Open** button to copy the image into your worksheet. If Excel does not readily identify the file type, it displays the Convert File dialog box. Select the type of image you are importing and click **OK**.

Select the image you want to import in the Insert Picture dialog box.

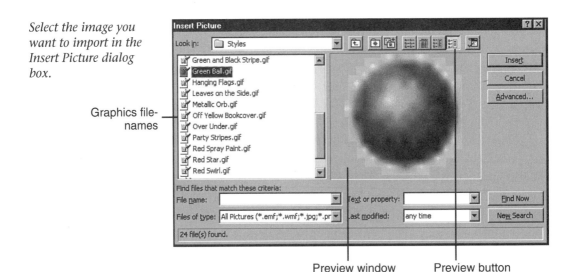

Graphics file-names

Preview window   Preview button

Drawing Your Own

"Everyone's a critic," says the actor. "Everyone's an editor," says the writer. "Everyone's an artist," says... the software developer? Yep. Even if you're awful, Excel gives you the tools to create art that can impress even the most jaded critic—your mom.

The Drawing toolbar contains a great selection of drawing tools. There are tools for drawing lines, boxes, circles, arrows, and just about any variation of those that you can imagine. You can fill in shapes with patterns and colors, change border styles, and have a whale of a good time getting your images just right.

To access the Drawing toolbar, click the **Drawing** icon on the Standard toolbar, or open the **View** menu, select **Toolbars**, and choose the **Drawing** toolbar. Excel displays the Drawing toolbar at the bottom of your screen.

On the Drawing toolbar, you'll find 18 icons hiding a plethora of drawing tools, each designed to provide hours of drawing pleasure.

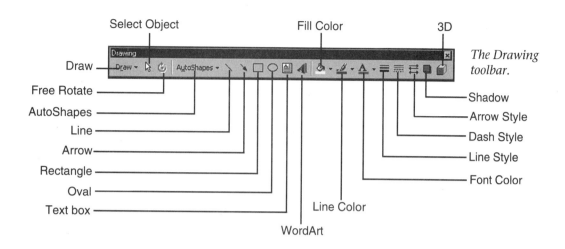

The Drawing toolbar.

Basic Shapes, Slings, and Arrows

Trying to master drawing in Excel by reading about it is like trying to learn to play the piano without touching a keyboard. We can tell you all you need to know, but you still need to get in there and fiddle about. So here are a few dry directions to help out when you feel the urge to fiddle (not, we ask, while major Italian cities are on fire).

It's time to have some fun. But first we'll do a quick rundown of some of the available options in the Drawing toolbar.

Excel's Drawing toolbar buttons

Button	Name	Description
Draw ▾	Draw	To draw or not to draw? Not really. Draw provides a means for manipulating figures that are already on the worksheet.
▨	Select Object	Select the object to be altered.
↻	Free Rotate	Turns the mouse pointer into something resembling a ringworm, which, when used to grab "pivot points," can be used to rotate some 3D objects.
AutoShapes ▾	AutoShapes	All the shapes you "auto" have and then some. It's new for Excel 97. Read about it later in this chapter.

continues

Excel's Drawing toolbar buttons Continued

Button	Name	Description
	Line	It's straight. Make it rotate from a center point by holding down the Ctrl key while you draw.
	Arrow	Point away. Eliminate jaggy lines by holding down the Shift key while you draw.
	Rectangle	Make it a perfect square by holding down the Shift key while you draw.
	Oval	These aren't AutoShapes. Think of these as the drawing tools for people with lots of time. Perfect circles happen if you hold down the Shift key.
	Text Box	Sometimes it is better to say it in words. Use this feature to add text to your graphics.
	WordArt	New for Excel 97. We say only nice things about this a little later in this chapter.
	Fill Color	Fills in your cell background with color.
	Line Color	Adds color to the lines in your cell.
	Font Color	Adds color to your writing.
	Line Style	Thick, thin, double, triple. Take your pick.
	Dash Style	Draw a line first, and use this icon to change it.
	Arrow Style	Alters the thickness and style of your lines, dashes and arrows.
	Shadow	Adds a shadow to your smile as well as boxes on your spreadsheet.
	3D	Changes the perspective of 3D objects on your worksheet. Not so scary without the glasses.

The Drawing Room

Drawing in Excel is not exactly drawing. It's more a case of choosing objects, placing them on your worksheet, and then maneuvering them to fit your needs. For the most part, you simply click a shape—choose Line, Arrow, Rectangle, or Oval, for example—and watch your pointer change to a small cross. Move your pointer to the work area of your spreadsheet and position it where you want the shape to begin. Then hold down the left mouse button and drag the shape to the size and position you want.

Shape Up

AutoShapes contains virtually every shape you "auto" have on a spreadsheet and then some. Select arrows: Make 'em straight or circular, or give them a certain waggle.

AutoShapes

Rather than set yourself up for a painful repetitive stress injury as you try to mouse your way through drawings, use AutoShapes and place perfectly drawn hearts, starts or squiggles in your document. Let the guys getting paid the big bucks deal with their own injuries.

To use them, click the **AutoShapes** icon. From the submenu, select your shape. They range from wiggly lines and flowchart symbols to stars and banners. With over 120 shapes to choose from, you "auto" find something that suits your needs. Place the selected shape on your document the same way as you would any of the other, more ordinary, shapes.

Art Linkletters

WordArt gives power to your text. Turn your letters into Leonardos.

An AutoShape.

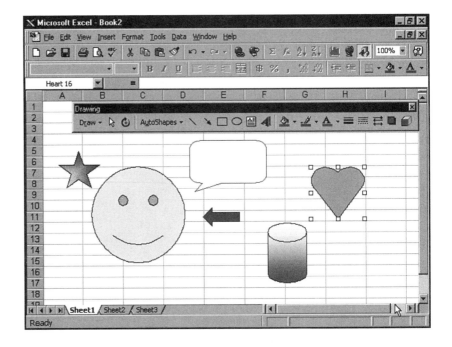

WordArt

To paraphrase a popular song (and to keep you up at night wondering what song it might be): The guys who spray things on the highway overpass have nothing on this, baby.

Click WordArt to splash your banner across the spreadsheet in a style that can't be missed. Write your message in tall 3D letters, wrapped, squeezed, pinched, arched, or splattered in bright colors. Other 3D effects let you vary the light source and point of view.

Click the **Insert WordArt** icon, and the WordArt Gallery dialog box appears.

The WordArt Gallery.

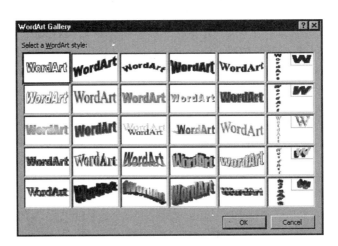

Double-click any one of the configurations. The Edit WordArt Text dialog box will appear on your screen. Type in the text box something like **The Beatles sang *For You Blue* on the *Let It Be* album** and click OK.

Your text appears in your worksheet and the WordArt toolbox is displayed.

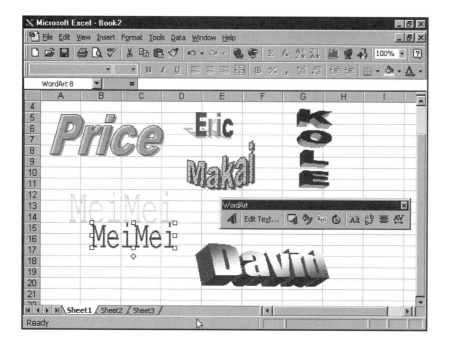

The WordArt toolbox.

You've now entered the world of presentation graphics. The best advice we can give is to go ahead and play. Click, drag, and draw your way into graphical proficiency. You're not going to harm anything. It is, after all, nothing more than a magnetic recording on a spinning disk. And you do make backup files, don't you?

Basic Training

When you're drawing one of these shapes, don't sweat the details. Just place it in your document. You can always reposition, lengthen, or shorten it later. To do that, just click the shape, and then drag the black squares, called vertexes, that appear at the ends of the line or shape.

You can change the characteristics of a created shape by selecting it (a single click) and then double-clicking it. When you do, the Format AutoShape dialog box appears.

Each shape has its own Color and Lines tab with options related to changing the appearance of that particular shape. On the Color and Lines tab for the arrow shape, for example, you can reformat Excel's arrows to make them longer, fatter, greener, double-headed, and so on.

203

Resize a shape by dragging one of the vertexes.

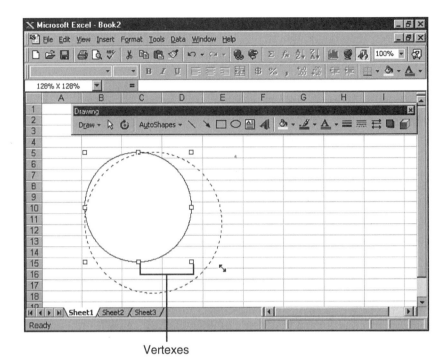

Vertexes

Use the Colors and Lines tab to change the attributes of a shape.

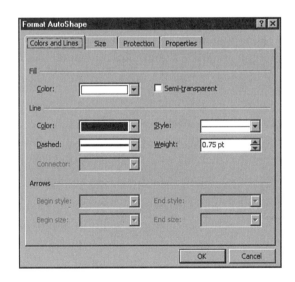

World's 'a Changin'

Another way to get to the Format Object dialog box is to select the text box or graphic you want to adjust, open the **Format** menu, and select **AutoShape**. The Format AutoShape dialog box appears on your screen. Easier yet, just double-click the object itself.

The Format AutoShape dialog box has three other tabs labeled Protection, Properties, and Size. Use the Protection tab to protect or unprotect an object from unwanted changes. (See Chapter 12, "Keep It Clean, Keep It Accurate, Keep It Safe," for more information on cell protection.) The Properties tab lets you choose what happens to the object if you move or change the underlying cells. You can move the object and resize it with the cells, move it without resizing it, or neither move nor resize it. Use the Print Object check box on this tab to indicate whether or not you want the object printed when you print your worksheet. The Size tab allows you to scale and rotate your object.

Labeling Graphics

You can label your graphics image by placing a text box in your image and typing your label or comments into it. Simply click the **Text Box** button on the Drawing toolbar, then drag the changed cursor diagonally across a section of the screen to draw a box. Then start typing. If you want to adjust the font type and size, select the text box and right-click it. Select **Format Text Box** from the shortcut menu. The Format Text Box dialog box will appear on your screen. Select from the formatting options to make changes.

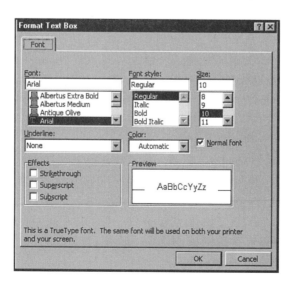

Make your font type, size, and other format selections here.

To make changes to background color, font color, or to add shadows or 3D effects, just select the text box and choose the appropriate icon from the Drawing toolbar.

Manipulating from Within

You'll make most of the changes to your graphic objects using the controls in the Drawing Toolbar described previously. However, you have a few other options for manipulating graphics.

Proportions

You can't do much to manipulate an imported graphics file from within Excel. You'll find it faster and safer to make changes to your object directly from your dedicated graphics package before you import it.

But you can easily make one change to any graphic from within Excel: sizing adjustments. Click the graphic you want to resize, and a box appears around the graphic with *sizing handles*, small squares located at the corners and midpoints of the box. Click a sizing handle with your mouse pointer, and drag the side or corner of the graphic to its new size. As you drag, the proportions of the image change in the direction you drag the border. To maintain constant proportions as you resize imported graphics, hold down the **Shift** key as you drag one of the sizing handles.

Drawn Objects

To maintain constant proportions as you resize imported graphics, hold down the **Shift** key or the **Ctrl** key as you drag one of the corner sizing handles.

Moving Objects

To move an object within a worksheet, click it with the mouse and drag it to where you want to it to be. To select two or more objects and move them as a set, you have two options. Either hold down the **Shift** key and click each object you want to move, or click the **Select Objects** icon and drag your pointer across all the objects you want to include in the set. When the multiple objects are selected, hold down the **Shift** key and drag the objects as a group to the new location.

The easiest way to move a graphic to another worksheet or workbook is to select the object and use the **Cut** and **Paste** buttons on the Standard toolbar.

Copying Objects

To copy an object within a worksheet, select it, press and hold down the **Ctrl** key, press the right mouse button, and drag the copied graphic to the new location. The original stays put.

The easiest way to copy to another worksheet or workbook is to select the object and use either the **Copy** and **Paste** buttons on the Standard toolbar, or the quick key combinations for copying (**Ctrl+C**) and pasting (**Ctrl+V**).

Exporting

Just as you can import a graphic from another program into an Excel worksheet, you can copy any graphics image in your Excel document (including Excel charts) into another program. To do so, select the image you want to export, hold down the **Shift** key, open the **Edit** menu, and select **Copy Picture**. Then, using the other program's menu commands, paste your image into the other application.

The Least You Need to Know

Graphics are a great way to brighten up your worksheets. Here are the things you should remember about using them:

➤ Most of your graphics will be imported. They look better than the ones you'd draw in Excel, and you have a wide variety to choose from.

➤ Some days you won't be able to resist drawing your own object. Excel's drawing tools are very basic, but they're adequate.

➤ To make changes to a graphic, select it. Then double-click it and make your changes in the Format Objects dialog box.

➤ You can resize, move, rotate, copy, bend, stretch, and mutilate objects to any place on your worksheet.

Top of the Charts

"If it wasn't so rare, we'd all be well done." Or so we were assured by a certain science teacher. A very funny joke we thought, until the day one of our classmates brought in a picture of a person who had actually spontaneously combusted.

The teacher tried to calm the class down. He reasoned with us, explaining that, statistically, the chances of it happening to any one of us were virtually nonexistent. But we weren't listening.

Seeing that his pleas were falling on deaf ears, he began drawing on the boards with bright, bold-colored markers. He drew a great bold line representing most of humanity and a small dot representing the members of humanity that spontaneously combust. We got the picture. The chaos abated, and we returned to our seats for the rest of class. But it was a full week before any one of us would sit close to another human being.

Choosing Charts

Why use charts? Because the impact is immediate. Rows and columns are accurate, sure, but they're emotionless. Even when dressed up for readability, they don't jump out and tell you anything. You know: There's a sum... and look over there: an average! Given enough time, your audience could figure out what it is about the numbers that excites you. But do you, or do they, really want to wait?

Charts reach out and grab your viewers by the throat. That thick sky-blue ribbon heading for the heavens—that's sales. The red ribbon snaking along at a low level along the bottom—that's cost. This is exciting. This is immediate. This is what charts are all about.

Charts made in Excel have the additional advantage of being able to change as you change the underlying data. Because the charts and the actual data are linked, the chart changes are automatic. So once you create a chart, you never have to go back and change it—unless you want to.

There are more than 120 basic charts to choose from in Excel, and that's before you do any customization. The chart you choose depends on what you're trying to emphasize (or de-emphasize).

Looking for Mr. Good Bar... and Other Types of Charts

In this section, we describe some of the more popular charts available in Excel. Later, we'll tell you how to create and modify simple charts of your own and how to create really, really complicated charts—the kind that impress novices and confuse experts.

➤ *Area* charts are great for piling it on... the data, that is. Area charts illustrate the breadth of change as opposed to a rising or falling rate of change.

➤ *Bar* and *column* charts emphasize variations. The far-reaching bar is generally the most impressive performer. If reaching for the stars is what counts, these charts can emphasize how well you're doing (or not doing).

➤ *Pie* charts and *doughnut* charts are for more than just law enforcement figures. They provide an excellent way to show how parts—such data as resources and income—relate to the whole.

➤ *Line* charts are great for showing where you've been, where you are, and where you're going.

➤ *XY (Scatter)* charts don't look good onscreen. But if you want to know at a glance how lots of data fall into patterns, these are the charts you need.

➤ *Radar* charts gather the values in a series of numbers and visualize a coverage area.

➤ You'll find 3D *surface* charts useful in "what if" applications. Resembling topographic maps, they make useful visual aids in determining ideal data combinations.

➤ *Three-dimensional Bar, Area, Column, Line,* and *Pie* charts are all functionally similar to their 2D counterparts. However, they offer greater visual impact and clarity.

Creating a Chart

It's not necessary to decide the kind of chart you want before you create it; however, it does help to have an idea of what it is you want to do. There are plenty of ways to change your selection later if the chart type you choose doesn't work out.

Creating a chart in Excel is very much an automated process. Still, it's nice to know where you're headed and what's happening on your trip. You can move and resize charts at will. If you change the worksheet data on which the chart is based, Excel updates the chart immediately to reflect the change. (Okay, almost immediately. Let's not quibble over a few milliseconds.)

To create a chart, you start with chartable data arranged in a tabular format. Any column(s) or row(s) of numbers will do. Charts work best if you've labeled the rows and columns. The following figure shows a range of cells that contain chartable data. Each of these items of data will become a data point on the chart.

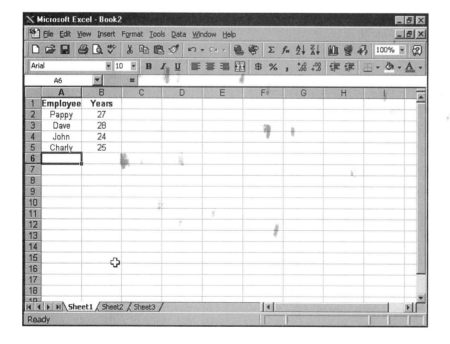

Chartable data arranged in a table.

Follow these steps to create your own chart:

1. Select the rows and columns you want to include in your chart, including any labels. With the cells still active, start the Excel Chart Wizard by clicking on the **Chart Wizard** icon on the Standard toolbar. The Chart Wizard—Step 1 of 4 dialog box appears on your screen.

Chart Wizard—
Step 1 of 4.

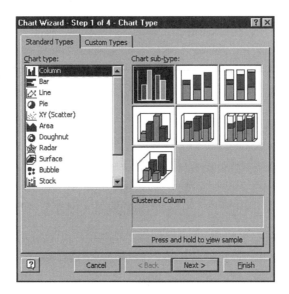

2. Choose a chart type. Don't agonize over which chart type to use at this point; you'll be able to change it later. For now, click any item in the Chart type menu and then select one of the available sub-types from the Chart sub-type box. After you've made your selection, click **Next** to get to Step 2.

   Click the **Data Range** chart to select the items to be represented in your chart. Since you've already selected a range, click **Next**, and go to Step 3.

3. The Chart Wizard—Step 3 of 4 dialog box allows you to make changes to titles, axes, gridlines, legend, and labels. Click the appropriate tab to make changes. Your change will be displayed in the preview box, giving you an opportunity to try out different variations before making a commitment. Click **Next** when you have finished adding your final touches, and move to Step 4.

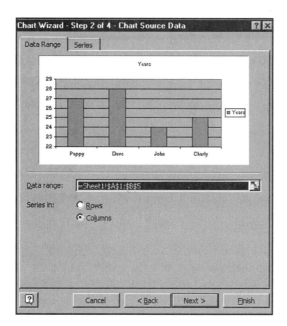

*Chart Wizard—
Step 2 of 4.*

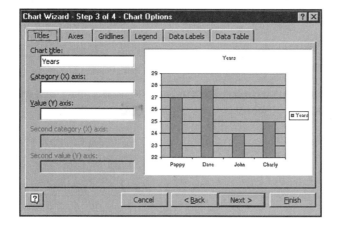

*Chart Wizard—
Step 3 of 4.*

Navigating in Chart Wizard

You can select the **Back** button at any time to back up a step and change a selection.

Chart Wizard—
Step 4 of 4.

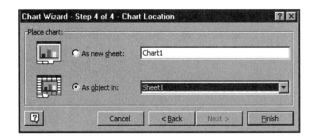

4. The final Chart Wizard dialog box will allow you to place your chart—as a new sheet or as an object—in the current worksheet. Make your choice, then press the **Finish** button to view your new chart.

If you put your chart on a separate sheet, it's easy to return to your place of origin. Just click its worksheet tab at the bottom of your screen. You have other viewing options, as well. By default, the chart is sized to fill the available space on your screen. To see what the chart would look like on the printed page, pull down the **View** menu and deselect the Sized With Window command. Excel automatically re-enables the Zoom feature with which you can zoom in or out. Additionally, you can preview the page from the **Print Preview** option on the **File** menu.

Quick and Easy Chart: Excel Knows Best

When time's a-wastin' and almost any chart will do, just select the data and labels you want included and press the **F11** key. Excel chooses which chart it thinks will best represent the selected data, creates the new chart, and opens it on a new chart sheet automatically. If you don't like it, you can always change it.

In the unlikely event that Excel admits it doesn't know what's best for your data, the Chart Wizard begins.

Creating Charts from Noncontiguous Cells

Cells do not have to be adjacent to be included in charts. To create a chart with cells from different areas of your worksheet, select the first group of cells you want to include in the chart. Press and hold the **Ctrl** key and select an additional group of cells from another area of your worksheet. You can do this more than once if necessary. Open the **Insert** menu, select **Chart**, and select either **As New Sheet** to place the chart on a new chart sheet or **On This Sheet** to create an embedded chart. Then proceed as usual.

214

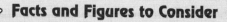

Facts and Figures to Consider

Besides the fact that throwing too many things on a single chart can render that chart a worthless hodgepodge of colorful blocks, there are some other limitations to consider. Truth is, though, that few worthwhile charts will even come close to these maximum limits:

4	Line weights
8	Line styles
12	Drummers drumming
16	Area patterns (onscreen)
255	Worksheets that a chart can refer to
255	Data series in a chart
255	Fonts in a chart
666	Evil software programmers
4,000	Data points per series
32,000	Data points for all data series
56,448	Pattern and color combinations

And one final finger-pointing number (meaning that no one is willing to accept responsibility): the total number of charts that your worksheet can link is limited by your available memory.

Morning-After Modifications

You've made your chart... but it's UGLY! It's INCOMPLETE! Who ya gonna call?

Meet the Toolbar

That sound you hear ain't the fat lady singing, so this mustn't be over yet. When your chart appears on the screen, it will be accompanied by a Chart toolbar.

There are several icons available, all designed for making additional changes to your chart. (Our favorite is the X button in the upper right-hand corner. It'll clear the screen of this toolbar without affecting the chart.) The first box selects any element of the chart so that you can manipulate it. Use the second icon to format the Chart Object selected in the first box. The third button changes the type of chart you've selected. The Legend button adjusts the definitions. We explain legends later in this section. The Data Table

215

button shows the values in a grid below the chart. By Row and By Column change the worksheet orientation. And the final two buttons change the layout of the text labels you add to your chart.

Adding Data to a Chart

You can usually add new data to an existing chart without too many complications. First, enter your new data where it belongs on your worksheet and select the cells you want to add to the chart. Move the pointer toward the edge of the selected cells until it becomes an arrow, and then click the left mouse button and drag the pointer into the chart. Excel automatically updates the chart to include the new group.

Chart toolbar.

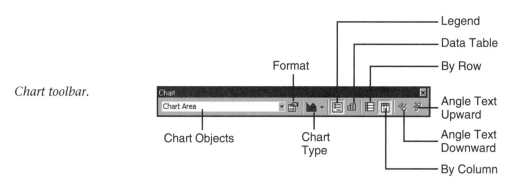

If for some reason Excel is unable to add the new data directly to the chart, the Paste Special dialog box appears onscreen. Enter the extra information as required and click **OK**.

What Becomes a Legend?

To create a legend, make up a story about a band of merry men who live in trees, wear pantyhose, rob from the rich, and star in hit movies. To place a legend of a different sort in your Excel chart, read on.

Adding a legend is simple. To place a legend on an embedded chart, right-click on the chart area. Select **Chart** options from the submenu. The Chart Options dialog box will appear.

Click the **Legend** tab. Choose the location for your legend by selecting the appropriate radio button listed in the Placement options.

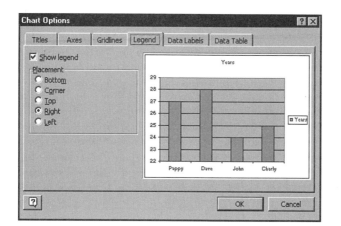

The Chart Options dialog box—Legend.

Data Labels

The process for adding data labels is similar to adding legends. Double-click the chart, and select **Chart Options**. When the Chart options dialog box appears, click the **Data Labels** tab. Select from the available options and click **OK**.

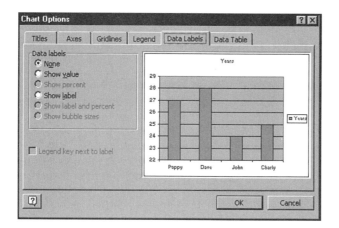

The Chart Options dialog box—Data Labels.

Between the Gridlines

Mother nature or menopause? We're not certain of the cause, but there may be times when you just can't seem to leave your chart's gridlines alone. Excel takes care of you with the Format Gridlines dialog box, a nifty feature for folks with lots of spare time. You can access it by double-clicking on the hairy edge of the grid lines in your current chart.

217

The Format Gridlines dialog box.

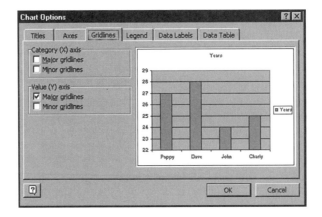

Select the **Patterns** tab to modify the axis. Under the Line options, select **Automatic**, the default setting; **None**, which makes the axis invisible; or **Custom**, which allows you to choose the line Style, Color, and Weight.

Select the **Scale** tab to change tick-mark values for either axis.

Sermon on the Charts

Earlier in this chapter, you learned to create simple charts. Now we discuss charts that have a bit more body: three-dimensional, combination, radar, scatter, and surface charts.

Width and Depth

Use these complex charts when you're dealing with complicated sets of data. For example, you might use them when you're comparing the costs of various kinds of vegetables with the costs of various kinds of meat; when you're dealing with scores of data points (say, sales volumes) across a period of time and want to see where they group; or when you're trying to prove a correlation (such as the weights of various mammals with their gestation periods).

Let's walk through creating a complex chart. First, enter your complex data sets using as many rows and columns as you need. We advise limiting yourself to no more than two sets, with seven or eight data points per set. Anything more complicated becomes difficult to read. Label your rows and columns, and then select all (or both) sets of data.

To actually create the chart, go through the Chart Wizard process as before.

3D or Not 3D

A 3D chart is a great choice for presentations, and best of all, special glasses are not required!

If you can look at a chart from only one angle, it's not 3D. It's just a 2D picture trying to look like 3D. In a genuine Excel 3D chart, you can turn or twist figures and look over, under, or behind them.

Excel provides for manipulating the 3D chart. Double-click the wall of a chart and grab one of the selection handles that appears along the edges of the chart. The mouse pointer changes to a small cross, and as you start to move the chart, it temporarily changes into a line drawing that you can twist and spin by dragging with the mouse from within the chart box.

Printing

Printing a chart is no different than printing a worksheet. Pull down the **File** menu and select the **Print Preview** command. Excel shows you the layout of the selected page.

Reshape and resize your embedded charts as necessary before you print. By default, Excel automatically sizes charts you created on separate sheets to fill the page. However, you can resize and rescale the chart if you want.

When you're satisfied with the chart's appearance, click the **Print** button on the Standard toolbar to start printing.

The Least You Need to Know

Thanks to Chart Wizard, the complicated process of creating a chart is reduced to following the relatively comprehensive onscreen instructions. This is what you need to remember about charts:

➤ Charts have immediate impact.

➤ Charts are linked to cells in a worksheet. When you change the contents of the cells, Excel updates the charts automatically.

➤ The Chart Wizard walks you through the creation of a chart step by step.

➤ You can modify or add to charts at a later date.

Mapping Your Future

There we were, late to a dinner appointment in the heart of Philadelphia, one of us driving, and the other trying to navigate.

"What does this say? North to Eustice?"

"No, it's one past Ulysses. I think."

"Can we stop to ask directions?"

"Grrrrrr…"

The navigator heaved a sigh and wondered when, exactly, men would learn what women have always known: Quit talking meaningless numbers. Get a map!

Excel's Mapping Function

Where in the world is... ?

With Excel's geographic maps, you can show at a glance where your highest sales or your lowest costs are. Show with graphic symbols the relative staff sizes of your Atlanta, Montreal, and Zaire offices. Graphically compare Hong Kong's export volumes to those of Taipei, Beijing, and Hubei.

Excel-generated maps let you visualize your worksheet results. And with the visual aids, your data, trend, and relationship analyses become easier.

Whatever you want to show on a geographic map, you can do with the Excel mapping function.

What's Available

Find It

If you need to locate a file, the easiest way is to use the Find applet. Click the **Start** button on your Windows 95 taskbar, and select **Find**, **Files or Folders**. A dialog box appears. In the Named box, type all or any part of the filename. Click **Browse** to specify where Windows should begin searching. Start the search by clicking the **Find Now**.

When you locate the file you're searching for, double-click it to load it.

The Map feature—or module—is based on an extensive database of maps and demographic information. To see the demographics of the Map module, open the workbook called MAPSTATS.XLS. (The location of this file varies, depending on your setup. In our latest incarnation of Excel, it was located in a folder called C:\Program Files\Common Files\Microsoft Shared\Datamap\Data. Say that three times fast without breathing!)

The most recent release of Excel 97 contains the following maps:

➤ Australia

➤ Canada

➤ Europe

➤ Mexico

➤ North America

➤ Southern Africa

➤ UK and ROI Countries

➤ U.S. with AK & HI insets

➤ World Countries

Need More Maps?

You can purchase additional maps from the software developer MapInfo Corporation at One Global View, Troy, NY, 12180-8399, USA. For telephone orders in the United States, call (800) 488-3552 toll-free; for international orders, call (518) 285-7110. Or you can fax MapInfo Corp at (518) 285-6070 or contact them via email at sales@mapinfo.com. Their Web page is http://www.mapinfo.com.

You can find a catalog of other maps in the map Help file, a separate Help file available within the Map module.

Maps as Graphics

Geographic maps become graphic objects on your Excel worksheet. You can place them, move them, and resize them just as you would any of the graphic objects we've described in the last two chapters.

There are a few differences, however:

➤ Maps are huge.

The underlying map commands make any worksheet you put them in very large. This means that once you embed a map, your worksheet runs more slowly and takes up a lot more hard disk space than it did before.

➤ Maps are complex.

When you update the data underlying a map, you need to execute a separate command to update the actual map. Excel doesn't do this automatically as it does with charts.

Those are the cautions. Here's how to get around them:

➤ Completely assemble your entire worksheet before you start to deal with maps.

➤ Make sure that your data is in place and in good tabular format before you even attempt to draw your map.

➤ Consider putting your map on a separate worksheet to speed up data entry and manipulation on the original sheet.

➤ Make sure you have lots of free hard disk space before you start creating maps and saving files.

In this chapter, you'll learn how to create and manipulate a map, update it, and change its appearance. Let's get started!

Create the Map

Creating the map involves two procedures: setting up the data and using the Map module.

Data Setup

Your map data works best when it's arranged as a two- or three-column table. Other layouts work, but they're more awkward.

Spreadsheet data can be mapped geographically.

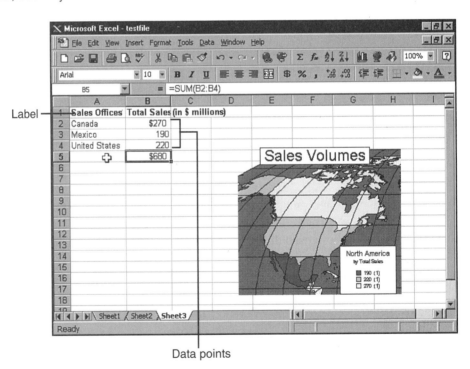

Put labels at the top of each column. Then put your locations (geographic areas, regions, states, countries, postal codes, cities, whatever) in the left column and the corresponding data points (sales figures, profit, expenses, staff size, market size, saturation percentages, or anything else that can be represented numerically) in the second column. If you have a second set of data points, list those in the third column.

Some locations (such as U.S. states, Canadian provinces, European countries, UK regions, and Australian states) can be abbreviated. Look in the Excel workbook MAPSTATS.XLS for the acceptable abbreviations. If you use postal codes, you must format them as text. If you leave them formatted as numbers, the leading zeros will not show.

Select the cells that contain your map data, including the column labels, and get ready to create.

Unfolding the Map: Using the Map Module

 With the relevant cells selected, click the **Map** icon on the Standard toolbar. Your mouse pointer turns into a cross hair.

This is your cue to select the area on your worksheet where you want the map to appear. Click at one corner of the desired area and drag your mouse pointer to the opposite corner. A blank rectangle appears on your screen, and the hard disk starts cranking as it looks for the information you need for your map.

If Excel finds an exact match for all of your geographic labels in its map database (found in the workbook MAPSTATS.XLS), you go directly to the next step in map creation. If not, it displays the Multiple Maps Available dialog box shown in the following figure. The box at the bottom lists multiple Excel maps that are available. Select the appropriate map and click **OK**.

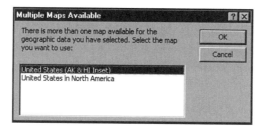

Choose the appropriate map from the Multiple Maps Available dialog box.

A preliminary map appears onscreen, and if your geographic areas were available in the map database (MAPSTATS.XLS or other add-in maps), your data points are graphed. If your geographic areas don't appear on the map, you need to create a custom push-pin map. See the section "Pin Maps" later in this chapter.

Controlling the Damage

After Excel draws your preliminary map, it displays the Microsoft Map Control dialog box (see the following figure).

225

*The Microsoft Map
Control dialog box.*

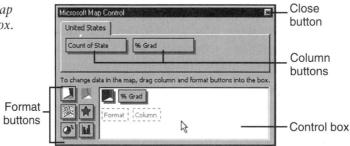

Close button

Column buttons

Format buttons

Control box

This dialog box contains three items: Column buttons at the top that match the column labels you assigned when you set up the data; format buttons on the left that you'll use to lay out your map; and a control box that contains buttons labeled Format and Column. (These labels are simply place markers; they don't serve any function other than to show you where your buttons belong.) If you used multiple columns of data, you'll see multiple column buttons in the control box.

You can change the way your data is graphed by dragging different format buttons onto the existing format button in the control box. The format buttons are

 ➤ *Value Shading.* Uses various shades of a single color to represent your data on the map. Change the value ranges or color while value shading is in use by going to the Map menu and selecting Value Shading Options. In the Format Properties dialog box, define the ranges and change the color.

 ➤ *Category Shading.* Uses various colors to represent data. To change the colors associated with each data point while category shading is in use, go to the Map menu and select Category Shading Options. In the Format Properties dialog box, highlight any listed category and modify its color.

 ➤ *Dot Density.* Scatters a representative number of dots across the corresponding geographic area. To change the size or value of the dots while they're being used, go to the Map menu and select Dot Density Options.

 ➤ *Graduated Symbol.* Uses a various-sized symbol—such as a dot—on each geographic area to represent data. To change the symbol while it's being used, go to the Map menu and select Graduated Symbol Options. In the Format Properties dialog box, click Modify Symbol.

 ➤ *Pie Chart.* Displays pie chart–formatted data in each geographic area. Change associated options while a Pie Chart is active from the Map menu, the Pie Chart Options command.

 ➤ *Column Chart.* Shows bar graph–formatted data for each area. Change associated options while a Column Chart is active from the Map menu, with the Column Chart Options command.

You can also change the column upon which your data is based or add another column. Drag a different column button into the control box, over the existing column button, and Excel changes your map formatting accordingly.

When you finish making changes, click the **Close** button (the **X** in the upper-right corner) to confirm your choices.

Loose Change

Inevitably, at some point you'll want to change something—your underlying data, the features of your map, or your entire presentation. All of that is done quite simply.

But changes may be confusing until you discover that the Map module is virtually a separate piece of software from Excel. When the Map module is operational, it has its own menus, its own toolbar buttons, even its own Help files. What this means is that you will make some changes from within Map, and you'll make others from the worksheet.

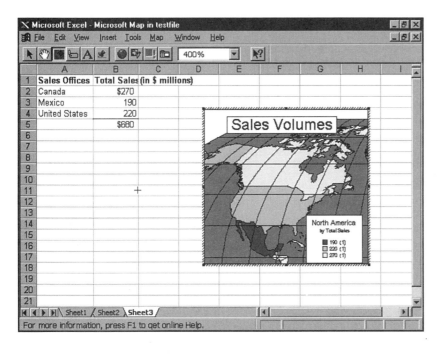

The wide striped frame shows that the map is active.

When the Map module is active, a wide striped frame surrounds your map. When it's inactive, the worksheet is active, and the map has a regular Excel frame.

The following sections outline the things you can change from outside the map (when the worksheet is active and the map is inactive) and those you can change within the Map module.

Changes from the Outside

From the Excel worksheet, you can change the size and position of the map, delete the map altogether, or change the data within your map.

Size and Position

You can move or resize your map or change its position as you would any graphic object. Select your map by clicking it once to make it an active Excel object. Do not click twice; that's how you restart the Map module.

You can now grab any of the sizing handles—the small squares on the perimeter of the box—to resize the map. Move the map by clicking on a sizing handle and dragging until it's in the proper position.

Another Option

You can also resize maps (but not move them) from within the active Map module. Just click and drag the sizing handle.

Delete Map

To delete your entire map, click it once to make it an active Excel object. When the map is selected, press the **Delete** key on your keyboard. The map disappears.

Changing Map Data

You can update the data in your worksheet without harming your map. Simply edit as usual by overwriting the cell or editing in the Formula bar.

Remember that Excel does not update maps automatically as it does charts. So every time you change parts of the worksheet data that underlie the map, you need to refresh the map display. Go to the Map menu and select **Refresh**.

While you're waiting, read about the changes you can make from within the Map module.

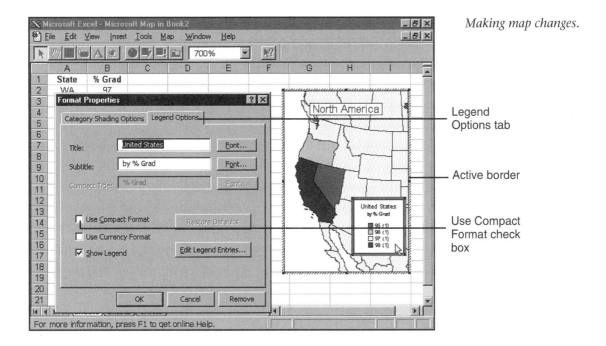

Making map changes.

Active Changes

When the Map module is active, you can make changes to features, text, view, and graphics.

When you activate the Map module by double-clicking on it, you see that it has its own toolbar for making other changes. These toolbar buttons are essential for making changes within the Map module. (If the Map toolbar isn't visible, go to the View menu and select Toolbar.) The following table shows the Map toolbar and tells you what each button does.

The Map toolbar buttons

Button	Name	Description
	Select Objects	Changes your mouse pointer back to an arrow shape, which allows you to select an object for modification.
	Grabber	Lets you shift the location of your map within its frame. (We explain how to use this tool in the later section "A Map with a View.")
	Center Map	Lets you designate a point as the center of the map.

continues

The Map toolbar buttons Continued

Button	Name	Description
	Map Labels	Lets you create text labels.
	Add Text	Prints text directly on the map.
	Custom Pin Map	Enables you to spotlight certain areas of your geographical map.
	Display Entire	Forces the entire map to fit in your designated frame size.
	Redraw Map	Updates the map when you've made changes to the underlying data.
	Map Refresh	Updates the data on the map to reflect changes made to the spreadsheet.
	Show/Hide Microsoft Map Control	Recalls the Data Map Control dialog box.
	Zoom Control	Lets you zoom in or out on your map.

The following sections explain in more detail some of the changes you can make from within your Excel Map module.

Changing Map Features

When you want to change features on your map (such as lakes, cities, countries, or highways), you need to make the Map module active. Click or double-click the map until the active border is visible. When your map is active, you can double-click anywhere on the actual map to call up the Map Features dialog box shown in the following figure.

The Map Features dialog box.

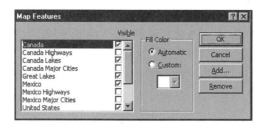

The Visible area contains a list of check boxes for available map features. Check the check boxes of the features you want to make visible, and remove the check from the check boxes of the features you want to hide. Choose colors and symbols for your map in the center box. Select the Custom option if you want to choose your own color and style. Select the Automatic option to let Excel use its best judgment. We predict you'll want to choose your own.

Just Words

You can make several changes to the text features of your map. These include:

➤ *Modifying legends.* By default, Excel displays legends in Compact Format, which shows as little as possible. To change to the expanded format, double-click the legend box on your map (the area that describes your graphic symbols). The Edit Legends dialog box appears. Uncheck the Use Compact Format option, and Excel creates an expanded legend. Other options in this dialog box allow you to edit and format the text of your legends. You can change the default by opening the **Tools** menu, selecting **Options**, and unchecking the Compact Legends by Default check box in the Data Map Options dialog box.

➤ *Adding labels.* To add labels to the geographic areas on your map, click the **Map Labels** button on the Map toolbar. The Map Labels dialog box appears, asking you to choose which features you want to label. Select from the pull-down list of map features (items like the Great Lakes) or click the **Values From** option button to get labels from your worksheet columns. Click **OK** to return to the map. Then the pointer becomes a crosshair, and you're ready to begin. As you move the crosshair over various regions of your map, labels appear under the crosshair. Click the left mouse button when you're satisfied with the placement of one label, and then continue placing others throughout your map. When you finish, choose the **Select Objects** toolbar button to turn off the Map Labels tool.

➤ *Adding text.* To add other text to your map, select the **Add Text** button and click in the place on your map where you want to add text. Then type in the text. You can change the text formatting by reselecting it, right-clicking, and choosing **Format Font** from the shortcut menu.

Text in the Blocks

Make sure you're satisfied with the size of your map before you insert new text. If you later change the zoom factor (explained in the next section), Excel changes the text size accordingly.

➤ *Changing the title.* You can amend the map's title by selecting the existing title and typing in a new name.

A Map with a View

If you want to see a more detailed view of a certain area, you can zoom in on that specific portion of your map. To do so, click the **Zoom Percentage of Map** button on the Map toolbar. Select the magnification level and Excel will adjust the map magnification by zooming in or out. Fine-tuning the magnification is simple. Just type in a different number.

When you zoom in on your map, it may not be centered properly in the frame. You can use the Grabber toolbar button to reposition the map within the frame. To do so, click the **Grabber** button, and the mouse pointer changes to a hand shape. Then position the mouse pointer anywhere on the map, hold down the left mouse button, and drag the map to its new location within the frame. If you want to fit the entire map within your frame, select the Display Entire tool.

If you dislike a view change you've made, you can return to your last view by opening the View menu and selecting Previous.

Customize the Graphics

To format the dot density, value shading, category shading, or graduated symbols you created originally, pull down the **Map** menu and choose the appropriate option. Depending on the format options you chose for your map, your Map menu might display the Category Shading Options command, the Dot Density Options command, or various other choices as the last command on the menu. When you click the option, a related dialog box appears, asking you for your color, sizing, values, summary, and visibility choices. Make your choices, and click **OK** to make them effective.

Redo the Map

The Redraw Map button on the Map toolbar enables you to quickly display minor changes you make to the map.

Use the Map Refresh button whenever you make changes to the underlying data on your Excel worksheet. The Show/Hide Data Map Control button gives you access to the Data Map Control dialog box you saw at the beginning of this chapter so you can change your original choices.

Pin Maps

When you need to mark elements on your map (key cities, countries, recreation sites, or target markets, for example), try using the Pin Map function. Just click the **Custom Pin**

Map button on the Map toolbar. Your pointer changes to a pushpin shape. Position the pointer in the location you want to mark and click your left mouse button. A pin appears on your map!

When you finish adding pins, reselect the **Select Objects** button. To delete a pin, click it with the **Select Objects** pointer and press the **Delete** key on your keyboard.

To move pins, use the **Select Objects** tool, then click and drag them to a new location.

A Call for Help

Because the Map module runs as a separate piece of software, you'll need to view the related Help files separately from those found in Excel itself. Fortunately, that's easy to do. When the Map module is active, press **F1**. That's it. You get full access to Map's Help files.

The Least You Need to Know

The Excel Map feature enables you to create geographic representations of your data. These are the things you'll want to remember about mapping:

➤ Set up your map data in columns with labels.

➤ Go to the MAPSTATS.XLS workbook to see the abbreviations and demographic data available for your maps.

➤ The Map feature runs as a separate piece of software within Excel, which means that you must make most changes to your map from within the activated Map module.

➤ The only changes you can make to the map when the module is not active are resizing, repositioning, and deletion.

➤ To read the Map Help files, you must first create a map. Then double-click the map and press **F1** to call up Map Help.

Part 4
Like a Database

*North paired with South,
Mae paired with West,
Client paired with the
correct accounts…a dream?
No it's a database.*

*In this section, you learn how to work with databases and import, manipulate, and
analyze data from other applications.*

List Management

Top Ten Reasons to Read This Chapter

10. Siddhartha traveled thousands of miles to get information this good.

9. What else are you going to do in the bathroom?

8. It's an Access avoidance activity.

7. You'd feel guilty if you skipped it.

6. It's the only chapter written entirely in the nude.

5. This chapter read backward is McCartney's biography.

4. It's the only chapter good enough to have a top ten list.

3. You might find small, intentional misspellings.

2. We promise that if we're going to hide a sex scene in this book, it'll be in this chapter.

1. Because if you don't, people will think you read this page solely for the sexual content.

This Thing Called List

You can't shop without them; politicians couldn't tell their friends from their enemies if these didn't exist; and you'd be reading the next chapter right now if Excel didn't have them. What are they? They're lists, of course. A bunch of vaguely related items under a common heading.

Most of the time you probably take lists for granted. Oh, yes you do. Lost the 10 pounds yet from your New Year's resolution list?

Excel's different. Excel takes lists seriously. Enter a list in Excel, and it begins to think it is a powerful database program. It treats columns of data as though they were fields in a database and looks at rows as the equivalent of records. (If you don't know a thing about databases, don't worry. A *field* is simply all the related information in a column, and a *record* is just a single row of information—such as your name, rank, and serial number—listed below the column—er, field—labels.)

Excel isn't a database program, but it may perform adequately enough to make a separate database program unnecessary for your work. In this section of the book, we'll treat Excel as though it really were a database performer. Nobody ever said that a piece of software couldn't initiate its own wish list.

Why You're Reading This Chapter

Database management programs give you a record of everything about something, and then let you yank out the good bits later on. Famous databases include the phone book, the ugly pages of the *Wall Street Journal*, the public library's card catalog (remember those?), box scores from baseball games (remember those?), your checkbook, and the *TV Guide*.

In this chapter, you'll learn how to create a database-like list in Excel and how to search your list to compile data based on your own criteria (such as "TV shows featuring Tony Danza"). You'll also learn how to make automated additions to your list.

Making a List

You don't have to learn any special tricks, buried commands, passwords, or secret handshakes to create a database, or list, in Excel. Simply enter some labels at the tops of your columns and type the entries below them. That's all there is to it—sort of.

There are a few guidelines that you probably ought to follow. There are lots of 'em, but they're not complicated or even critical. It's just that doing so will make life sweeter and easier for both you and the folks manning the telephones at the Excel customer support desk.

➤ Make sure your list is made up of several columns of data (which we'll call *fields* of data in this section), with labels at the top of each column (field).

➤ Each field (column) must contain items of related information. In other words, one field may contain names or addresses or figures or percentages or labels or social security numbers or the fat contents of fast-food meals. But you never want to mix different kinds of information in the same column.

➤ If you're going to play database games, don't create more than one list on a worksheet. Hey, we don't make up the rules—at least not all of them. Anyway, this is a rule with reason. Some Excel features don't function properly if you have more than one list on a worksheet. This is not to be confused with the limit on the number of records or fields you can use. Excel treats contiguous columns as a single list. You can use as many records and fields as your worksheet can hold, which is a mere 16,384 records and 256 fields.

➤ Leave a buffer zone of at least one blank column and one blank row between your list and other data on the worksheet. Workbooks are not a contact sport; this separation enables Excel to differentiate between your list and randomly scattered data.

➤ If you absolutely must have other data on the same worksheet as your list, avoid putting it to the side or bottom of your list because later, when you attempt to filter, that data may get hidden. Instead, use a practice some refer to as diamond-backing (yeah, like the snake). The following figure shows an example of diamond-backing in a worksheet. To do some diamond-backing of your own, enter blocks of unrelated information in a diamond pattern so that you can later add, delete, and hide columns and rows without disturbing information in other blocks.

➤ Make the first row of your list into column labels—also called field names. Excel is going to treat that first entry as a label whether you like it or not, so you may as well play along. It does become important later on when sorting data, creating reports, and performing other kinds of automatic manipulation.

➤ Choose fancy fonts and crazy colors for your labels. This is not actually a requirement, but setting off the field labels from the rest of the data can make a long list a little easier to read.

➤ Don't use dashes or blank rows to separate your labels from your data. This is an actual requirement. Excel assumes that blank cells are not a part of the contiguous set. (If it were up to Excel, Alaska would be handed over to Canada right now.)

➤ When entering your data, remember that all characters (even spaces) count when it comes to sorting, filtering, and other kinds of data manipulation.

➤ If you have protected cells or formulas in your list, unprotect them. If you don't, you might run into difficulties doing some database work. Or you might not. But they're not fatal.

Diamond-backing lets you add data to your worksheet safely.

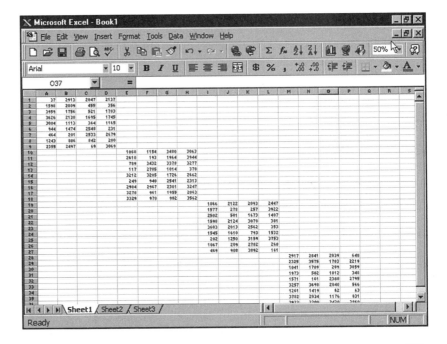

Copy It!

Because some database features don't get along well with formulas, you might want to change all your formulas to text or numbers. Of course, that would destroy your formulas, so here's a better way.

Select your entire list and click the **Copy** button on the standard toolbar (or press **Ctrl+C**) to copy it to the Windows Clipboard. Then open a new worksheet, pull down the **Edit** menu, and select **Paste Special**. In the Paste Special dialog box, click the **Values** option button to copy all your formula values as figures. Your original worksheet remains unchanged.

List Management and Other Sleight-of-Hand Tricks

The problem with lists is that nobody has yet found an effective way of stopping them from growing. Before you know it, a small list of a few hundred entries suddenly shoots up toward the thousands of entries. By then, there's too little time and not enough paper to handle the list without some sort of help.

Professional help comes at a high cost, though. People actually earn college degrees in this stuff. In fact, if the guy standing next to you in the bookstore is thumbing through a database book, offer him a compassionate smile. Then walk to the counter, buy this book, and be glad you got out of the store safely. This section covers all you really need to know about databases.

Data Forms

Let's say you've already done everything you can do. You entered your list in a worksheet following the rules we described above, you assigned great labels, and it looks good in general. So now is a good time to ask the question of the ages: What can Excel do for you?

One thing it can do is give you a cool, easy way to add even more data to your list. This feature is called the Data Form. The Data Form makes it easier for you to add, change, and delete data. As an added bonus, it lets you hunt for certain items based on specific criteria. Think of it as a look-up function, and we'll keep the hype to a minimum.

If you haven't already created a list to play around with, do so now. You need fields of related data with labels at the top. Once you've laid out your list correctly, you're ready to try Data Form.

First, click any cell in your list to make it active. Then open the **Data** menu and select **Form.** A dialog box appears with the name of your current worksheet in the title bar (see the following figure).

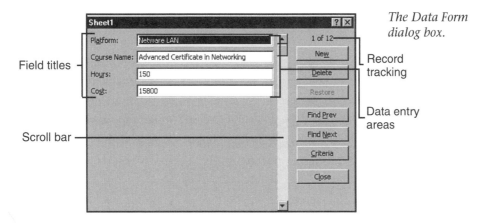

The Data Form dialog box.

Field titles

Scroll bar

Record tracking

Data entry areas

Excel creates the data form for you based on your list and field label information. To enter new records, just click **New** and input the information in the blank data entry areas. To remove a record, click the **Delete** button.

241

You can edit the text in any field except those that are protected or that contain Excel formulas. Simply find the data you want to edit, click in its data entry area, and edit the text. If you change your mind about an edited change, click the **Restore** button before you leave the record.

To navigate quickly through your entire data list, use the scrollbar or select the **Criteria** button. The Criteria option allows you to search your list for records that match the parameters you assign. For example, if you had a database of telephone numbers, you could search all records that match (801)*, where (801) is the area code and * is a wild card for anything that follows. Use the asterisk (*) as a wild card for multiple characters at the end of a string of characters, and the question mark (?) as a wild card for single characters within a string. You can look for records that match your criteria by clicking the **Find Prev** and **Find Next** buttons.

When you finish entering and editing data, click the **Close** button.

AutoTemplates

In the beginning, lists were created by hand. In those days, you took a sharpened number-two pencil, scribbled all pertinent data on yellow legal pads, and scurried back to your desk to enter it in your computer.

Thankfully those days are behind us, in most cases. With Excel, you can keep data from various sources in a master database. And you can create darling little workbooks for other people, so that they can collect your data for you. Then, from time to time, you can gather up those workbook juniors, and let Excel add their data to your master database automatically.

Excel's AutoTemplates are database input forms created for a specific task. The input form, or AutoTemplate, might look like an invoice, a receipt, an order form, or an index card. Certain cells in the form—you'll decide which cells—are linked to your master database. Entries made in the linked cells can then be automatically added to your database list as a new record (the data in a single row of an Excel database list).

All that remains now is to create a template. Sounds scary—and the truth is, it probably would be if not for the Template Wizard.

Prep Time

Once again we're off to see a wizard for help and guidance in performing a function the Excel way. We'll open two new workbooks to get things started. The Template Wizard takes you through AutoTemplate construction with a minimum of pain and suffering—but there are a few preliminary steps that you must take.

Begin by creating a brand new workbook that will contain your database list. Click the **New Workbook** button on the standard toolbar to get started. Then put labels at the top of the fields (or columns) in your list. The following figure shows a sample database list. The data from the input form will eventually be entered as a new record (or row) into this workbook. Click the **Save** button on the Standard toolbar to save the database workbook.

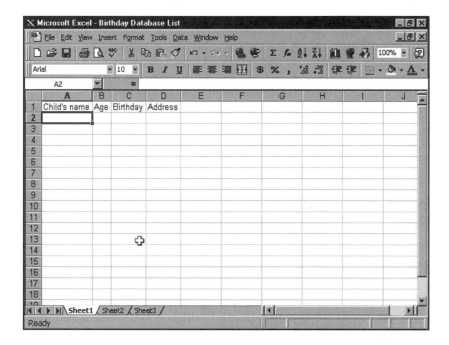

The database list with field labels.

Next, open a whole new workbook and create your input form. Using your database list as a guide, create an input form (such as a sales receipt or an order form) that features places for all of the data you want recorded in your database. Make it look any way you like; you can add pretty pictures, curly letters, and explanatory comments if it suits you, but be sure to label the cells in the input form in the same way as they are labeled in your database list.

You can create as many additional labels as you like in your input form, but, of course, their contents won't be recorded in your database workbook (unless you update the workbook). Once again, save the input form by clicking the **Save** button.

The input form, with labels that correspond to the database.

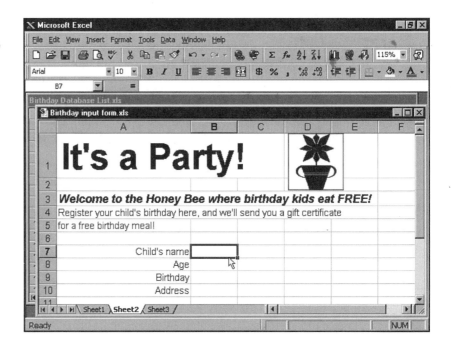

The Template Wizard: Five Steps to Template Nirvana

So you've created your input form. The layout is beautiful; the instructions are concise; you've included text comments and arrows and text boxes. All that's left now is to link this form to your database workbook. Then you can sit back and watch as the data starts marching in.

Now quit your humming and let's get started on this thing. It's time to call the wizard.

Step 1. Start by opening that template workbook—the input form—you created. Then open the **Data** menu and select **Template Wizard**. The first Template Wizard dialog box (shown in the following figure) appears.

Select the name given to the template workbook and click **Next.** (If the template workbook is not open or does not appear on the selection list, close the Template Wizard by selecting the Cancel button, open the template workbook, and start again.) The Template Wizard—Step 2 of 5 dialog box appears.

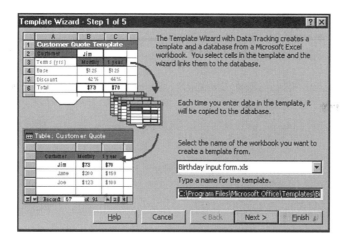

The Template Wizard—Step 1 of 5 dialog box.

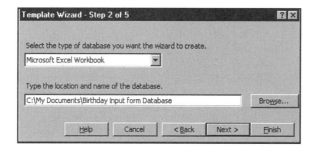

The Template Wizard—Step 2 of 5 dialog box.

Step 2. Confirm that the name and location of the database workbook are correct or type the correct name and location if necessary. You may need to click the Browse button to open a dialog box that will help you locate your database workbook. Another option in the dialog box enables you to select the type of workbook you want to create. This is an Excel-centric chapter so stick with the default— The Excel Workbook Database. Click **Next** to move on to the dialog box shown in the next figure.

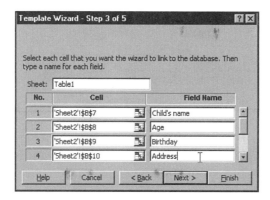

The Template Wizard—Step 3 of 5 dialog box.

Step 3. In this step, you select the cells that will be linked to your database. Only data from the input form linked cells is recorded in the database workbook. Enter the cell addresses from the input form (either manually or by clicking on them with the mouse pointer) in the cell column. If the selected cell is properly labeled—that is, if a label appears in an adjacent cell—the label will automatically appear in the Field Name box. Click **Next.**

Step 4. This step is useful only if you've been doing this stuff for a while and have a backlog of old input forms. If you do, go ahead and repent for past sins. But be prepared. If you answer yes, you'll be expected to name names... of the workbooks. There is some help. A preview area is available to make sure only correct values are copied. Normally, though, you'll simply click the **No, skip it** option button and continue. Click **Next.**

The Template Wizard—Step 4 of 5 dialog box.

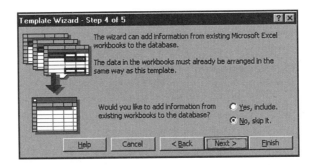

Get Your Kicks

The Add Routing Slip button in the Template Wizard—Step 4 of 5 dialog box—enables you to create a mailing list for your new template. This way you can automatically send new workbooks created with the new template to the people you select.

Step 5. Template Wizard displays the name and location of the new template. At this point you can select **Finish** to finish the process, **Cancel** to discard your work, or **Back** to modify your original selections.

There. You've finished your AutoTemplate.

Collection Plate

Now you can use your AutoTemplate input form to collect one record at a time. The AutoTemplate input form is slightly different from your original input form because it has a new name (which ends in .XLT instead of .XLS, and which is probably located in your Templates folder). Open the input form as you would any other workbook. Input the information into the template. (If you're on a network and want other users to input information into the same template, simply make the template workbook available to them in a common directory.)

Save the template using either the **Save** command or the **Save As** command if you want to assign a unique name to the worksheet. When you save or close the template, Excel asks if you want to add the data to your database as a new record or to replace the last record, or if you simply want to ignore it. Normally you will want to create a new record.

Now you can enter the data for the next record by simply overwriting the one that was saved. Open the database workbook at any time to check on the progress of your database.

Sorting

A database is a living, vibrant thing with data constantly streaming in from several sources. Without a mechanism to straighten it out, your list represents a slice of time: Records appear in the same order in which they arrived. This could be valuable as a time capsule, but it does not always make it convenient when you need to look for a particular entry. With Excel, you can sort data stored in columns or rows, a feature that no long list should be without.

To sort all rows or columns in a database, select any cell in the list you want to sort. Select Sort from the Data menu, and the Sort dialog box appears.

Enter your sorting criteria in the Sort dialog box.

Excel automatically selects all cells that are part of your database (all connecting rows of cells). Choose your sorting criteria from among the options in the Sort dialog box, and then click OK.

➤ To sort only a particular row or column, select the row or column headers you want to sort. Then select **Sort** from the Data menu. Excel asks you to confirm that you

247

want to sort only the selected rows or columns. After you make your selection, the Sort dialog box appears. Criteria selection options are the same.

➤ You can sort by as many as three columns at a time, as indicated by the three text boxes in the Sort dialog box. For each column you want to sort by, enter its label in the text box and choose whether you want the results displayed in ascending or descending order. If you choose Ascending, Excel sorts text from A to Z or sorts numbers from smallest to largest; if you choose Descending, Excel sorts text from Z to A or sorts numbers from largest to smallest.

➤ To sort by more than three columns, begin the sorting process by first selecting the three least-significant columns. Then repeat the sort function selecting the next-least-important column each time. Continue this cycle until all columns have been sorted.

➤ Fortunately, Microsoft anticipated those trying times when the header is to the left and the data is to the right, and they're no longer trying. Select any cell from among the group to be sorted, pull down the **Data** menu, and select **Sort**. Click the **Options** button in the Sort dialog box, and the Sort Options dialog box appears. Select the **Sort left to right** button in the Orientation box.

The Sort Options dialog box.

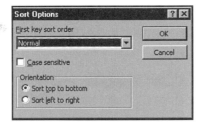

The Least You Need to Know

In this chapter, we had a brief meeting with Excel's dark side, attempting to walk the walk of the database. Don't forget these points:

➤ There are no complicated tricks to creating a database, or *list,* in Excel. Simply place a label at the top of your column and fill in the entries below it.

➤ Use the Data Form as an easy method of entering or altering data in a list. Select any cell from your list and choose Form from the Data menu.

➤ Let Template Wizard create a template from your workbook and link it with your database list.

➤ Use AutoFilter to break the onscreen list into workable chunks.

➤ You can sort data by as many as three columns by selecting Sort from the menu.

Chapter 20

Retrieving and Consolidating Data

In This Chapter

> ➤ The data day business of imports

> ➤ Go get 'em

> ➤ Query-vents

> ➤ Last ditch imports

> ➤ Giving it all away

> ➤ Consolidation must-knows

> ➤ Terrific tips for tracking trivia

Yeah, we've heard dog stories. Heroic stories about dogs who climb mountains to lie on the chests of unsuspecting travelers lost in the snow. Courageous stories of dogs who rescued their owners from burning buildings. Tear-jerking stories of dogs who lie on the chests of their dead owners for seven or eight years.

Well, the authors of this book have owned a dog or two in their respective lives. Smart dogs, dumb dogs, St. Bernard dogs, little yappy dogs... and we're here to tell you:

Not one of them actually responded when ordered to fetch.

That's why we've got cats.

Whole Lotta Data Going On

You might not believe it if you've caught the myopic vision of this book, but not everyone uses Excel. There's a whole world out there of vendors competing for a place in your wallet… er, heart. As a result, you may sometimes find yourself in a position where the data you want already exists in a non-Excel file.

You could reinvent the wheel and enter the data manually into an Excel worksheet. Or you could simply retrieve the data using one of Excel's import tools and convert it to a format you can use. The choice is yours; but personally, we prefer the path of least typing.

In this chapter, we show you how to bring data into Excel from other places.

Bringing Home the Data

Just because a file is different doesn't mean importing it will be difficult. Excel can import some files almost as easily as if they were native Excel workbooks.

You can open the following file types very easily in Excel without any special manipulation:

➤ Data Interchange Format

➤ dBASE files

➤ Lotus 1-2-3

➤ HTML documents

➤ Microsoft Excel

➤ Microsoft Excel 4.0 charts

➤ Microsoft Excel 4.0 macros

➤ Microsoft Excel 4.0 workbooks

➤ Microsoft Works 2.0

➤ Quattro Pro DOS

➤ Quattro Pro Windows

Doesn't Match Up?

This list was a current sampling at the time this book was put together. Your mileage—and list of import filters—may vary.

To import one of the files in this list, pull down the **File** menu and select **Open**. The standard Open dialog box appears.

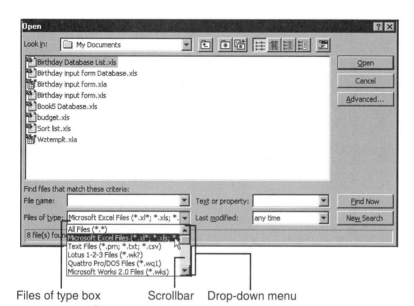

Select the type of file you want to import.

Files of type box   Scrollbar   Drop-down menu

In the lower left corner of the dialog box is the Files of type box. Click its down arrow, and a drop-down menu appears, listing the names of various file types. If the type of file you are opening appears on the list, simply select it. Excel displays all files of the selected type in the dialog box display area. Select and open the file as you would a regular Excel workbook.

Fit to be Tied—In

Even if a file type doesn't appear in the Files of type list of the Open dialog box, you may still be able to import a usable version. The following procedure works on files that contain straight text, and on some that contain variations of straight text. If the last procedure didn't work, try this.

Choose **Open** from the **File** menu again, and select **Text Files** from the Files of type list in the Open dialog box. Select your file. Excel asks if you want to import the file as a text file. Click **OK**, and stand ready to meet the Text Import Wizard.

The Text Import Wizard - Step 1 of 3 dialog box.

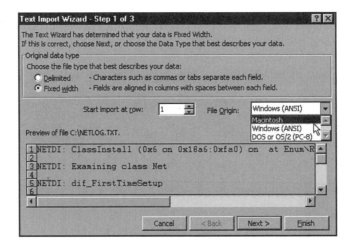

The Text Import Wizard leads you through a three-step process that ought to import your data to Excel in as near a standard layout as possible. It helps, of course, if your text is already lined up in neat rows and columns. A display window in the Text Import Wizard dialog box gives you a preview of what your imported file will look like in Excel. Follow the wizard's instructions to import the file and get back to Kansas.

When All Else Fails

No matter how many filtering options you install, you will eventually come across a file type that no one has seen before and that Excel cannot possibly import. In those rare cases, search for a common middle ground. Perhaps the mystery application itself can export its files into a format Excel can read, such as a text file.

Export Data from Excel

It's not always the other guy's fault.

You're the kid with the new toy—this latest and greatest version of Excel. If your co-workers need to access your data to perform work on their machines, chances are they won't be able to read your files. After all, your software was still a Beta when theirs were coming of age.

Facilitate them a little... especially if it's the boss you're swapping files with. Excel can save worksheets in formats other than its own.

To save a worksheet in a non-Excel format, pull down the **File** menu and select **Save As**. As you might expect, the Save As dialog box appears.

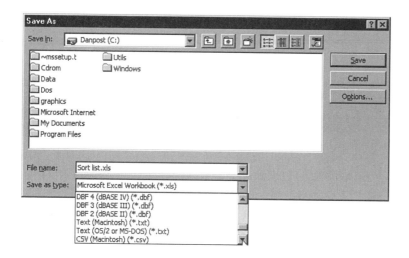

The Save As dialog box.

Near the bottom is a Save as Type box. Click its down arrow to see which formats are available. Select the format in which you want to save the file, enter the filename in the File name box, and click the **Save** button.

Unfortunately, not all saves are equal. Some formats save the whole workbook, while others save only the active worksheet. This means that in some cases you'll be required to save every worksheet of a workbook as a separate file. C'est la vie. The following table lists which programs save what and how.

Good save

Format	Filename Extension
Formats That Save the Entire Workbook	
Excel 4.0 workspace	.XLW
Excel 5.0 template	.XLT
Excel 5.0 workbook	.XLS
Excel 5.0 workspace	.XLW
Excel 7.0 workbook	.XLS
Lotus 1-2-3 release 3.x (worksheets and chart sheets only)	.FM3, .WK3
Lotus 1-2-3 release 4.0	.WK4

continues

Good save Continued

Format	Filename Extension
Formats That Save Only the Active Worksheet	
dBASE II, III, and IV	.DBF
DIF (Data Interchange Format)	.DIF
Excel 2.x formats	.XLC, .XLM, .XLS, .XLW
Excel 3.0 formats	.XLA, .XLC, .XLM, .XLS, .XLT, .XLW
Excel macro	.XLM
Lotus 1-2-3	.WKS, .WK1
Quattro Pro (DOS)	.WQ1
Quattro Pro for Windows	.WQ*
SYLK (Symbolic link format)	.SLK
Text	.TXT
Text, comma-separated values	.CSV
Text, formatted	.PRN

Consolidation

Until now, this chapter has focused on exchanging data with the great unknown outside the world of Excel. Consolidation works from the inside out. You use consolidation to summarize data from multiple worksheets in a single cell on another worksheet.

Here's an example of consolidation in practice. Daily worksheets contain daily reports. On Monday, top salesmen Larry, Moe, and Curly sold $200 worth of goods, and you record it on a Daily worksheet. At the end of the week, you want to consolidate all the Daily worksheets into weekly reports, which we'll call Weeklies. In our example, when we add all the sales for the period, the Weekly worksheet would show that for the week ending 9/7/97 Larry, Moe, and Curly had sold $300 worth of goods. These guys are awful. Later you'll consolidate the data from all of the Weeklies into yearly reports, which we'll call Yearlies. Yep, you guessed it. The Yearlies show that the dynamic trio sold only $900 worth of goods for the whole year. You might consider hiring new salesmen at this point or you might want to continue consolidating different factors. Carry on this process of consolidation for as long and in as many different directions as you want.

A Must See

Although consolidation tables are useful for pulling in data from multiple sources, they lack the flexibility of Pivot Tables. Pivot Tables are covered in Chapter 21, "Pivot Tables," coming soon to a chapter near you.

The Work of Consolidation

You can use either of two methods to consolidate data:

➤ Consolidate by position when data and labels are in the same position on both the source and destination documents.

➤ Consolidate by category when labels and data are not in the same position on both the source and destination documents.

To consolidate by position, begin by selecting the upper left cell of the destination worksheet. Open the **Data** menu and select **Consolidate,** and the Consolidate dialog box appears.

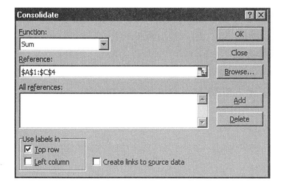

The Consolidate dialog box.

➤ In the **Function** drop-down list, select the **summary function** you want to use for your consolidation.

➤ In the Reference box, enter the **location of the areas** you want to consolidate. Click **Add** for each additional entry in the Reference box. Check the **Create Links to Source Data** box if you want Excel to update your consolidated data whenever a change is made to the source data. When you finish making your selections, click **OK.**

➤ To consolidate by **category,** begin by selecting the **upper left cell** of the destination worksheet. Open the **Data** menu and select **Consolidate,** and the Consolidate dialog box appears.

➤ In the Function drop-down list, select the summary function that you want to use for your consolidation. In the Reference box, enter the areas you want to consolidate, including the data labels in the selection. Click **Add** for each additional entry in the Reference box.

➤ In the Use Labels In box, check the box that indicates where the labels are in the source area. (Check both boxes if applicable.) Click the **Create Links to Source Data** box if you want Excel to update your consolidated data whenever a change is made to the source data. When you finish making your selections, click **OK**.

Now you've got yourself a fine little consolidation table. Enjoy!

The Least You Need to Know

Retrieving and consolidating data gives you a way to control information. This is what you should put together:

➤ Excel can import the most common file types without any difficulty. Just select the file type from the Files of type drop-down list in the Open dialog box.

➤ You can import less common file types, but the procedure is more complicated.

➤ Obscure file types have to be converted to a common format by the originating software.

➤ Consolidate data from multiple worksheets to make it more readable.

Chapter 21

Pivot Tables

In This Chapter

➤ Pivot to heel

➤ Get it together

➤ Make it work

➤ Twist and shout

➤ Change it all about

➤ Undulating undertakings

"Say that again!" she demands.

"If you marry your stepfather's father, you become the mother of your own parents. And if you are your mother's mother, you are your own grandmother. See?"

She's only six years old, but she's starting to catch on. She screws up her face, looks completely puzzled, and says, "Now tell me one more time."

Intro to Pivot Tables

It's more than just rows or columns of meaningless numbers. It's data. Somehow, some way, all those numbers relate to one another. Your mission—accept it or not—is to find out how. You have to determine whether the large sales staffs are more productive than the smaller ones, and whether paying a high commission gets better results than paying a lower commission. Of course, those answers might vary depending on what country you're operating in and what the product line is.

Pivot tables show all these relationships in a single place and switch them around to see what factors correspond with which results. Bend, spindle, and mutilate your tables into a cohesive vision from which you can create charts and maps that are more effective than they ever could have been with the simple rows and columns of your pre-pivot worksheet.

How They Work

Pivot tables work by showing you new relationships between categories. Madonna and Dennis vs. Madonna and the personal trainer vs. the personal trainer and Dennis... well, you see how relationships can be confusing. Normally, spreadsheets show relationships in two dimensions: Dimension 1 is a budget category, and Dimension 2 is a dollar figure (your budget). But what if you want to add a third dimension, say, a rating for how critical the budget item is. Food and shelter get an A rating, genuine vinyl siding (say what?) gets a B rating, and Abba CDs get a C rating.

With a pivot table, you can drag columns to rows and rows to columns, and—like a supermarket tabloid—make otherwise unseen relationships very apparent.

Definitions

Before we get too deeply into this, there are a few terms you'll need to understand:

➤ *Pivot Table.* A table you create to show interactive relationships between many kinds of things. A pivot table lets you drag columns and rows back and forth.

➤ *List.* The underlying database (arranged in columns, with labels at the top of each column) that is the source of the pivot table's data.

➤ *Field.* Each column of a typical Excel database list.

➤ *Record.* Each row of a typical Excel database list.

➤ *Source Data.* The data in the list or lists upon which a pivot table is based.

➤ *Pivot Table Data.* All the summarized data out in the middle of the table.

➤ *Pivot Table Control.* Your pivot table looks very much like a regular table, except that the row and column labels turn into buttons that you can drag to other locations. These buttons are called controls.

➤ *Summary Functions.* All the calculations Excel performs on the data out in the middle of the pivot table (it's summarized, calculated, subtotaled, and grand-totaled).

➤ *Page Field.* Individual fields of data that you've instructed the pivot table to break out into separate pages and display one at a time.

➤ *Group.* To subdivide categories of data and regroup the subdivisions. If Africa and Europe were categories, for example, all the separate countries in each location could be grouped together.

It's a Setup

Begin your pivot table by setting up a list the same way you did in Chapter 19, "List Management." Note, however, that pivot tables are particularly adept at using data that can be broken out by category, subcategory, and sub-subcategory. The more ways Excel can group the data in your database list, and the more often the same words or figures appear in different categories, the more interesting your pivot tables will be.

Enter your list data in columns, or fields, with a label at the top of each column. (These labels will eventually appear in your pivot table as button-like controls.) The following figure shows a sample database list that could be used as the source data for a pivot table.

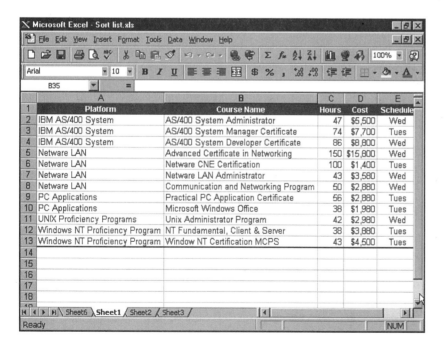

Create a database list.

Heed these additional rules when creating lists for your pivot tables:

➤ Column labels are not optional. Without them, your pivot table won't work.

➤ Avoid including totals and subtotals in the portions of your database that are included in the pivot table. (You don't have to use the entire worksheet in your pivot table, and calculations off to the side generally won't cause any problems.)

➤ Formulas work better in pivot tables than they did in the Data Forms you saw in Chapter 19. The whole point of the pivot table is to change the relationships between data. Formulas can handle the stress.

➤ If you've used filters in your list, the pivot table ignores them and uses all the data.

Now you know the ground rules. Let's make a pivot table!

The Creation Story

Once again, you can rely on the help of a wizard. Follow these steps to create your own pivot table:

Step 1. To create a pivot table from a database list, first make the worksheet containing your list the active sheet. Then select the entire list or the segment that contains the information you want to review in pivot table form. Be sure to include the column labels when you make your selection. Open the **Data** menu and choose the **PivotTable Report...** option. The PivotTable Wizard—Step 1 of 4 dialog box appears.

The PivotTable Wizard—Step 1 of 4 dialog box.

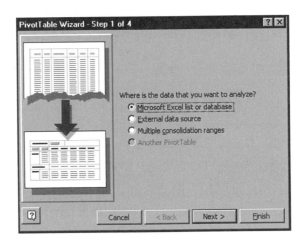

The Microsoft Excel List or Database option is automatically selected. You also have the option of importing data from an external data source (see Chapter 19), from multiple consolidation ranges (Chapter 20, "Retrieving and Consolidating Data"), or from another pivot table. For now, we'll use only the Excel list as a data source. Click the **Next** button to proceed to the next step.

Step 2. In the PivotTable Wizard—Step 2 of 4 dialog box, Excel asks for the range of the data you're using.

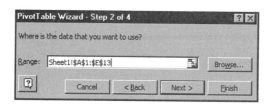

Enter the range address of the list in the Step 2 of 4 dialog box.

The range address of the selected cells appears in the Range text box with absolute references, as indicated by the dollar signs attached to each of the references.

You can change the selection by entering a new reference or address, by clicking the **Collapse Dialog** icon and dragging over a new range directly in the worksheet, or by using the Browse dialog box. To access the Browse dialog box (which looks exactly like the Open dialog box you use to open a workbook), select the **Browse** button. If you choose another Excel file from the Browse dialog box, Excel creates your pivot table from that data instead of from the information on your current worksheet.

Collapse Dialog Icon

Excel's asking for the address of some cells, and you can't remember where they are. Not a problem. Use the Collapse Dialog Icon to revisit your worksheet, and use the mouse pointer to select the cells. The addresses of the highlighted cells appear automatically in the original dialog box.

Step 3. We'll continue with the current worksheet. With your range selected, click the **Next** button. Predictably, the Step 3 of 4 dialog box appears.

Step 3 is where you do all the hard work of creating the pivot table. Decide whether you want your original column labels—which are now called field buttons—to appear in your pivot table as row labels, as column labels, as data to be summed or counted, or as separate pages called page fields. You can change these assignments later if you want, so it's okay to be a little haphazard for the time being.

Do You Use All of Them?

No, you don't need to use all of the field buttons. If you're well acquainted with your data, you'll understand immediately which items you want to see the relationships for.

*The PivotTable
Wizard—Step 3 of 4
dialog box.*

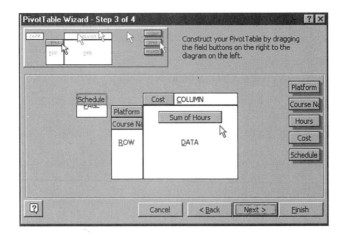

When you drag field buttons into the page, row, and column areas, nothing changes. But
when you drag them into the data area—and you must put at least one button in the data
area—the pivot table wants to perform some calculations on it. After you've done the
drag, double-click the button you dragged to the data area. The PivotTable Field dialog
box appears.

*PivotTable Field
dialog box with
options selected.*

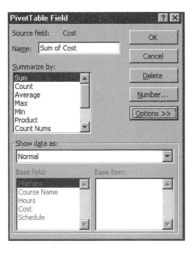

In the Summarize By area, you see a list of 11 ways the pivot table can perform mathematical and statistical calculations. Pick any of them and click **OK**; you can change it
later if necessary.

Check This Out...

Those Amazing Calculations

Here are some quick descriptions of each of the 11 mathematical and statistical calculations available in the pivot table:

Sum. Sum of values in underlying data. The default function for numeric data fields.

Count. Number of records or rows in underlying data. The default summary function for data fields that contain something other than numbers.

Average. Average of values in underlying data.

Max. Largest value in underlying data.

Min. Smallest value in underlying data.

Product. Product of underlying data.

Count Nums. Number of records or rows in underlying data that contain numeric data.

StdDev. Estimate of standard deviation of a population, based on sample of underlying data.

StdDevp. Standard deviation of a population, based on entire population of underlying data.

Var. An estimate of variance of a population, based on sample of underlying data.

Varp. Variance of a population of data, based on entire population of underlying data.

Click the **Options** button to choose from the nine options in the Show Data as box. These options allow you to customize your data display in the following ways:

➤ *Difference From.* Shows all data in the data area as the difference between Base Field and Base Item you select. (You choose the Base Field and Base Item in the corresponding boxes in this dialog box.)

➤ *% Of.* Shows all data in data area as a percentage of Base Field and Base Item.

➤ *% Difference From.* Same as Difference From, but shows difference as a percentage of Base data.

➤ *Running Total In.* Shows data for consecutive items as a running total. Select field with items you want shown in a running total.

➤ *% Of Row.* Shows data in each row as percentage of total of the row.

➤ *% Of Column.* Shows all data in each column as percentage of the total of the column.

➤ *% Of Total.* Shows data in data area as percentage of grand total of all data in pivot table.

➤ *Index.* Shows data by using following equation: $((\text{value in cell}) \times (\text{Grand Total})) / ((\text{Grand Row Total}) \times (\text{Grand Column Total}))$.

Step 4. Click the **Next** button, and ta-da! It's Step 4 of 4!

Format your pivot table with the options in the Step 4 of 4 dialog box.

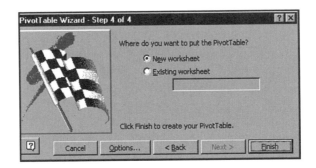

Click the **Options** button to open the PivotTables Options dialog box.

PivotTable Options dialog box.

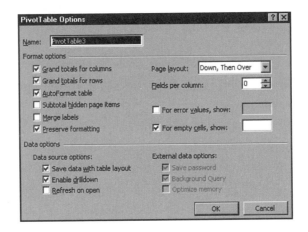

Formatting options that control how your pivot table will look are available by clicking the **Format options** and the **Data options** check boxes. For our single simple sample table, make sure the following options are checked. In the Format options section, check Grand totals for columns, Grand totals for rows, AutoFormat table, Preserve formatting, and For empty cells, show. In the Data Options, check **Save data with table layout**, and **Enable drilldown**.

After you've checked the options, click **Finish**, and you're ready to start pivoting.

The Hokey Pokey

Your new pivot table looks something like the following figure. The information in the pivot table is grouped by category (in this case, by area). Within each category are secondary groupings.

Now let's see how to make some changes.

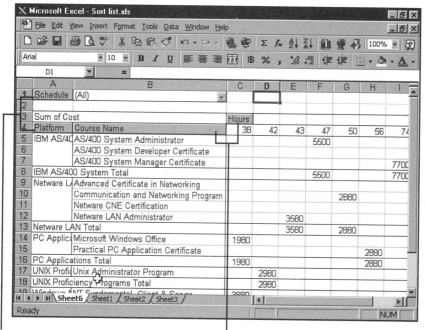

Your typical pivot table.

Row field controls

Column field controls

The Toolbar

When Excel displays your new pivot table, it also displays the PivotTable toolbar, shown in the following figure. If the PivotTable toolbar doesn't appear automatically, force an appearance by opening the View menu, selecting Toolbars, and choosing PivotTable. We'll consider each of the buttons on the PivotTable toolbar as we discuss ways to change the pivot table.

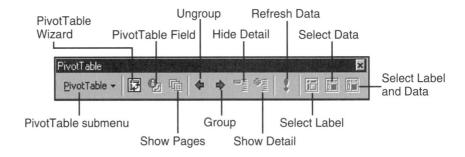

The PivotTable toolbar.

PivotTable Wizard

PivotTable Field

Ungroup

Hide Detail

Refresh Data

Select Data

Select Label and Data

PivotTable submenu

Show Pages

Group

Show Detail

Select Label

For now, dock your toolbar by dragging it off the work area of your worksheet. The toolbar changes shape. Stay calm. None of the icons are lost.

Make It Pivot

Now that you've got your table ready, the fun begins. You can change the layout of your pivot table simply by grabbing any field control and moving it to a different row or column or to a different place on its current row or column. As you do so, the shape of your pointer changes to reflect column or row shapes, depending on where you drag. You may also see some other pointer shapes, which we explain later in this chapter.

This figure shows the same pivot table after we moved some controls around. Notice that the data is simply reorganized into new views to show different relationships. You can make changes as often as necessary to see every possible relationship of your data.

The modified pivot table.

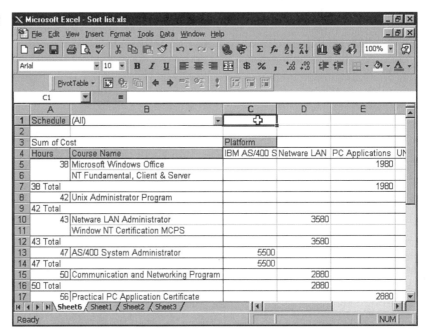

You can make changes to the setup of any field by selecting the field control button and double-clicking the **PivotTable Field** button on the PivotTable toolbar. When you do, the PivotTable Field dialog box appears.

The PivotTable Field dialog box.

In this box you can change the location—the orientation—of your field control, change the way the summaries are calculated, select items in your field you want to hide, or delete the field altogether.

Page Fields

Sometimes, when the data gets just too complicated, you'll want to break your data out even further and view separate pivot tables for each record in your field. That's what page fields are for. Page fields simply add one more dimension to your pivot table analysis. Here's how they work.

In the PivotTable Wizard—Step 3 of 4 dialog box, you had the option to drag fields into the page field box. Now that your table is in place, you can recall the wizard by clicking the **PivotTable Wizard** button on the toolbar. Then simply drag your field labels into the page field box and click **Finish**.

Alternatively, instead of recalling the wizard, you can just drag existing field controls up to the upper left corner of your pivot table. The pointer shape changes from a row or a column to a series of steps. Release the pointer, and you've got yourself a page field control.

Using page fields.

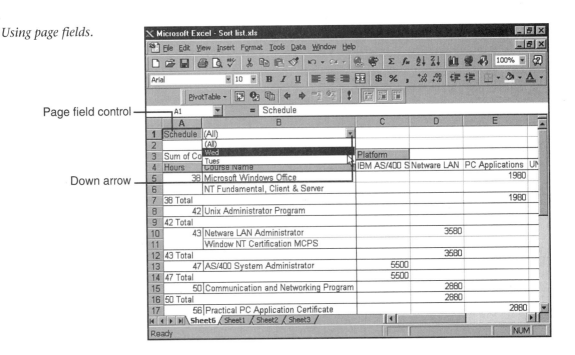

Page field control ──

Down arrow ──

Page fields are always located two full rows above the main body of the pivot table. To use the page fields, click the down arrow of the page field control on your pivot table. A drop-down list appears, and you can select a view. At the bottom of the list is the All option, which gives you a consolidated view.

You can click the **Show Pages** button on the Query and Pivot toolbar to copy each page field to its own separate worksheet. Click **OK** to see worksheet tabs at the bottom of your screen for the new worksheets.

Refining the View

The pivot table is supposed to simplify the way you view your data. Often, though, the pivot table introduces so much new information that you get confused all over again. The next three sections tell you about options that can make your life easier.

Delete Fields

Maybe you've just tried too hard. Drive the irrelevant fields out of your life forever (or until you change your mind, whichever comes first) by dragging the field control off the main body of your pivot table. When the pointer changes to a large X over a bar, release the mouse button, and the field disappears.

You can get it back by recalling the PivotTable Wizard (click the **PivotTable Wizard** icon on your PivotTable toolbar) and dragging the field control back in. Then click **Next** and **Finish**.

Group and Ungroup Fields

You can consolidate items in a category with the grouping command. To do so, select two or more items in a column or a row that can be grouped together. For example, if you have a column of items numbered 1 through 4, you might want to combine 1 with 2 to create the first group, and combine 3 with 4 to create the second group.

You needn't select every cell in the column from the group; a representative sample from each column will do. To select noncontiguous cells, click the first cell, press and hold down **Ctrl**, and click additional cells. With at least two cells selected, choose the right-arrow **Group** icon from the PivotTable toolbar. The following figure shows the sample pivot table after grouping fields.

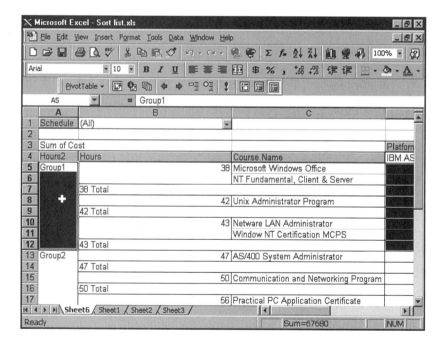

A grouped field.

A new field, with the new groupings, appears to the left of your original field with the new groupings. You can drag this field around the table as you would any other.

To remove the new groupings, select a representative cell in the field and click the left-arrow **Ungroup** icon. When you've ungrouped every grouping, the entire field disappears.

Hide 'Em

You can collapse your pivot table into manageable views by hiding the details. To hide the details of a particular field (including its subtotals and subcategories), select the field control and click the **Hide Detail** icon on the PivotTable toolbar.

Reverse the process by reselecting the field control and clicking the **Show Detail** icon.

Making Changes

You've changed the format, changed the options, even swapped the columns and rows. Can there be any more?

Sure! Believe it or not, there are still more changes you can make to your new pivot table.

Changing the Source Data

If you add new information to your original database list, you'll want to update the pivot table to reflect those changes. There's a simple way to do this and a more complicated way, but which method you use depends on what kinds of changes you're making.

If you're changing only the existing data numbers, and not adding or deleting rows or columns, you can do the simple update. Make your changes to the database, return to the pivot table, and click the **Refresh Data** icon on the PivotTable toolbar. Excel updates your changes automatically.

On the other hand, if you're changing the number of rows or columns in the database list, changing the pivot table is a little more complex. The following steps outline the procedure.

1. Make your database changes, return to the pivot table, and select any cell in the pivot table to make it active.

2. Pull down the **Data** menu and choose **PivotTable Report**. The Step 3 dialog box reappears.

3. Click the **Back** button to return to Step 2. In the Step 2 dialog box, amend the database range to include the new rows or columns.

4. Finish the steps in the dialog boxes as you did originally, and your changes appear in the revised pivot table.

Retrieving More Fields

In the unlikely event that your pivot table isn't complicated enough, you can add more fields for further analysis.

Just click the **PivotTable Wizard** icon on the PivotTable toolbar. Excel returns you to Step 3 of the wizard, where you can add, subtract, and customize your fields to your heart's content. Click the **Finish** button in the dialog box to return to the pivot table.

Changing Number Format

Changing numbers formats is as easy as click-click-click. Select the cell to change. Click with the right mouse button. Select **Format Cell** from the mini-menu that appears on your screen.

Check This Out...

Gone but Not Forgotten

As you rearrange the pivot table you'll notice that cells lose their new formats when they are shifted to another location. Fear not. You can re-format the cells in their new location. And all is not lost. Should you return the cells to their original alignment, whatever special formatting you may have done will return.

Sorting Fields

Excel can sort your pivot table fields alphabetically or numerically or by a combination of the two, and it can sort from top to bottom or bottom to top.

To sort a field, click the button for the field you want to sort. Then select one of these sort icons from the standard toolbar at the top of your Excel screen:

 Sort Ascending

 Sort Descending

When you select Sort Ascending, Excel sorts the text fields in alphabetical order (A to Z) and sorts numbers from lowest to highest. The Sort Descending button reverses these orders (Z to A and highest to lowest). Within a field, Excel sorts items in this order: numbers, text, logical values, error values, and blank cells.

The Name Game: Renaming Fields

You can rename a pivot table field in one of two ways:

➤ Make the change in the original database list. Then return to the pivot table, click an active cell, and click the **PivotTable Wizard** toolbar icon. The Step 3 dialog box appears. Click **Back** to go back to Step 2. Then recapture the cell range, click

Next, and drag the field labels back into position. Click **Finish** to exit the dialog box. The field is renamed when you return to the pivot table.

➤ Make the change in the pivot table, without changing the underlying database list. Just click the field name to make it active, and edit the name in the formula bar above the column headers or in the cell itself. Then return to the pivot table and click the **Refresh Data** icon on the PivotTable toolbar.

Deleting the Table

You can delete the entire table without affecting the underlying source data. To do so, select the entire pivot table. Then open the **Edit** menu and select **Clear/All**.

What? You didn't really want to delete it? Press **Ctrl+Z** to bring it back.

The Least You Need to Know

Pivoting lets you twist your data into all new views. This is what you'll want to remember about pivot tables.

➤ Pivot tables let you look at data in multiple dimensions.

➤ Pivot tables work best with data that has multiple layers and identical subcategories repeated throughout.

➤ Build your database list first, and then create the pivot table using the **Data, PivotTable** command.

➤ You can drag field labels to other places on the rows or columns to see new relationships.

➤ Pivot tables can be formatted to perform a variety of mathematical and statistical calculations.

Chapter 22

The What-If Conundrum

In This Chapter

➤ First and goal

➤ Final solution

➤ Making a scene

➤ Zounds, Batman! A zinger at the problem-solving zenith!

By the time you read this, our "The Book's Finished and Now We Can Sleep" party will have been long past. That much we know. But as we write, we still haven't decided how many guests, how many bottles of 7-Up, or how many bags of charcoal briquettes we're going to need. Guess it's time to pull out a worksheet and figure it out, right?

What Is What-If?

This chapter is for people who like to read magazines—and books—from back to front. Throughout this book, we've been teaching you how to get from a set of variables to a result. In this, the last real chapter of the book, we tell you how to turn it around: how to go from a result to a whole bunch of variables.

This chapter introduces you to some advanced Excel features that you will use when you want to do some planning. In other words, when you still have time to influence the variables.

Go ahead and ask Excel all those burning questions in your life. What if I could earn a little more money? What if I made a few more charitable donations? How would that affect my taxes? What if my worthless son-in-law repaid the $8,000 I loaned him last year? Excel let's you do your planning with a set of "what-if" features that'll have you on the phone calling in your IOUs in no time flat.

Each of the assumptions you make (about future interest rates, commission rates, sales figures, tax rates, or your income level, for example) is called a variable. In this chapter, we discuss Excel's Goal Seek feature, which you use when you want Excel to adjust a single variable to help you achieve a predetermined result; the Solver feature, which you use when you can adjust multiple variables; and the Scenario Manager, which gives you the power to save lots of different scenarios (suppositions about future events).

Working Backward: The Excel Goal Seek Function

Theoretically, when you shop for refrigerators or used cars, you're out there comparing prices. "We have enough money to buy a 1983 Hyundai," you tell your spouse. Your spouse nods in assent as you pull into the lot. Three hours later, you leave with a late-model Miata and five years of payments. Why?

You fell for goal-seeking, a mechanism whereby you twist the facts to fit a predetermined ending—in this case, the old "The monthly payment is just a little higher, and we've got this trade-in, and even though we have to make payments well into the next millennium, well, we'd probably have to pay for repairs on the older car, so it all works out the same" routine.

Excel's Goal Seek function works backward from the usual formula routine. Normally, you input a formula and read the results. With Goal Seek, you choose the result, and the formula adjusts the factors to make the result come out the way you say.

This is how it works. Suppose you're working on commission, and you write a formula in cell B3 that calculates your expected income for next year, based on your sales figures and commission rate.

The formula in cell B3 will calculate next year's expected income.

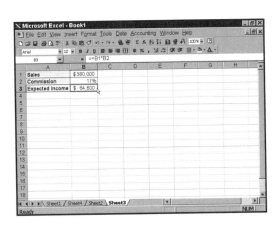

The income figure is a little on the low side. You can keep playing with the sales figures and commission rates until the income figure looks right, or you can use Goal Seek.

To use Goal Seek, click the cell that shows your income, cell B3, open the **Tools** menu, and select **Goal Seek**. The Goal Seek dialog box appears (see the following figure).

The Goal Seek dialog box.

In the Set cell box, you enter the cell reference address for which you want to set a value. Because you already selected cells, its address appears automatically. In the To value box, enter your dream number. Then enter the address of the cell you are willing to adjust in the By changing cell box. (In our example, because your sales figure is calculated from other figures, you can change either the commission rate or the sales volume.)

When you finish entering the necessary data, click **OK**. Goal Seek makes the required adjustment. If only your boss would change your commission rate that easily....

Solving Problems

Okay, Goal Seek works for simple problems—but yours are more complex, right?

When you've got multiple variables to consider, you need something stronger. To find the ideal solution within parameters you define, use Solver.

Using Solver

With Solver, you set up your "what-if" situation by actually changing multiple variables in an existing worksheet. Therefore, you need to have your worksheet already set up.

Add Solver

Before you try to use Solver, make sure it's installed on your system. To determine whether Solver has already been installed, see if the Tools menu contains the Solver command. If it doesn't, you have to install it.

Open the **Tools** menu and select **Add-Ins**. Select **Solver** from the list in the Add-Ins dialog box. If Solver isn't listed in the dialog box, you'll have to re-run the Excel Setup altogether.

In our "expected income" example, we want to increase the expected income, but can't increase the commission percentage above 20 percent. We use Solver to find both the change in commission and the change in expected sales to arrive at the new expected income. To use Solver, select the cell in which you'll do your solving work, in our example, cell B3. Then choose **Solver** from the Tools menu. The Solver Parameters dialog box (shown in the following figure) appears.

Your selected cell address, B3, appears in the Set Target Cell box. To select the smallest possible value for the target cell, click the **Min** option button. To select the largest possible value for the target cell, select the **Max** option button. To set your own value for the target cell, click the **Value** option button and enter a value in the box provided.

The Solver Parameters dialog box.

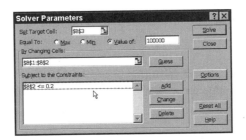

In the By Changing Cells text box, enter the reference addresses of all the cells you will allow Solver to change in order to achieve your target value, in our example, cells B1 to B2. If you want Solver to determine which cells to change, click the Guess button instead. Then enter any constraints (you have four choices: greater than, less than, equal to, or integer) in the Subject to the Constraints box. In our example, the constraint is that the commission rate in B2 can't be greater than 20 percent. Click the **Solve** button. Solver calculates the solution and displays the Solver Results dialog box.

Free Sample

Excel comes with a sample workbook that illustrates Solver's problem solving capabilities. You can find the workbook Solvsamp.xls in the Examples\Solver folder under your Excel installation folder.

Solvsamp.xls contains seven worksheets. Each worksheet includes a brief description of the problem, shows the target cell, and indicates which cells and constraints are changing.

Now you've got some decisions to make. To retain the solution values, select the **Keep Solver Solution** option button in the Solver Results dialog box (as shown in the following figure). Alternatively, you can select Restore Original Values to replace the solution values with the original values.

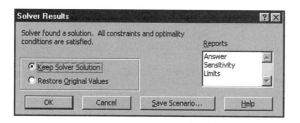

Tell Solver what you want to do with the results of the calculation.

If you think you might need the solution values later, click the Save Scenario button to save the Solver settings. The Save Scenario dialog box appears, prompting you to enter a name for the saved scenario.

Scenario Management

Excel lets you define and save different scenarios (the set of suppositions you make about your data). Once you save a scenario, you can easily recall it and play the what-if game a thousand different times, a thousand different ways. Excel's Scenario Manager makes the storing and recalling of scenarios an orderly process.

You can create a scenario in either of two ways:

➤ You can save the results of a Solver calculation as a scenario by selecting the **Save Scenario** button in the Solver Results dialog box.

➤ You can create a scenario manually. This is the more flexible method, and the one you'll be using most often.

To create a scenario manually, you must first make your worksheet changes. Adjust any of the figures to reflect your fantasies. Go crazy, because your changes won't affect the underlying worksheet. Once your changes are complete, access the Scenario Manager. Go to the **Tools** menu and select **Scenarios**. The Scenario Manager box opens with several options. Click **Add**, to bring up the Add Scenario dialog box.

The Add Scenario dialog box.

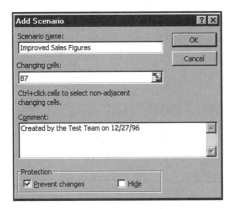

Enter the name of your fantasy scenario. Then remind yourself of what you changed by recording the location of the changed cells—up to 32 of them—in the **Changing cells** box. To select non-adjacent cells, hold down the **Ctrl** key while you click the cells. Enter your **Comments**, select your **Protection** preferences, and click **OK**. The Scenario Values dialog box appears. Make your changes as indicated, and click **OK** to return to the Scenario Manager. Clicking **Close** saves your changes.

To recall a scenario, just click again on **Scenarios** from the **Tools** menu. View, Delete, Edit, Merge or Summarize your scenarios as often as you'd like.

That's It! Now You've Mastered Excel!

The Least You Need to Know

Now you're an Excel Expert, guaranteed. Just remember these final points:

➤ Use the Goal Seek feature to solve simple problems involving only one variable.

➤ Use Solver when you have more than one variable to change or when you want to set other limits on cell modifications.

➤ You can save your Solver scenarios with Scenario Manager so you can retrieve them at a later time.

➤ Each scenario can have as many as 32 different cell changes.

Part 5
What Good Is Excel?

If you answered, "It'd make an Excel-ent doorstop," you'd be wrong.

Excel is more than just a fancy calculator: It's a scratch pad, financial planner, checkbook balancer, master budgeter, database, and friend of the earth (it saves trees). It will enable you to tuck your fingers and toes away forever as you use it to save valuable hours running your business, paying bills, and budgeting your way to the getaway vacation of your dreams.

This section answers the "What good is…" question by demonstrating several useful applications. It's an Excel-ent beginning.

Chapter 23

Tracking Your Life and Your Business

In This Chapter

➤ Take control of your checkbook and your online banking

➤ Quick tricks for budgeting

➤ The dreaded tax return

➤ What are you worth? Financial statements and analysis

We like to think we're smarter than animals. Sometime it's hard to tell. In North America alone, the number of people who have devised algorithms to solve problems of space, motion, time, and income taxes is far outnumbered by those who forgot to carry the 1.

Fortunately, we're smart enough to use tools to cover for those momentary lapses. Excel, for example, is particularly good at determining the exact number of gallons of special-blend turquoise paint you'll need for your living room—or for calculating the sum of the medical bills when your spouse faints at the sight of a turquoise living room.

In earlier chapters, you learned the theory behind various Excel features. Now it's time to put what you've learned to practical use.

All Your Eggs in One Handy Basket: Your Personal Finances

Even if you use Excel primarily for your small business, it's a good idea to use it for tracking your personal finances as well. Both lenders and equity investors will want information about the financial position of your business, and also about the personal financial situation of its owners.

Because you've managed your personal finances all your life, you're probably in the habit of tossing off budgets and checkbook reconciliations on scraps of paper. But once you begin to keep electronic records, you'll find you save time, eliminate repetitive entries, and get more useful information than you ever had with a pen-and-paper calculation.

Electronic budgets, for example, give you the advantage of doing "what-if" calculations, such as "What if I make double payments on my department store charge cards for the next six months? What do I save in interest charges? Can I afford to triple the payments? Will I annoy the clerk?"

This section shows you how to use Excel to reconcile your checkbook, track your bank accounts, analyze your financial activity, prepare a budget, develop a personal financial statement, and calculate your tax return.

Reconciling Your Checkbook

Not only is the electronic reconciliation more accurate than the old pen-and-paper method; it also gives you the basis for analyzing your expenditures, tracking your deductible expenses, and verifying your income.

To set up a workbook for reconciling your checkbook, create two worksheets—one for tracking your checkbook and one for reconciling the checkbook. The following figures show examples—first the Check Tracking worksheet and then the Reconciliation Record worksheet.

Check This Out...

The Name Game

Naming worksheets is simple. Just point at the worksheet name (that is, Sheet1), and click the right mouse button. A pop-up menu appears. Select **Rename**, and type the new worksheet name. Press **Enter**, and you've got a new name.

On the Check Tracking worksheet, create columns that duplicate your checkbook register.

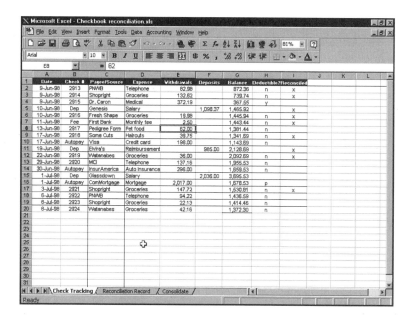

The Check Tracking worksheet.

The Reconciliation worksheet.

The Check Tracking worksheet contains only one formula: the running balance, in column G. The Balance formula in cell G3 [=+G2-E3+F3] starts with the previous balance, and subtracts the withdrawal or adds the deposit. Copy the formula each time you add a new entry to the worksheet.

One-upsmanship

Doing an electronic checkbook reconciliation gives you the freedom to go wild. Feel free to include additional columns for information such as the nature and the deductibility of your expenses. When tax time rolls around, you'll have everything you need in one place.

To simplify your reconciliation, be sure to name the columns for Withdrawals, Deposits, Balance, and Reconciled, as shown in the following figure.

Name columns on the Check Tracking worksheet to simplify the reconciliation.

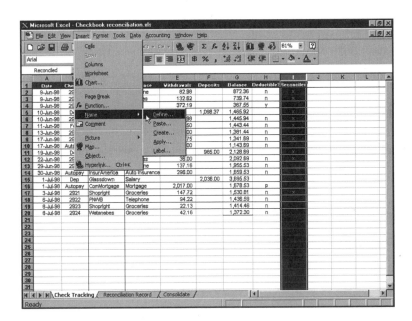

Setting up the Reconciliation Record worksheet is easy. The first figure, Account Ending Balance, comes from your monthly bank statement, and is the only figure you have to re-enter each month.

The second figure, Deposits Made (cell F3), is the total of all the unreconciled deposits. Here's the formula (the example workbook is named Checkbook reconciliation.xls—your formula should show *your* workbook's name):

> **=SUMIF('Checkbook reconciliation.xls'!Reconciled,"<>x",'Checkbook ➥reconciliation.xls'!Deposits)**

In the third cell, Checks, Withdrawals, and Charges Outstanding (cell F4), subtract the total of all your unreconciled checks by using the following formula:

=-SUMIF('Checkbook reconciliation.xls'!Reconciled,"<>x",'Checkbook
➥reconciliation.xls'!Withdrawals)

The Account Balance (cell F5) is the sum of the first three cells:

=SUM(F2:F4)

The Checkbook Balance calculation (cell F6) is the number from the last cell of your
running balance on the Check Tracking worksheet:

=OFFSET('Check Tracking'!G1,(DCOUNTA('Checkbook
➥reconciliation.xls'!Balance,1,'Checkbook reconciliation.xls'!Balance)),0)

The Difference calculation (cell F7) is simply the Account Balance subtracted from the
Checkbook balance:

=F6-F5

If the number is zero, you're reconciled!

The reconciliation formulas are somewhat complex, but they'll enable you to continue
adding to your checkbook register throughout the months without any manual
recalculation.

Tracking Your Online Bank Accounts

Do your banking online? Capture that information in Excel and you'll be able to track
and analyze your expenditures at any time.

Different banks use different software, of course, so capturing that information may be a
bit tricky. The simplest method is to export the data from your bank's software to Excel.
Check the command menus to see whether there is an "export" feature.

Your bank's software may not export data directly to Excel, but it should enable you to
save your data in *some* common format. Look for options such as "Quicken-compatible"
or "text-delimited." In most situations, this data can be easily imported into Excel.

Import-ant Tip

Importing foreign data into Excel? Go to the **File** menu and select
Open, and then at the bottom of the Open dialog box, select the
foreign file type from the **Files of Type** option. In addition to Excel
files, you can open text (.TXT), Lotus 1-2-3, Quattro Pro, Microsoft
Works, dBASE, HTML, SYLK (.SLK), and Data Interchange Format (.DIF) files.

A third alternative is to copy (Ctrl+C) and paste (Ctrl+V) a window of banking data directly into an open Excel worksheet.

Analyzing Your Financial Activity

Whether your banking and expenditure records are entered manually from your check register, or electronically from your online banking service, you'll end up with essentially the same data. Analyzing it is fairly simple.

In our example, we continue using the same Checkbook reconciliation workbook, and draw information from the Check Tracking worksheet.

Assign budget categories (such as automobile, clothing, entertainment, and so on) in a column to the left of each expenditure (see, for example, the Expense column in the first figure in this chapter). Then use Excel's Consolidate feature to summarize your expenditures in each category.

To use Consolidate, open a new worksheet in your workbook and name it **Consolidate**. Click a blank cell (in our example, cell A2), and then go to the **Data** menu and choose **Consolidate**.

Good Housekeeping

Make a habit of labeling columns before doing any calculations. Being obsessive about labeling saves time later when you discover your scratch calculations are actually useful.

From the dialog box, choose **Function: Sum**. In the Reference box, list the range name or cell references that contain the columns for your budget categories and expenditures. (In our example, we named the two-column Expense-Withdrawals range on our Check Tracking worksheet "Consolidation," and simply inserted the range name.)

Click the **Add** button, and check the **Use Labels In Left Column** box. Click the **OK** button, and watch Excel consolidate all the data from your first worksheet onto your second worksheet. Use Excel's Chart Wizard to graph the data, as we've shown here.

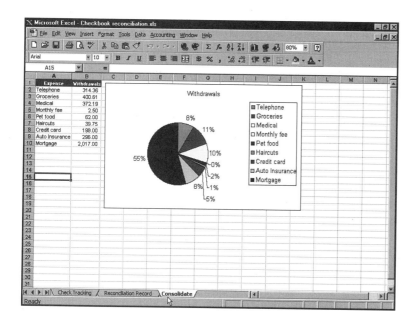

The Consolidate worksheet lets you analyze your financial position.

Preparing a Budget

There was a time when your friendly authors budgeted like everyone else: We made a list of income and expenses, and hoped the income outweighed the expenses. Unfortunately, the "make a list" system was of little use, in large part because after the work was done, the real numbers rarely matched actual income or expenditures. Then what?

Now our budgeting is more complex—and vastly more useful. If you want to use Excel to make a simple list, feel free! It'll do a marvelous job for you. But if you'd rather create something a little more useful, consider our budgeting system:

Open a new workbook and make two worksheets: Budget—planned, and Budget—actual. All the preliminary work is done in the Budget—planned worksheet.

Our budget has three parts: Financial Position, Resources, and Outgo. Begin by labeling the Budget—planned worksheet, as shown in the following figure. Row 1 contains 14 column labels: Category, Source, and the 12 months of the year.

The Budget—planned worksheet contains preliminary budget plans.

	A	B	C	D	E	F	G	
			Jul-98	Aug-98	Sep-98	Oct-98	Nov-98	Dec
1	Category	Source						
2	Financial Position							
3	Resources minus Outgo		$ 779.00	$ 921.40	$ 1,063.80	$ 1,206.20	$ 1,348.60	$ 1,4
4	Resources							
5	Current	Cash on hand	190.00					
6		Checking account balance	792.00	779.00	921.40	1063.80	1206.20	13
7	Total Current		$ 982.00	$ 779.00	$ 921.40	$ 1,063.80	$ 1,206.20	$ 1,3
8	Income	Jack -- IDT		3690.00	3690.00	3690.00	3690.00	36
9		Jill -- Tremont		4220.00	4220.00	4220.00	4220.00	42
10		Rent -- West Ave.		600.00	600.00	600.00	600.00	6
11		Interest -- Commercial bank		83.33	83.33	83.33	83.33	
12		Jack -- Shop		1200.00	1200.00	1200.00	1200.00	12
13		Misc. income	50.00	200.00	200.00	200.00	200.00	2
14	Total Income		$ 50.00	$ 9,993.33	$ 9,993.33	$ 9,993.33	$ 9,993.33	$ 9,9
15	Total Resources		$1,032.00	$10,772.33	$10,914.73	$11,057.13	$11,199.53	$11,3
16	Outgo							
17	Percentage	Charity	5.00	999.33	999.33	999.33	999.33	9
18		Savings/Investment	7.50	1,499.00	1,499.00	1,499.00	1,499.00	1,4
19		Tax payments	10.50	2,098.60	2,098.60	2,098.60	2,098.60	2,0
20	Fixed monthly	Auto payment		365.00	365.00	365.00	365.00	3
21		Cable TV		27.00	27.00	27.00	27.00	
22		Child care	55.00	220.00	220.00	220.00	220.00	2
23		Health insurance		750.00	750.00	750.00	750.00	7
24		Mortgage payment		2012.00	2012.00	2012.00	2012.00	20
25	Fixed semi-annual	Auto insurance		216.67	216.67	216.67	216.67	2

Month to Month

Rather than label columns with the months January through December (ho-hum), here's a way to make your column labels dynamic. Your budget can always begin with the current month, and show your projections for the year following.

The formula for the current month, in this example, cell C1, is [=TODAY()]. Each of the 11 subsequent months increases the previous calculation by 30.42 days (1/12th of a year). So cell D1 gets the formula [+C1+30.42]. Copy cell D1 all the way to column N.

To format the labels as dates, select the entire row, go to the **Format** menu, and choose **Cells.** Under the **Number** tab, choose **Date,** and select a **Mon-Yr** format. Next, create labels for columns A and B.

In cell A2, create the label **Financial Position.** Just below it, in cell A3, create the label **Resources minus Outgo.** We'll fill in the calculations later.

Now it's time to label the Resources portion of the worksheet. Cell A4 is labeled Resources. Beneath it, in cell A5, type **Current.** These current resources include money that is immediately available to you without penalty: cash on hand, your checking account balance, or a mutual fund account with checking privileges. Beginning in cell B5, list each of these Current resources. In our example, we list Cash on hand, and in cell B6, Checking account balance. In the next cell, A7 in our example, insert the **Total Current** label.

The following section is for income. Label cell A8 **Income**, and to the right, in column B, list each regular income source. In our example we label cell A14 **Total Income**, and below that we find **Total Resources**, the combined current and income figures.

Finally, create labels for the Outgo portion of the budget—expenses, contributions to savings or investment plans, charitable contributions, and set-asides for major purchases. Cell A16 in our example is labeled Outgo. Expenditures are grouped into five sections with labels in column A:

➤ *Percentages*. These include items that you pay as a regular percentage of your income (savings, charitable donations, income tax payments).

➤ *Fixed monthly expenses*. These include payments, mortgage payments.

➤ *Fixed semiannual expenses*. These include auto insurance and tuition.

➤ *Variable monthly expenses*. These include utilities, entertainment, and groceries.

➤ *Variable semiannual expenses*. These include repairs, clothing, gifts, and vacations.

To the right of each section, in column B, list the actual expenditures, based on information gathered in the financial analysis you did in the previous section of this chapter.

Now it's time to insert the numbers and the formulas. Save the Financial Position portion for last, and skip directly to the Resources section, cell C5 in our example. Enter the actual number for Cash on hand. If you've created a Checkbook reconciliation worksheet, insert the actual cell address in cell C6 to reflect the current checking account balance. In cell C7, Total Current, find the sum of total current resources by clicking the **Autosum** button on the standard toolbar.

The Income portion shows figures for expected income for the current month. In other words, if today is the 15th day of the month, you'll input figures only for the income you normally receive in the second half of the month. Income you've already received was reflected in the Current section, above. In cell C14 in our example, we total the entire income section, including blank cells, with the formula [=SUM(C8:C13)].

The figure for Total Resources (cell C15) is the total of Current and Income [=+C7+C14].

Now jump down to the Outgo portion of the worksheet (see the following figure). Again, enter only the figures that reflect expected expenses for the remainder of the current month. The Percentage expenditures in our example are a portion of income. Charitable contributions, for example, are 10 percent of income [=0.1*C14]. Continue inputting figures and formulas for the current month's remaining expenses. On the last line of the worksheet, cell C50 in our example, total all expenditures for the current month, including blank cells [=SUM(C17:C49)].

The Outgo portion of the budget—planned worksheet shows expected expenses.

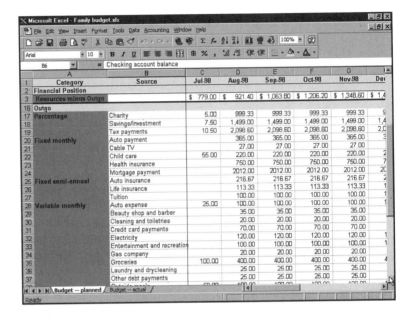

Finally, jump back to the top of the worksheet, and input the formula to calculate your financial position (cell C3). The formula is simply Total Resources less Total Expenditures [=+C15-C50]. If the number is positive, you're doing well. If it's negative, you'll have to either increase your income or decrease your expenditures.

There's your budget for the current month.

Next month requires just one change: Your financial position at the end of the current month (cell C3) is your Current position at the beginning of the next month. We choose to place this number in the Checking account balance area (cell D6) using the formula [+C3]. Copy the current month's Current total (cell C7) to next month (cell D7).

Input next month's income figures in cells D8 through D13 as required. Copy the Total Income and Total Resources formulas from C14:15 to cells D14:15.

At this point, you'll want to work your way down the worksheet to input expenditures.

Watch Your Financial Position

While working your way down the worksheet, you'll want to continue watching your Financial Position to make sure your expenditures stay within your income. To keep your Financial Position visible on the screen, try freezing the view. Position your mouse pointer in cell C4, then go to the **Window** menu and select **Freeze Panes**. From here on, your labels and your financial position will stay visible on the screen as you scroll around the remainder of the worksheet.

Enter the expenditures for the following month in the remainder of column D, and copy the Total Expenditures formula from C50 to D50.

Once you've finished next month, you can easily copy column D to columns E through N to finish out the year.

After you're satisfied with your planned budget, copy the contents of the entire worksheet to the blank Actual worksheet. As you continue keeping your budget through the months, make modifications to the Actual worksheet.

Developing a Personal Financial Statement

Looking for a lender? Hope to find an investor for your small business? In either event, you'll need to assemble some financial information to demonstrate that you're a sound risk.

The personal financial statement has two parts: the balance sheet and the income statement.

Accounting 101

The *balance sheet* describes your *assets* (such as your home) and *liabilities* (such as your mortgage). The number left over when you subtract liabilities from assets is your *net worth*.

The *income statement* identifies your sources of income and your expenses, called *contingent liabilities*. The number left over when you subtract expenses from income is your *retained income*.

Our sample personal financial statement consists of a workbook with six worksheets. The front sheet, which we named Personal Financial Statement, shows both the Balance Sheet and the Income Statement (see the following two figures).

The Balance Sheet is the top portion of the Personal Financial Statement.

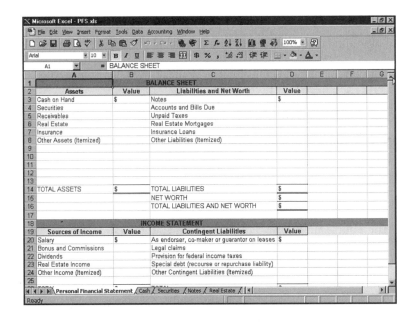

The Income Statement appears at the bottom of the Personal Financial Statement.

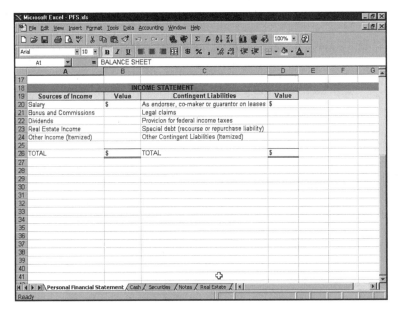

Most of the entries on the Balance Sheet are backed by other worksheets in the workbook. The Cash on Hand entry (cell B3) comes from the Cash worksheet, as shown in the following figure.

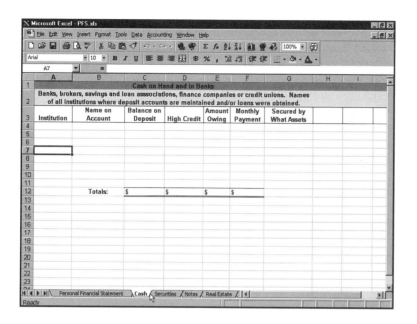

The Cash worksheet records cash on hand.

There's a separate worksheet called Securities backing up the Securities entry in cell B4.

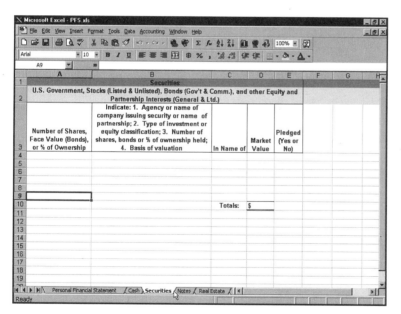

Record stocks, bonds, and other securities on the Securities worksheet.

The Receivables figure (cell B5) and the Accounts and Bills Due figure (cell D4) on the Balance sheet come from the Notes worksheet.

293

Accounts and bills due appear on the Notes worksheet.

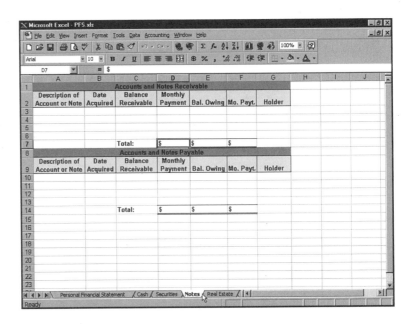

You'll list information on Real Estate (cell B6 on the Balance sheet) and Mortgages (cell D6) on the Real Estate worksheet.

Real estate holdings and mortgages appear on the Real Estate worksheet.

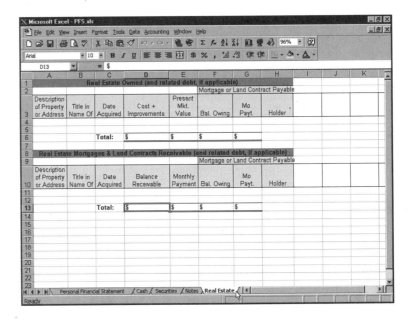

Finally, the Insurance (cell B7) and Insurance Loans (cell D7) figures on the Balance sheet are listed on the Insurance worksheet.

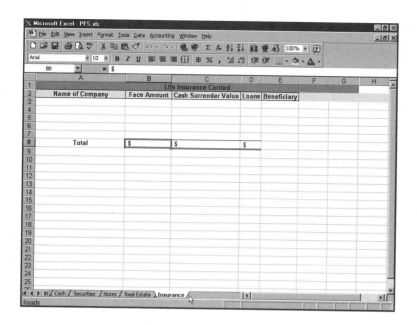

List insurance policies and loans on the Insurance worksheet.

The Balance Sheet calculations are simple. Total Assets (cell B14) is a simple sum [=SUM(B3:B13)]. Total Liabilities (cell D14) is also a sum [=SUM(D3:D13)]. Your Net Worth is the difference between assets and liabilities [=+B14-D14]. The figure in cell D16, Liabilities and Net Worth, equals the Assets figure in B14—hence the name Balance Sheet.

The Income Statement follows the Balance Sheet. If any of the Income Statement figures require explanation, add additional worksheets (go to the **Insert** menu and choose **Worksheet**) to break out the data.

Preparing Your Tax Return

We're big fans of the two leading commercial tax preparation products, and would recommend them to anyone. Even so, it's worth keeping Excel open in the background while preparing your tax return—whether electronically or manually.

Start an Excel workbook called TAXES*nn*.XLS (where *nn* is the year) to store detailed tax information that doesn't appear on your tax return.

For example, if you own a rental home, you'll want to open a worksheet to record all the receipts and expenses related to that home in a single place. The IRS isn't interested in knowing whether you purchased that replacement faucet at Home Depot or at Sears, or whether you bought seven gaskets or three—but Excel will cheerfully remember for you.

Check This Out...

Details, Details!

Excel enables you to record more detail, and perform better calculations, than you can in commercial tax software. And your Excel worksheets are more accessible than the detailed information in tax prep software, enabling you to format, analyze, copy, access, and print your data at will.

Likewise, use separate worksheets to record employee expenses, deductible automobile expenses, medical and insurance expenses, casualty losses, child care costs, property taxes and other deductible expenses related to your home, office, investments, and more.

You're better off recording them all in Excel worksheets than you would be detailing them in the limited resources of your tax preparation software.

Business Sense for Business Cents

Much of what you do as a business owner is identical to what you do in your personal financial situation. You create budgets, develop financial statements, track bank accounts, pay taxes, and analyze your financial position.

Additionally, though, you're probably developing business plans, recording daily transactions, preparing additional reports, generating payroll, and even working with a double-entry accounting system. While there are a number of dedicated commercial software products on the market designed specifically to handle business accounting, you should recognize that you can do all your accounting—and often do it better—in Excel.

If your business is very small, you may even find that Excel is a superior, less cumbersome choice than full-blown commercial accounting products, with their invoice generation, payroll, time-tracking, and job-costing features. (If your business is somewhat larger, though, you'll find commercial accounting packages such as Intuit's QuickBooks or QuickBooks Pro very useful. Chapter 24, "Small Business Financial Manager," teaches you how to integrate them with Excel to tap into its unique analysis features.)

In this section, we describe a few of the business uses of Excel.

Financial Statements

As you build your accounting system, you'll find that Excel's primary strength is its ability to pull together information from a variety of sources.

Generally, it's easiest to keep all your accounting data in a single workbook, and to assign different tasks to different worksheets within the workbook. The balance sheet goes on one worksheet, the revenue projections on another, analytical graphs on another, and so on.

Multiple Submissions

If you're working with submissions from multiple departments, or pulling information from databases, word processing documents, or other sources, Excel is up to the task.

To pull a figure—say, a departmental salary projection—from a separate workbook, just open both workbooks, position your pointer in the cell where you want the information to appear, and type **+**, then press **Ctrl+F6** to switch to the other workbook. Select the cell where the information is found, and press **Enter**. The salary projection is now available in your new workbook, and automatically updates itself each time you make changes to the old workbook.

Similarly, if you need to place an object—say, a bitmapped graphic or a document you created in Microsoft Word—into your worksheet, use Excel's Insert, Object command to cause the object to appear on your worksheet. As you make changes to the object, the updates appear automatically in Excel.

Because every business has its own accounting reports, we'll illustrate here the most common one: the balance sheet.

The balance sheet for a business—particularly one that carries an inventory—is significantly more complex than it is for an individual, as you can see by the following figure.

In our example, we use a balance sheet with several columns. In the Assets section, calculations performed in column B carry over to column C, and from there to column D, to arrive at a total for Current, Fixed, and Other Assets.

The Liabilities section in our example requires only two columns for calculations, reflecting Current and Long-Term Liabilities.

The Equity—or Capital—section summarizes Owner's Investment, Net Profit or Loss (Retained Earnings), and Drawings or Dividends.

As you prepare your other financial statements—general ledger, trial balance, profit and loss, income statement, cash flow, transaction reports, journals, payroll, A/R (Accounts Receivable), A/P (Accounts Payable), and reports specific to your business—you'll discover that Excel's capability to integrate numbers from one report to the next eliminates errors and simplifies all your financial work.

Setting up the business balance sheet.

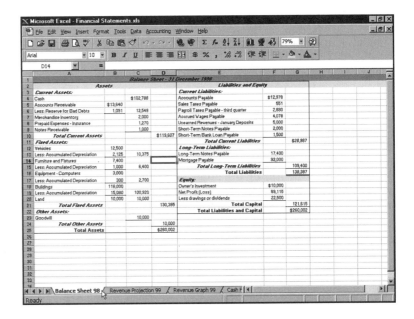

Financial Analysis

After you have access to all your financial data, Excel is a wizard at analyzing it.

What you're looking for when you do analysis is a quick picture of where you stand.

Excel's Charting feature is key to generating visual images of your financial position. You might, for example, decide to produce a graph of your month-to-month income (see the following figure) or chart changes in your quarterly profitability.

If you're looking for more fundamental analysis, use Excel to produce basic business ratios that describe your financial position.

Set up a separate worksheet in your accounting workbook for calculating business ratios. The numbers you'll want to analyze come directly from the financial reports you've produced, primarily your balance sheet and income statement. Those calculations are described in the following sections.

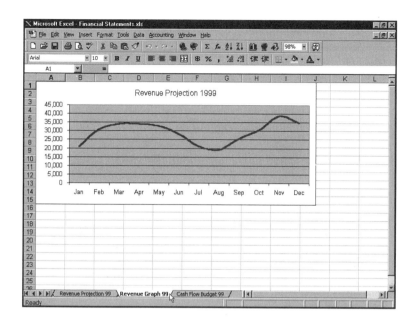

Use charting to create visual graphs of your financial data.

Efficiency Ratios

How good are your business assets at generating income? Use these common efficiency ratios to find out:

➤ *Accounts Receivable Analysis*

  ➤ *Average Daily Sales*. This is Annual Sales divided by 360.

  ➤ *Average Collection Period*. This is the amount of time you're extending credit. Formula: Accounts Receivable Balance divided by Average Daily Sales.

  ➤ *A/R-to-Sales Ratio*. This is the predictor of cash flow problems related to accounts receivable. Formula: A/R Balance divided by Monthly Sales.

➤ *Asset Turnover Analysis*

  ➤ *Fixed Asset Turnover*. This is the analysis of how well fixed assets help in generating sales. Formula: Sales divided by Fixed Assets.

  ➤ *Total Asset Turnover*. This is the measure of how total business assets generate revenue. Formula: Total Sales divided by Total Assets.

➤ *Inventory Analysis*

  ➤ *Average Daily Cost of Goods Sold*. This is the price of creating inventory. Formula: Annual Cost of Goods Sold divided by 360.

➤ *Inventory-to-Sales Ratio.* This predicts potential cash flow problems as they relate to inventory. Formula: Inventory Balance divided by Monthly Sales.

➤ *Turnover.* This is the amount of time it takes to convert inventory to cash. Formula: Inventory Balance divided by Average Daily Cost of Goods Sold.

Liquidity (Working Capital) Ratios

How liquid is your business? Use these ratios to track your ability to stay solvent in the short term:

➤ *Current Ratio.* This is a measure of short-term solvency. Formula: Current Assets times Current Liabilities.

➤ *Quick Ratio,* or *Acid Test.* This is a measure of real short-term solvency. (Current Assets minus Inventory) times Current Liabilities.

Profitability Ratios

Is your company as profitable as it could be? These ratios will tell you where you stand:

➤ *Gross Profit Margin.* Formula: Gross Profit divided by Sales.

➤ *Net Profit Margin.* Formula: Net Income divided by Sales, expressed as a percentage.

➤ *Operating Profit Percentage.* This is the measure of how much you're earning in your primary business operations. Formula: Operating Income divided by Sales.

➤ *Return on Assets.* This is an analysis of how well your assets generate income. Formula: Net Income divided by Total Assets.

➤ *Return on Equity.* This is the determination of how well your investment is doing. Formula: Net Income divided by Owner's Equity.

Solvency Ratios

Solvency ratios tell you how well you're able to meet your obligations in the longer term:

➤ *Debt to Assets.* This is a measure of debt financing. Formula: Total Liabilities divided by Total Assets.

➤ *Debt to Equity.* This is a measure of leverage. Formula: Total Liabilities divided by Owner's Equity.

➤ *Fixed Costs Coverage*. This is a measure of ability to meet fixed obligations such as debt repayments, leases, and preferred stock dividends. Formula: Net Income (before taxes and fixed charges) divided by Fixed Charges.

➤ *Interest Coverage*. This is a measure of ability to cover interest charges alone. Formula: Operating Income divided by Interest Expense.

The Least You Need to Know

In this chapter you learned that Excel can take advantage of your banking software, help organize your finances, and budget your next vacation. Now, if you could only calculate the raise you deserve. This is what you learned in this chapter:

➤ Gaining control of personal finances with the help of Excel worksheets is not as difficult as it may first appear.

➤ You can take advantage of your bank's online software by importing account information directly into Excel.

➤ All the tools you need to create custom, full-featured business accounting applications can be found in Excel.

➤ It really is possible to reconcile a checkbook.

Chapter 24

Small Business Financial Manager

In This Chapter

➤ Getting started

➤ Importing accounting information

➤ What Small Business Financial Manager (SBFM) can do for you

As a small business owner, you're well aware of the value of time. Yes, you'd *like* to read all 300-plus pages of a cleverly written book in one sitting, but you'll probably put it off until tomorrow. For now, you just want to get back to work.

The Small Business Edition of Microsoft Office features just what you're looking for: an application to get you up and running right away. It's called Small Business Financial Manager, and we're going to show you how to use it—right now!

Getting Started

To use Small Business Financial Manager, your business must do three things:

1. Use the Accrual basis for accounting, not the Cash basis.

2. Use a 12-period accounting system—not quarterly or annual.

3. Use one of the commercial accounting software packages listed following as the basis of its accounting system.

Opening the Books

This chapter assumes you know a bit about accounting. If not, we'd have to include a tutorial on how to use the accounting packages from which the data is drawn—and that's, well, a whole 'nother series of books.

Small Business Financial Manager doesn't replace commercial accounting software. Instead, it supplements it. Picture your accounting package—QuickBooks, Peachtree, DacEasy, or any of a long list of products we detail later—as a database. SBFM extracts data from your accounting package and massages it to produce a variety of reports and analyses.

Small Business Financial Manager is not a separate piece of software. It is, rather, a complex add-in for Excel.

Microsoft updated Small Business Financial Manager to version 98 at the end of March 1998, which changed the list of accounting packages it supports.

You may use the older Small Business Financial Manager 97 if you do your accounting in one of the following commercial packages:

➤ ADP One-Write-Plus Accounting with Payroll for DOS, 4.0

➤ Computer Associates ACCPAC Plus for DOS, 6.1

➤ Computer Associates Simply Accounting for Windows, 3.0

➤ DacEasy Accounting for DOS, 6.0

➤ Great Plains Accounting for DOS, 8.0

➤ Intuit QuickBooks, 3.1

➤ Peachtree Accounting for Windows, 3.0

➤ Peachtree Complete Accounting for DOS, 8.0

➤ Platinum Series for DOS and Windows, 4.02

➤ State of the Art Business Works for DOS and Windows, 9.0

➤ State of the Art M*A*S 90 Evolution/2, 1.5

➤ Timeline MetaView, 3.0

If you use one of the following packages, you should upgrade to Small Business Financial Manager 98:

➤ ADP One-Write-Plus for DOS, 4.03

➤ Computer Associates ACCPAC Plus Accounting for DOS, 6.1a

➤ Computer Associates Simply Accounting, 3.0, 4.0, or 5.0

➤ DacEasy Accounting for DOS, 5.0

➤ Great Plains Accounting for DOS, 8.0, 8.1, or 8.2

➤ Intuit QuickBooks or QuickBooks Pro for Windows, 3.1, 4.0, or 5.0

➤ Peachtree Accounting for Windows, 3.0, 3.5, and 5.0

➤ Peachtree Complete Accounting for DOS, 8.0

➤ Peachtree Complete Accounting for Windows, 4.0

➤ Platinum Series, 4.1 or 4.4

➤ State of the Art BusinessWorks for Windows, 9.0

➤ State of the Art M*A*S 90 Evolution/2, 1.51

➤ Timeline MetaView Analysts/Server, 2.3, 2.4, or 2.5

Microsoft promises to list additional or updated accounting packages and filters at its Small Business Edition Web site, www.microsoft.com/office/sbe, although it hadn't done so at the time of this writing. The site is somewhat complex, so go to the **Search** tool, and search on the term "financial manager" to view files specifically related to SBFM.

If you own the older (97) version of SBFM, we strongly recommend combing through the Web site to locate upgrades, bug fixes, and additional templates. In fact, that's a good practice to get into, regardless of the software application you own.

Installing Small Business Financial Manager

Before installing new software, you should first close all other applications. To install SBFM, you must first have Excel 97 installed on your hard drive.

Here's the installation procedure:

1. Insert the Office 97 CD (disc 1) into your CD-ROM drive, and select the **Run** command from the **Start** menu on your taskbar.

2. From the Look In line of the Run dialog box, select your CD-ROM drive (normally D:/) and click the **Autorun** file.

3. In the Small Business Edition dialog box, position your mouse pointer over the **Small Business Financial Manager** icon and click.

4. A series of brief dialog boxes will appear asking you to input information about your company and your CD-ROM.

5. When the Financial Manager Setup dialog box appears, click the large **Custom** button. From the Custom dialog box, choose the accounting software applications you use—or might use in the future—and click **OK**.

6. Select additional options from any subsequent dialog boxes, and then watch as SBFM installs itself on your hard drive.

To open SBFM, locate the **Microsoft Small Business Financial Manager** icon under the **Program** folder on your **Startup** menu, and click. The SBFM window will appear onscreen.

The opening screen for Small Business Financial Manager displays several clickable options.

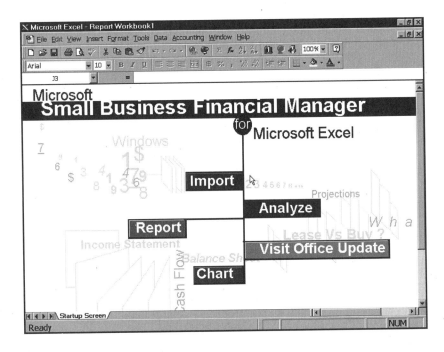

Warning: This Thing Contains Macros!

As SBFM opens, you may encounter a dialog box warning that the workbook contains macros. Click the **Enable Macros** option, and the SBFM opening window will appear.

Importing Accounting Information

After you've posted your accounting information from within your accounting software—but before you've closed out the period—you can import it into SBFM.

The importing process extracts raw data from your accounting software and stores it in Microsoft Access format. (You don't need to have a copy of Access on your machine to run the Import Wizard or use the extracted data.) In the examples that follow, we use sample data from Intuit QuickBooks Pro, v. 5.0, a best-selling business accounting package.

SBFM doesn't import everything from your accounting package, but it does import, at a minimum, the posted general ledger transactions. If available, it will also import your chart of accounts, posted detail transactions and associated data, and customer information. It will also import data from sales invoices and inventory balances.

Clean It Up

If possible, before you import, check that your accounting data is clean and compact. That means running any integrity or validation checks provided as part of the accounting package, and using the data compacting feature, if one is available.

Now you're ready to import. Click the **Import** button on the SBFM opening screen, or go to the **Accounting** menu and choose **Import Wizard**. The Import Your Accounting Data dialog box will appear, as shown in the following figure. Select the **Import** option (in the future, you'll use the Update option), and click **Next**.

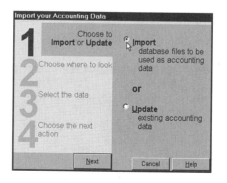

The Import your Accounting Data dialog box will—guess what?—import your accounting data.

Step 2 tells SBFM where to look for the data (see the next figure). If you know where the data is stored, choose the **In Specific Folders** option. Otherwise, select the **Look on "My Computer"** option to tell SBFM to search the entire machine. Click **Next**. If SBFM has to search a large disk, this process may take a moment or two.

Step 2 of importing your accounting data.

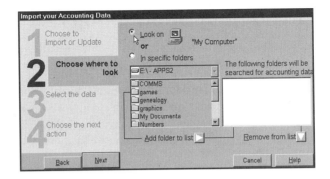

Step 3 asks you to select the data, as shown in the next figure. Choose the correct company, and click **Next**. The import process can be lengthy, but generally takes no more than 30 seconds or so.

Step 3 of importing.

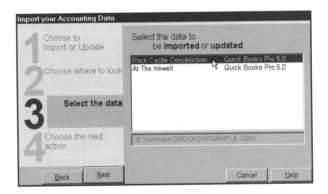

Step 4 gives you several options, as shown next. Select **Remap Your Accounting Data** at this stage, because you want to be certain your accounts were imported into the correct categories before you create reports or analyses.

Importing, step 4.

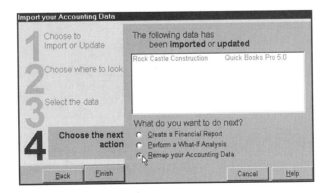

Click **Finish**. The Map Your Accounts dialog box appears, with a Windows Explorer-like screen listing your account groupings. By clicking the plus or minus signs, you can expand or shrink the categories to see or hide the underlying information. If some of the accounts ended up in the wrong groupings, click them one by one and drag them, with the left mouse button held down, to the correct groupings.

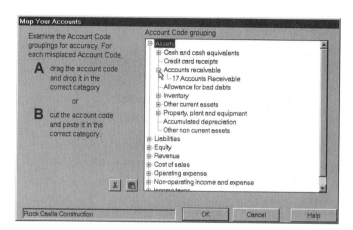

Mapping your accounts hides or reveals your account categories.

On the Map

If you forget to remap in step 4, open the **Accounting** menu and choose **Remap Data**. Then click and drag your accounts to the proper categories as usual.

When you're satisfied that all the groupings are correct, click **OK**. The original SBFM opening screen reappears, and you're ready to work!

What SBFM Can Do for You

As you saw on the opening screen, Small Business Financial Manager has five functions. In addition to the Import function covered earlier, SBFM can go directly to the Web to find Office software updates, and it can create three kinds of financial aids: Reports, Analyses, and Charts.

Financial Reports

Financial Manager creates seven familiar financial reports, some of which will already appear as reports in your business accounting package. SBFM's Report Wizard will create a trial balance, balance sheet, income statement, cash flow report, changes in stockholders' equity report, sales analysis, and business ratios. (See Chapter 23, "Tracking Your Life and Your Business," for a discussion of business ratios and several financial reports.)

To create any of the seven reports, click the **Report** button in SBFM, or go to the **Accounting** menu and choose **Report Wizard**. The Create a Financial Report dialog box appears with a list of financial reports and company names. Choose the report you want to create, and click **Next**.

Seven different kinds of reports are available from the Create a Financial Report dialog box.

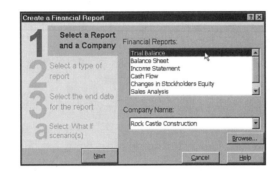

In step 2, select the type of report, if applicable, and click **Next**. Step 3 requires you to select an ending date for the report from a list of options and click **Finish**.

Your completed report is added as a new worksheet in a familiar Excel format. Most of the reports appear in the form of pivot tables, discussed in Chapter 21, "Pivot Tables." You're free to manipulate the pivot tables to view the data in other configurations. Most reports also display outline icons in the top rows and left columns. Click the plus and minus signs to expand and hide data as required.

Custom Financial Reports

Financial Manager also permits you to develop your own financial reports based on account information you imported from your accounting software. The custom reporting feature is extremely limited, however, giving you access to only a few of your accounts.

Nevertheless, if you'd like to give it a shot, here's the procedure:

1. First, create a new worksheet. Go to the **Insert** menu and select **Worksheet**. Create column and row labels as desired, and then point to a blank cell where you want the account information to appear.

2. Go to the **Accounting** menu and select **Insert Balance**. The Insert Account Balance dialog box appears, as shown here.

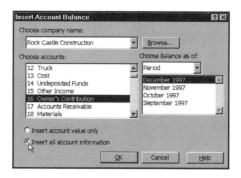

Develop your own financial reports from the Insert Account Balance dialog box.

3. Choose the account you want to see on your custom report, select the desired date information, and decide whether you want to see the account balance alone, or all the available account information.

4. Click **OK**, and account balance data appears on your new worksheet.

Financial Analyses

With Small Business Financial Manager, you can perform several analyses on your imported data. To choose a tool, click the **Analyze** button on the SBFM opening screen, or go to the **Accounting** menu and choose **Select Analysis Tool**. The Select a Financial Manager Analysis Tool dialog box appears, giving you four options:

➤ *Business Comparison Reports*, for comparing your business to others in your general industry category to see how you stack up.

➤ *Projection Wizard*, to forecast business growth.

➤ *Create Projection Reports*, based on results from the Projection Wizard.

➤ *What-If Analysis*, to create alternate scenarios based on new assumptions for profitability, accounts receivable, accounts payable, inventory, expenses, sale of assets, new loans, loan payoffs, and buying versus leasing.

Choose your analysis tool, select desired options from subsequent dialog boxes, and watch as SBFM prepares new analyses based on historical data and your assumptions about the future.

Charts

The final feature of SBFM is a small selection of analytical charts. Click the **Chart** button on the opening screen, or go to the **Accounting** menu and select **Chart Wizard**. The Create a Financial Chart dialog box appears with four chart options:

➤ Revenue-Expense Trend

➤ Sales Composition

➤ Balance Sheet Composition

➤ Cash Flow Trend

Select the desired chart and the company name, and click **Next**. Step 2 requires you to choose a chart type. Click **Next** to proceed to step 3, where you'll select a date for the chart. Click **Finish**, and the new chart appears on its own worksheet.

Analytical charts appear on their own worksheet.

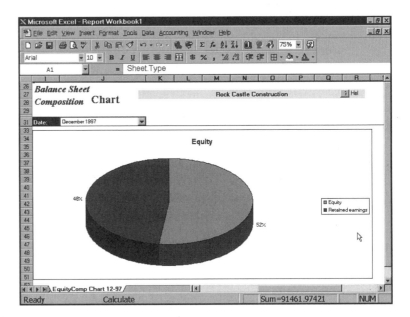

The Least You Need to Know

With Small Business Financial Manager, you'll be able to apply the analytical powers of Excel to data imported from other sources.

➤ Remember to check out the Microsoft Small Business Edition Web site, `www.microsoft.com/office/sbe`, for update information.

➤ You can create financial reports with the Report Wizard. Options include: trial balance, income statement, sales analysis, and more.

➤ SBFM features a what-if function, making it easier to analyze alternative scenarios for various situations.

➤ You can easily create analytical charts with the Chart Wizard.

Part 6
Stuff at the Back of the Book

This section contains the usual back-of-the-book appendix-type information. You know, stuff like technical support, reference guides, and a glossary.

Please note that this book read backward provides absolutely no clues as to the whereabouts of Paul McCartney.

Installation and Technical Support

Installation

To install Microsoft Excel 97, you need to have the following on your computer:

➤ Windows 95 or Windows NT version 3.51 or higher

➤ At least 20MB of available hard disk space

Installation from CD

To install Excel from a CD-ROM, follow these steps:

1. Insert the CD in your CD-ROM drive. Close the door. On most systems, a feature called Autorun should automatically start the installation process. If not:

2. Click the **Windows 95 Start** button and select **Run** from the Start menu. The Run dialog box will appear. The Open option in the Run dialog box should automatically display the correct information for running Setup—disk, folder (if applicable), and program name.

3. If this information is correct, click the **OK** button. If the information is not correct or if you are uncertain, click the **Browse** button. Select the drive letter assigned to your CD-ROM (usually D:\) and search for the Setup program for Excel (or Microsoft Office 97, if you're installing Excel from Office). After you click the Setup program, Windows will return to the first Run dialog box. Click the **OK** button.

4. The Excel (or Office) installation routine begins. Select the **Typical** installation to have Excel perform the installation automatically. If you want to be sure all your options are available, however, choose **Custom** installation and select **All**.

Installation from Floppy Disk

To install Microsoft Excel 97 from floppy disks, follow these steps:

1. Insert Disk #1 in your drive.

2. Click the **Windows 95 Start** button and select **Run** from the Start menu. The Run dialog box will appear. The Open option in the Run dialog box should contain the correct information for running setup—disk, folder (if applicable), and program name.

3. If this information is correct, click the **OK** button. If the information is not correct or if you are uncertain, click the **Browse** button. Select the drive that you inserted floppy disk #1 into (usually A:\) and select the **Setup** program. Windows will return to the first Run dialog box. Click the **OK** button.

4. The Excel (or Office) installation routine begins. Select the **Typical** installation to have Excel perform the installation automatically.

Technical Support

The Microsoft Corporation provides standard technical support between the hours of 6:00 a.m. and 6:00 p.m. Pacific Time. The number to call for technical support is (206) 635-7110.

This is not a toll-free call, so prepare yourself before you call. You should have these things handy before you start running up telephone charges:

➤ Software version numbers.

➤ Operating system version numbers.

➤ Hardware types and model numbers.

➤ The exact text of any onscreen messages.

➤ Prepare to describe what you were attempting to do when the problem occurred.

Online Support

Online support is available for Microsoft products from the major commercial online providers. Contact your online provider for details. For online support over the World Wide Web, visit Microsoft's home page at http://www.microsoft.com. Additionally, you might want to participate in Microsoft's Internet newsgroup at news://msnews.microsoft.com.

The Function Guide

Here, in living color, is a complete reference guide to every Excel function in the known universe.

Excel's functions in all their glory

Function (Syntax)	Description	Category
ABS(number)	Absolute value of a number	Mathematical
ACCRINT(issue, first_ interest, settlement, rate, par, frequency, basis)	Accrued interest for a security that pays periodic interest	Financial
ACCRINTM(issue, maturity, rate, par, basis)	Accrued interest for a security that pays interest at maturity	Financial
ACOS(number)	Arccosine of a number	Mathematical
ACOSH(number)	Inverse hyperbolic cosine of a number	Mathematical
ADDRESS(row_num, column_num, abs_num, a1, sheet_text)	Show a reference as text to a single cell in a worksheet	Lookup
AMORDEGRC(cost, date_ purchased, first_period, salvage, period, rate, basis)	Depreciation for each accounting period	Financial
AMORLINC(cost, date_ purchased, first_period, salvage, period, rate, basis)	Depreciation for each accounting period, French system	Financial
AND(logical1, logical2, ...)	TRUE if all arguments are TRUE	Logical
AREAS(reference)	Number of areas in a reference	Lookup
ASIN(number)	Arcsine of a number	Mathematical

continues

Excel's functions in all their glory   Continued

Function (Syntax)	Description	Category
ASINH(number)	Inverse hyperbolic sine of a number	Mathematical
ATAN(number)	Arctangent of a number	Mathematical
ATAN2(x_num, y_num)	Arctangent from x and y coordinates	Mathematical
ATANH(number)	Inverse hyperbolic tangent of a number	Mathematical
AVEDEV(number1, number2, ...)	Average of absolute deviations of data points from their mean	Statistical
AVERAGE(number1, number2, ...)	Average of all arguments	Statistical
AVERAGEA(value1, value2, ...)	Finds arithmetic mean	Statistical
BESSELI(x, n)	Modified Bessel function In(x)	Engineering
BESSELJ(x, n)	Bessel function Jn(x)	Engineering
BESSELK(x, n)	Modified Bessel function Kn(x)	Engineering
BESSELY(x, n)	Bessel function Yn(x)	Engineering
BETADIST(x, alpha, beta, A, B)	Cumulative beta probability density function	Statistical
BETAINV(probability, alpha, beta, A, B)	Inverse of cumulative beta probability density function	Statistical
BIN2DEC(number)	Change a binary number to decimal	Engineering
BIN2HEX(number, places)	Change a binary number to hexadecimal	Engineering
BIN2OCT(number, places)	Change a binary number to octal	Engineering
BINOMDIST(number_s, trials, probability_s, cumulative)	Individual term binomial distribution probability	Statistical
CEILING(number, significance)	Round a number to nearest integer or to nearest multiple of significance	Mathematical

Function (Syntax)	Description	Category
CELL(info_type, reference)	Information about formatting location, or contents of a cell	Information
CHAR(number)	Character specified by code number	Text
CHIDIST(x, degrees_freedom)	One-tailed probability of chi-squared distribution	Statistical
CHIINV(probability, degrees_freedom)	Inverse of one-tailed probability of chi-squared distribution	Statistical
CHITEST(actual_range, expected_range)	Test for independence	Statistical
CHOOSE(index_num, value1, value2, 1/4)	Choose a value from a list of values	Lookup
CLEAN(text)	Remove all nonprintable characters from text	Text
CODE(text)	Numeric code for first character in a text string	Text
COLUMN(reference)	Column number of a reference	Lookup
COLUMNS(array)	Number of columns in a reference	Lookup
COMBIN(number, number_chosen)	Number of combinations for a given number of objects	Mathematical
COMPLEX(real_num, i_num, suffix)	Change real and imaginary coefficients into a complex number	Engineering
CONCATENATE (text1, text2, …)	Join several text items into one text item	Text
CONFIDENCE(alpha, standard_dev, size)	Confidence interval for a population mean	Statistical
CONVERT(number, from_unit, to_unit)	Change a number from one measurement system to another	Engineering
CORREL(array1, array2)	Correlation coefficient between two data sets	Statistical
COS(number)	Cosine of a number	Mathematical
COSH(number)	Hyperbolic cosine of a number	Mathematical

continues

Excel's functions in all their glory Continued

Function (Syntax)	Description	Category
COUNT(value1, value2, ...)	Number of values in list	Statistical
COUNTA(value1, value2, ...)	Number of non-blank values in list	Statistical
COUNTBLANK(range)	Number of blank cells within a range	Information
COUNTIF(range, criteria)	Number of non-blank cells within a range that meet given criteria	Mathematical
COUPDAYBS(settlement, maturity, frequency, basis)	Number of days from beginning of coupon period to settlement date	Financial
COUPDAYS(settlement, maturity, frequency, basis)	Number of days in coupon period that contains settlement date	Financial
COUPDAYSNC(settlement, maturity, frequency, basis)	Number of days from settlement date to next coupon date	Financial
COUPNCD(settlement, maturity, frequency, basis)	Next coupon date after settlement date	Financial
COUPNUM(settlement, maturity, frequency, basis)	Number of coupons payable between settlement date and maturity date	Financial
COUPPCD(settlement, maturity, frequency, basis)	Previous coupon date before settlement date	Financial
COVAR(array1, array2)	Covariance, average of products of paired deviations	Statistical
CRITBINOM(trials, probability_s, alpha)	Smallest value for which cumulative binomial distribution is less than or equal to a criterion value	Statistical
CUMIPMT(rate, nper, pv, start_period, end_period, type)	Cumulative interest paid between two periods	Financial
CUMPRINC(rate, nper, pv, start_period, end_period, type)	Cumulative principal paid on a loan between two periods	Financial
DATE(year, month, day)	Serial number of a particular date	Time

Function (Syntax)	Description	Category
DATEVALUE(date_text)	Change a date in form of text to a serial number	Time
DAVERAGE(database, field, criteria)	Average of selected database entries	Database
DAY(serial_number)	Change a serial number to a day of the month	Time
DAYS360(start_date, end_date, method)	Number of days between two dates based on a 360-day year	Time
DB(cost, salvage, life, period, month)	Depreciation of an asset for a specified period using fixed-declining balance method	Financial
DCOUNT(database, field, criteria)	Count cells containing numbers from a specified database and criteria	Database
DCOUNTA(database, field, criteria)	Count nonblank cells from a specified database and criteria	Database
DDB(cost, salvage, life, period, factor)	Depreciation of an asset for a specified period using double-declining balance method or some other method you specify	Financial
DEC2BIN(number, places)	Change a decimal number to binary	Engineering
DEC2HEX(number, places)	Change a decimal number to hexadecimal	Engineering
DEC2OCT(number, places)	Change a decimal number to octal	Engineering
DEGREES(angle)	Change radians to degrees	Mathematical
DELTA(number1, number2)	Test whether two values are equal	Engineering
DEVSQ(number1, number2, ...)	Sum of squares of deviations	Statistical
DGET(database, field, criteria)	Extract from a database a single record that matches specified criteria	Database

continues

Excel's functions in all their glory   Continued

Function (Syntax)	Description	Category
DISC(settlement, maturity, pr, redemption, basis)	Discount rate for a security	Financial
DMAX(database, field, criteria)	Maximum value from selected database entries	Database
DMIN(database, field, criteria)	Minimum value from selected database entries	Database
DOLLAR(number, decimals)	Change a number to text, using currency format	Text
DOLLARDE(fractional_dollar, fraction)	Change a dollar price expressed as a fraction into a dollar price expressed as a decimal number	Financial
DOLLARFR(decimal_dollar, fraction)	Change a dollar price expressed as a decimal number into a dollar price expressed as a fraction	Financial
DPRODUCT(database, field, criteria)	Multiply values in a particular field of records that match criteria in a database	Database
DSTDEV(database, field, criteria)	Estimated standard deviation based on a sample of selected database entries	Database
DSTDEVP(database, field, criteria)	Standard deviation based on entire population of selected database entries	Database
DSUM(database,field, criteria)	Sum numbers in field column of records in database that match criteria	Database
DURATION(settlement, maturity, coupon, yld, frequency, basis)	Annual duration of a security with periodic interest payments	Financial
DVAR(database, field, criteria)	Estimated variance based on a sample from selected database entries	Database

Function (Syntax)	Description	Category
DVARP(database, field, criteria)	Variance based on entire population of selected database entries	Database
EDATE(start_date, months)	Serial number of date that is indicated number of months before or after start date	Time
EFFECT(nominal_rate, npery)	Effective annual interest rate	Financial
EOMONTH(start_date, months)	Serial number of last day of month before or after a specified number of months	Time
ERF(lower_limit, upper_limit)	Error function	Engineering
ERFC(x)	Complementary error function	Engineering
ERROR.TYPE(error_val)	Show number corresponding to an error type	Information
EVEN(number)	Round a number up to nearest even integer	Mathematical
EXACT(text1, text2)	Check to see if two text values are identical	Text
EXP(number)	E raised to power of a given number	Mathematical
EXPONDIST(x, lambda, cumulative)	Exponential distribution	Statistical
FACT(number)	Factorial of a number	Mathematical
FACTDOUBLE(number)	Double factorial of a number	Mathematical
FALSE( )	Logical value FALSE	Logical
FDIST(x, degrees_ freedom1, degrees_ freedom2)	F probability distribution	Statistical
FIND(find_text, within_text, start_num)	Search one text value within another (case-sensitive)	Text

continues

323

Excel's functions in all their glory   Continued

Function (Syntax)	Description	Category
FINV(probability, degrees_freedom1, degrees_freedom2)	Inverse of F probability distribution	Statistical
FISHER(x)	Fisher transformation	Statistical
FISHERINV(y)	Inverse of Fisher transformation	Statistical
FIXED(number, decimals, no_commas)	Format a number as text with a fixed number of decimals	Text
FLOOR(number, significance)	Round a number down, toward zero	Mathematical
FORECAST(x, known_y's, known_x's)	Value along a linear trend	Statistical
FREQUENCY(data_array, bins_array)	Frequency distribution as a vertical array	Statistical
FTEST(array1, array2)	Result of an F-test	Statistical
FV(rate, nper, pmt, pv, type)	Future value of an investment	Financial
FVSCHEDULE(principal, schedule)	Future value of an initial principal after applying a series of compound interest rates	Financial
GAMMADIST(x, alpha, beta, cumulative)	Gamma distribution	Statistical
GAMMAINV(probability, alpha, beta)	Inverse of gamma cumulative distribution	Statistical
GAMMALN(x)	Natural logarithm of gamma function, G(x)	Statistical
GCD(number1, number2, ...)	Greatest common divisor	Mathematical
GEOMEAN(number1, number2, ...)	Geometric mean	Statistical
GESTEP(number, step)	Test whether a number is greater than a threshold value	Engineering
GETPIVOTDATA(pivot_table,"cell_label")	Collect summary data from pivot table	Database
GROWTH(known_y's, known_x's, new_x's, const)	Values along an exponential trend	Statistical

Function (Syntax)	Description	Category
HARMEAN(number1, number2, ...)	Harmonic mean	Statistical
HEX2BIN(number, places)	Change a hexadecimal number to binary	Engineering
HEX2DEC(number)	Change a hexadecimal number to decimal	Engineering
HEX2OCT(number, places)	Change a hexadecimal number to octal	Engineering
HLOOKUP(lookup_value, table_array, row_index_num, range_lookup)	Look in top row of an array and return value of indicated cell	Lookup
HOUR(serial_number)	Change a serial number to an hour	Time
HYPERLINK(link_location, cell_display)	Shortcut to server, intranet or Internet	Lookup
HYPGEOMDIST(sample_s, number_sample, population_s, number_population)	Hypergeometric distribution	Statistical
IF(logical_test, value_if_true, value_if_false)	Specify a logical test to perform	Logical
IMABS(inumber)	Absolute value (modulus) of a complex number	Engineering
IMAGINARY(inumber)	Imaginary coefficient of a complex number	Engineering
IMARGUMENT(inumber)	Argument theta, an angle expressed in radians	Engineering
IMCONJUGATE(inumber)	Complex conjugate of a complex number	Engineering
IMCOS(inumber)	Cosine of a complex number	Engineering
IMDIV(inumber1,inumber2)	Quotient of two complex numbers	Engineering
IMEXP(inumber)	Exponential of a complex number	Engineering

continues

325

Excel's functions in all their glory   Continued

Function (Syntax)	Description	Category
IMLN(inumber)	Natural logarithm of a complex number	Engineering
IMLOG10(inumber)	Base-10 logarithm of a complex number	Engineering
IMLOG2(inumber)	Base-2 logarithm of a complex number	Engineering
IMPOWER(inumber, number)	Complex number raised to an integer power	Engineering
IMPRODUCT(inumber1, inumber2, ...)	Product of two to 29 complex numbers	Engineering
IMREAL(inumber)	Real coefficient of a complex number	Engineering
IMSIN(inumber)	Sine of a complex number	Engineering
IMSQRT(inumber)	Square root of a complex number	Engineering
IMSUB(inumber1,inumber2)	Difference of two complex numbers	Engineering
IMSUM(inumber1, inumber2, ...)	Sum of complex numbers	Engineering
INDEX(array, row_num, column_num) or INDEX(reference, row_num, column_num, area_num)	Use an index to choose a value from a reference or array	Lookup
INDIRECT(ref_text, a1)	Reference indicated by a text value	Lookup
INFO(type_text)	Information about current operating environment	Information
INT(number)	Round a number down to nearest integer	Mathematical
INTERCEPT(known_y's, known_x's)	Intercept of linear regression line	Statistical
INTRATE(settlement, maturity, investment, redemption, basis)	Interest rate for a fully invested security	Financial

Function (Syntax)	Description	Category
IPMT(rate, per, nper, pv, fv, type)	Interest payment for an investment for a given period	Financial
IRR(values, guess)	Internal rate of return for a series of cash flows	Financial
ISBLANK(value)	TRUE if value is blank	Information
ISERR(value)	TRUE if value is any error value except #N/A	Information
ISERROR(value)	TRUE if value is any error value	Information
ISEVEN(value)	TRUE if number is even	Information
ISLOGICAL(value)	TRUE if value is a logical value	Information
ISNA(value)	TRUE if value is #N/A error value	Information
ISNONTEXT(value)	TRUE if value is not text	Information
ISNUMBER(value)	TRUE if value is a number	Information
ISODD(value)	TRUE if number is odd	Information
ISREF(value)	TRUE if value is a reference	Information
ISTEXT(value)	TRUE if value is text	Information
KURT(number1, number2, ...)	Kurtosis of a data set	Statistical
LARGE(array, k)	K-th largest value in a data set	Statistical
LCM(number1, number2, ...)	Least common multiple	Mathematical
LEFT(text, num_chars)	Leftmost characters from a text value	Text
LEN(text)	Number of characters in a text string	Text
LINEST(known_y's, known_x's, const, stats)	Parameters of a linear trend	Statistical
LN(number)	Natural logarithm of a number	Mathematical

continues

Excel's functions in all their glory   Continued

Function (Syntax)	Description	Category
LOG(number, base)	Logarithm of a number to a specified base	Mathematical
LOG10(number)	Base-10 logarithm of a number	Mathematical
LOGEST(known_y's, known_x's, const, stats)	Parameters of an exponential trend	Statistical
LOGINV(probability, mean,standard_dev)	Inverse of lognormal distribution	Statistical
LOGNORMDIST(x, mean, standard_dev)	Cumulative lognormal distribution	Statistical
LOOKUP(lookup_value, lookup_vector, result_vector) or LOOKUP(lookup_value, array)	Look up values in a vector or array	Lookup
LOWER(text)	Change text to lowercase	Text
MATCH(lookup_value, lookup_array, match_type)	Look up values in a reference or array	Lookup
MAX(number1, number2, ...)	Maximum value in a list	Statistical
MAXA(value1,value2, ...)	Largest value in a list, including logical values	Statistical
MDETERM(array)	Matrix determinant of an array	Mathematical
MDURATION(settlement, maturity, coupon, yld, frequency, basis)	Macauley modified duration for a security with an assumed par value of $100	Financial
MEDIAN(number1, number2, ...)	Median of given numbers	Statistical
MID(text, start_num, num_chars)	Specific number of characters from a text string starting at position you specify	Text
MIN(number1, number2, ...)	Minimum value in a list of arguments	Statistical

Function (Syntax)	Description	Category
MINA(number1, number2, ...)	Minimum value in a list, including logical values	Statistical
MINUTE(serial_number)	Change a serial number to a minute	Time
MINVERSE(array)	Matrix inverse of an array	Mathematical
MIRR(values, finance_rate, reinvest_rate)	Internal rate of return where positive and negative cash flows are financed at different rates	Financial
MMULT(array1, array2)	Matrix product of two arrays	Mathematical
MOD(number, divisor)	Remainder from division	Mathematical
MODE(number1, number2, ...)	Most common value in a data set	Statistical
MONTH(serial_number)	Change a serial number to a month	Time
MROUND(number, multiple)	Number rounded to desired multiple	Mathematical
MULTINOMIAL(number1, number2, ...)	Multinomial of a set of numbers	Mathematical
N(value)	Value converted to a number	Information
NA( )	Error value #N/A	Information
NEGBINOMDIST(number_f, number_s, probability_s)	Negative binomial distribution	Statistical
NETWORKDAYS(start_date, end_date, holidays)	Number of whole workdays between two dates	Time
NOMINAL(effect_rate, npery)	Annual nominal interest rate	Financial
NORMDIST(x, mean, standard_dev, cumulative)	Normal cumulative distribution	Statistical
NORMINV(probability, mean, standard_dev)	Inverse of normal cumulative distribution	Statistical
NORMSDIST(z)	Standard normal cumulative distribution	Statistical

continues

Excel's functions in all their glory Continued

Function (Syntax)	Description	Category
NORMSINV(probability)	Inverse of standard normal cumulative distribution	Statistical
NOT(logical)	Reverse logic of argument	Logical
NOW( )	Serial number of current date and time	Time
NPER(rate,pmt,pv,fv, type)	Number of periods for an investment	Financial
NPV(rate, value1, value2, …)	Net present value of an investment based on a series of periodic cash flows and a discount rate	Financial
OCT2BIN(number, places)	Change an octal number to binary	Engineering
OCT2DEC(number)	Change an octal number to decimal	Engineering
OCT2HEX(number, places)	Change an octal number to hexadecimal	Engineering
ODD(number)	Round a number up to nearest odd integer	Mathematical
ODDFPRICE(settlement, maturity, issue, first_coupon, rate, yld, redemption, frequency, basis)	Price per $100 face value of a security with an odd first period	Financial
ODDFYIELD(settlement, maturity, issue, first_coupon, rate, pr, redemption, frequency, basis)	Yield of a security with an odd first period	Financial
ODDLPRICE(settlement, maturity, last_interest, rate, yld, redemption, frequency, basis)	Price per $100 face value of a security with an odd last period	Financial
ODDLYIELD(settlement, maturity, last_interest, rate, pr, redemption, frequency, basis)	Yield of a security with an odd last period	Financial
OFFSET(reference, rows, cols, height, width)	Reference offset from a given reference	Lookup

Function (Syntax)	Description	Category
OR(logical1, logical2, ...)	TRUE if any argument is TRUE	Logical
PEARSON(array1, array2)	Pearson product moment correlation coefficient	Statistical
PERCENTILE(array, k)	K-th percentile of values in a range	Statistical
PERCENTRANK(array, x, significance)	Percentage rank of a value in a data set	Statistical
PERMUT(number, number_ chosen)	Number of permutations for a given number of objects	Statistical
PI( )	Value of pi (3.14159)	Mathematical
PMT(rate, nper, pv, fv, type)	Periodic payment for an annuity	Financial
POISSON(x, mean, cumulative)	Poisson distribution	Statistical
POWER(number, power)	Result of a number raised to a power	Mathematical
PPMT(rate, per, nper, pv, fv, type)	Payment on principal for an investment for a given period	Financial
PRICE(settlement, maturity, rate, yld, redemption, frequency, basis)	Price per $100 face value of a security that pays periodic interest	Financial
PRICEDISC(settlement, maturity, discount, redemption, basis)	Price per $100 face value of a discounted security	Financial
PRICEMAT(settlement, maturity, issue, rate, yld, basis)	Price per $100 face value of a security that pays interest at maturity	Financial
PROB(x_range, prob_ range, lower_limit, upper_limit)	Probability that values in a range are between two limits	Statistical
PRODUCT(number1, number2, ...)	Multiply all arguments	Mathematical
PROPER(text)	Capitalize first letter in each word of a text value	Text
PV(rate, nper, pmt, fv, type)	Present value of an investment	Financial

continues

Excel's functions in all their glory   Continued

Function (Syntax)	Description	Category
QUARTILE(array, quart)	Quartile of a data set	Statistical
QUOTIENT(numerator, denominator)	Integer portion of a division	Mathematical
RADIANS(angle)	Change degrees to radians	Mathematical
RAND( )	Random number between 0 and 1	Mathematical
RANDBETWEEN(bottom,top)	Random number between numbers you specify	Mathematical
RANK(number, ref, order)	Rank of a number in a list of numbers	Statistical
RATE(nper, pmt, pv, fv, type, guess)	Interest rate per period of an annuity	Financial
RECEIVED(settlement, maturity, investment, discount, basis)	Amount received at maturity for a fully invested security	Financial
REPLACE(old_text, start_num, num_chars, new_text)	Replaces characters within text	Text
REPT(text, number_times)	Repeat text a given number of times	Text
RIGHT(text, num_chars)	Rightmost characters from a text value	Text
ROMAN(number, form)	Change an Arabic numeral to Roman, as text	Mathematical
ROUND(number,num_digits)	Round a number to a specified number of digits	Mathematical
ROUNDDOWN(number, num_digits)	Round a number down, toward zero	Mathematical
ROUNDUP(number, num_digits)	Round a number up, away from zero	Mathematical
ROW(reference)	Row number of a reference	Lookup
ROWS(array)	Number of rows in a reference	Lookup
RSQ(known_y's,known_x's)	Square of Pearson product moment correlation coefficient	Statistical

Function (Syntax)	Description	Category
SEARCH(find_text, within_text, start_num)	Search one text value within another (not case-sensitive)	Text
SECOND(serial_number)	Change a serial number to a second	Time
SERIESSUM(x, n, m, coefficients)	Sum of a power series based on formula	Mathematical
SIGN(number)	Sign of a number	Mathematical
SIN(number)	Sine of given angle	Mathematical
SINH(number)	Hyperbolic sine of a number	Mathematical
SKEW(number1, number2, ...)	Skewness of a distribution	Statistical
SLN(cost, salvage, life)	Straight-line depreciation of an asset for one period	Financial
SLOPE(known_y's, known_x's)	Slope of linear regression line	Statistical
SMALL(array, k)	K-th smallest value in a data set	Statistical
SQRT(number)	Positive square root	Mathematical
SQRTPI(number)	Square root of (number*pi)	Mathematical
STANDARDIZE(x, mean, standard_dev)	Normalized value	Statistical
STDEV(number1, number2, ...)	Estimated standard deviation based on a sample	Statistical
STDEVA(number1, number2, ...)	Estimated standard deviation based on a sample, including logical values	Statistical
STDEVP(number1, number2, ...)	Standard deviation based on entire population	Statistical
STDEVPA(number1, number2,...)	Standard deviation based on entire population of arguments	Statistical
STEYX(known_y's, known_x's)	Standard error of predicted y-value for each x in regression	Statistical

continues

Excel's functions in all their glory   Continued

Function (Syntax)	Description	Category
SUBSTITUTE(text, old_text, new_text, instance_num)	Substitutes new text for old text in a text string	Text
SUBTOTAL(function_num, ref)	Subtotal in a list or list or database	Mathematical
SUM(number1, number2, ...)	Sum all arguments	Mathematical
SUMIF(range, criteria, sum_range)	Sum cells specified by a given criteria	Mathematical
SUMPRODUCT(array1, array2, array3, ...)	Sum of products of corresponding array components	Mathematical
SUMSQ(number1, number2, ...)	Sum of squares of arguments	Mathematical
SUMX2MY2(array_x, array_y)	Sum of difference of squares of corresponding values in two arrays	Mathematical
SUMX2PY2(array_x, array_y)	Sum of sum of squares of corresponding values in two arrays	Mathematical
SUMXMY2(array_x, array_y)	Sum of squares of differences of corresponding values in two arrays	Mathematical
SYD(cost,salvage,life, per)	Sum-of-years' digits depreciation of an asset for a specified period	Financial
T(value)	Change arguments to text	Text
TAN(number)	Tangent of a given angle	Mathematical
TANH(number)	Hyperbolic tangent of a number	Mathematical
TBILLEQ(settlement, maturity, discount)	Bond-equivalent yield for a Treasury bill	Financial
TBILLPRICE(settlement, maturity, discount)	Price per $100 face value for a Treasury bill	Financial
TBILLYIELD(settlement, maturity, pr)	Yield for a Treasury bill	Financial
TDIST(x, degrees_freedom, tails)	Student's t-distribution	Statistical

Function (Syntax)	Description	Category
TEXT(value, format_text)	Format a number and convert it to text	Text
TIME(hour, minute, second)	Serial number of a particular time	Time
TIMEVALUE(time_text)	Change a time in form of text to a serial number	Time
TINV(probability, degrees_freedom)	Inverse of Student's t-distribution	Statistical
TODAY( )	Serial number of today's date	Time
TRANSPOSE(array)	Transpose of an array	Lookup
TREND(known_y's, known_x's, new_x's, const)	Values along a linear trend	Statistical
TRIM(text)	Remove spaces from text	Text
TRIMMEAN(array, percent)	Mean of interior of a data set	Statistical
TRUE( )	Logical value TRUE	Logical
TRUNC(number,num_digits)	Truncate a number to an integer	Mathematical
TTEST(array1, array2, tails, type)	Probability associated with a Student's t-test	Statistical
TYPE(value)	Number indicating data type of a value	Information
UPPER(text)	Change text to uppercase	Text
VALUE(text)	Change a text argument to a number	Text
VAR(number1, number2, ...)	Estimated variance based on a sample	Statistical
VARA(number1, number2, ...)	Estimated variance based on a sample, including logical values	Statistical
VARP(number1, number2, ...)	Variance based on entire population	Statistical
VARPA(number1, number2, ...)	Variance based on entire population of arguments	Statistical

continues

Excel's functions in all their glory   Continued

Function (Syntax)	Description	Category
VDB(cost, salvage, life, start_period, end_period, factor, no_switch)	Depreciation of an asset for a specified or partial period using a declining balance method	Financial
VLOOKUP(lookup_value, table_array, col_index_num, range_lookup)	Look in first column of an array and move across row to return value of a cell	Lookup
WEEKDAY(serial_number, return_type)	Change a serial number to a day of week	Time
WEEKNUM(serial_number, return_type)	Returns number of weeks within a year	Time
WEIBULL(x, alpha, beta, cumulative)	Weibull distribution	Statistical
WORKDAY(start_date, days, holidays)	Serial number of date before or after a specified number of workdays	Time
XIRR(values, dates, guess)	Internal rate of return for a schedule of cash flows that is not necessarily periodic	Financial
XNPV(rate, values, dates)	Net present value for a schedule of cash flows that is not necessarily periodic	Financial
YEAR(serial_number)	Change a serial number to a year	Time
YEARFRAC(start_date, end_date, basis)	Year fraction representing number of whole days between start_date and end_date	Time
YIELD(settlement, maturity, rate, pr, redemption, frequency, basis)	Yield on a security that pays periodic interest	Financial
YIELDDISC(settlement, maturity, pr, redemption, basis)	Annual yield for a discounted security such as a treasury bill	Financial
YIELDMAT(settlement, maturity, issue, rate, pr, basis)	Annual yield of a security that pays interest at maturity	Financial
ZTEST(array,x,sigma)	Two-tailed P-value of a z-test	Statistical

Excel Shortcut Keys

Shortcut keys (by key combination and feature)

Key Combination	Result
F1	Access Help system
F2	Activate a cell
F3	Issue Paste command
F4	Repeat most recent action
F5	Issue GoTo command
F6	Move to next pane
F7	Start spelling checker
F8	Extend a selection
F9	Calculate all formulas
F10	Move cursor to Main Menu bar
F11	Create automatic chart
F12	Open Save As dialog box or save named file
Shift+Ins	Insert (Paste) item that was copied or cut
Shift+Home	Select cells from active cell to left edge of current row
Shift+PgUp	Select cells from active cell to top of current column
Shift+Delete	Move selected cells
Shift+PgDn	Select cells from active cell down one screen page
Shift+F1	Get Help on a screen item
Shift+F2	Edit a cell
Shift+F3	Start Function Wizard
Shift+F4	Repeat most recent Find or GoTo

continues

Shortcut keys (by key combination and feature)   Continued

Key Combination	Result
Shift+F5	Issue Find command
Shift+F6	Switch to another Excel window
Shift+F8	Select multiple cells
Shift+F9	Calculate active sheet
Shift+F10	Open shortcut menu related to active cell or object
Shift+F12	Open Save As dialog box or save named file
Ctrl+B	Bold selected text
Ctrl+C	Copy selected item
Ctrl+D	AutoFill down
Ctrl+F	Open Find dialog box
Ctrl+G	Open GoTo dialog box
Ctrl+H	Open Replace (and Find) dialog box
Ctrl+I	Italicize selected text
Ctrl+N	Open New worksheet dialog box
Ctrl+O	Open Open worksheet dialog box
Ctrl+P	Open Print dialog box
Ctrl+R	AutoFill right
Ctrl+S	Open Save As dialog box or save existing file
Ctrl+U	Underline selected text
Ctrl+V	Insert (paste) item that was copied or cut
Ctrl+W	Close worksheet
Ctrl+X	Cut selected item
Ctrl+Y	Repeat AutoFill
Ctrl+1	Open Format Cells dialog box
Ctrl+2	Toggle bold on and off
Ctrl+3	Toggle italic on and off
Ctrl+4	Toggle underline on and off
Ctrl+5	Toggle strikethrough on and off
Ctrl+7	Toggle standard toolbar display on and off
Ctrl+8	Display Outline symbols or create outline

Key Combination	Result
Ctrl+0	Hide Columns
Ctrl+' (apostrophe)	Copy information from cell above active cell
Ctrl+' (single open quotation mark)	Resize Columns
Ctrl+; (semicolon)	Show serial number corresponding to current date
Ctrl+ –	Open Delete dialog box to delete rows, columns
Ctrl+Del	Move active cell to another location
Ctrl+down arrow	Move cursor down column, skipping blank cells
Ctrl+End	Move cursor to end of sheet
Ctrl+Home	Move cursor to cell A1
Ctrl+Ins	Copy selected item
Ctrl+left arrow	Move cursor to left, skipping blank cells
Ctrl+PgDn	Move backward through worksheets
Ctrl+PgUp	Move forward through worksheets
Ctrl+right arrow	Move cursor to right, skipping blank cells
Ctrl+up arrow	Move cursor up column, skipping blank cells
Ctrl+F2	Open Info window
Ctrl+F3	Define name
Ctrl+F4	Close window
Ctrl+F5	Restore window
Ctrl+F9	Minimize window
Ctrl+F10	Maximize window
Ctrl+F11	Start Macro sheet
Ctrl+F12	Open Open worksheet dialog box
Alt+Tab	Switch to another open program
Alt+D	Open Data menu
Alt+E	Open Edit menu
Alt+F	Open File menu
Alt+H	Open Help menu
Alt+I	Open Insert menu

continues

Shortcut keys (by key combination and feature)   Continued

Key Combination	Result
Alt+O	Open Format menu
Alt+T	Open Tools menu
Alt+V	Open View menu
Alt+W	Open Windows menu
Alt+ –	Open File menu
Alt+=	Sum the cells immediately above
Alt+\	Move cursor to left side of current row
Alt+;	Make cells visible
Alt+down arrow	Open AutoComplete dialog box
Alt+PgDn	Move one page to the right
Alt+PgUp	Move one page to the left
Ctrl+Shift+F	Access Font list
Ctrl+Shift+P	Access Font Size list
Ctrl+Shift+2	Format cell as time
Ctrl+Shift+3	Format cell as date
Ctrl+Shift+4	Format cell as currency
Ctrl+Shift+5	Format cell as percentage
Ctrl+Shift+6	Format cell as scientific
Ctrl+Shift+7	Outline selected cells
Ctrl+Shift+8	Select block that includes all cells with data
Ctrl+Shift+'	Copy from above
Ctrl+Shift+;	Display serial number corresponding to current time
Ctrl+Shift+=	Open Insert dialog box
Ctrl+Shift+ –	Delete Line selection
Ctrl+Shift+down arrow	Select entire column
Ctrl+Shift+right arrow	Select an entire row
Ctrl+Shift+F3	Open Create Names dialog box
Ctrl+Shift+F4	Repeat Find
Ctrl+Shift+F12	Open Print dialog box

Shortcut keys (by feature and key combination)

Feature	Key Combination
Activate a cell	F2
AutoFill down	Ctrl+D
AutoFill right	Ctrl+R
Bold selected text	Ctrl+B
Calculate active sheet	Shift+F9
Calculate all formulas	F9
Call up Help on a screen item	Shift+F1
Close window	Ctrl+F4
Close worksheet	Ctrl+W
Copy from above	Ctrl+Shift+'
Copy information from cell above active cell	Ctrl+' (apostrophe)
Copy selected item	Ctrl+C
Copy selected item	Ctrl+Ins
Create automatic chart	F11
Cut selected item	Ctrl+X
Define name	Ctrl+F3
Delete Line selection	Ctrl+Shift+ –
Display Outline symbols or create outline	Ctrl+8
Display serial number corresponding to current time	Ctrl+Shift+;
Edit a cell	Shift+F2
Extend a selection	F8
Find command	Shift+F5
Font list	Ctrl+Shift+F
Font size list	Ctrl+Shift+P
Format cell as currency	Ctrl+Shift+4
Format cell as date	Ctrl+Shift+3
Format cell as percentage	Ctrl+Shift+5

continues

Shortcut keys (by feature and key combination)   Continued

Feature	Key Combination
Format cell as scientific	Ctrl+Shift+6
Format cell as time	Ctrl+Shift+2
GoTo command	F5
Help system	F1
Hide Columns	Ctrl+0
Insert (Paste) item that was copied or cut	Shift+Ins Ctrl+V
Italicize selected text	Ctrl+I
Make cells visible	Alt+;
Maximize window	Ctrl+F10
Minimize window	Ctrl+F9
Move active cell to another location	Ctrl+Del
Move backward through worksheets	Ctrl+PgDn
Move cursor down column, skipping blank cells	Ctrl+down arrow
Move cursor to cell A1	Ctrl+Home
Move cursor to end of sheet	Ctrl+End
Move cursor to left side of current row	Alt+\
Move cursor to left, skipping blank cells	Ctrl+left arrow
Move cursor to Main Menu bar	F10
Move cursor to right, skipping blank cells	Ctrl+right arrow
Move cursor up column, skipping blank cells	Ctrl+up arrow
Move forward through worksheets	Ctrl+PgUp
Move one page to the left	Alt+PgUp
Move one page to the right	Alt+PgDn
Move selected cells	Shift+Delete
Open AutoComplete dialog box	Alt+down arrow
Open Create Names dialog box	Ctrl+Shift+F3
Open Data menu	Alt+D

Feature	Key Combination
Open Delete dialog box to delete rows, columns	Ctrl+–
Open Edit menu	Alt+E
Open File menu	Alt+–
Open File menu	Alt+F
Open Find dialog box	Ctrl+F
Open Format Cells dialog box	Ctrl+1
Open Format menu	Alt+O
Open GoTo dialog box	Ctrl+G
Open Help menu	Alt+H
Open Info window	Ctrl+F2
Open Insert dialog box	Ctrl+Shift+=
Open Insert menu	Alt+I
Open New worksheet dialog box	Ctrl+N
Open Open worksheet dialog box	Ctrl+F12 Ctrl+O
Open Print dialog box	Ctrl+P Ctrl+Shift+F12
Open Replace (and Find) dialog box	Ctrl+H
Open Save As dialog box or save existing file	Ctrl+S
Open Save As dialog box or save named file	F12 Shift+F12
Open shortcut menu related to active cell or object	Shift+F10
Open Tools menu	Alt+T
Open View menu	Alt+V
Open Windows menu	Alt+W
Outline selected cells	Ctrl+Shift+7
Paste command	F3
Repeat AutoFill	Ctrl+Y
Repeat Find	Ctrl+Shift+F4

continues

Shortcut keys (by feature and key combination)   Continued

Feature	Key Combination
Repeat most recent action	F4
Repeat most recent Find or GoTo	Shift+F4
Resize Columns	Ctrl+' (single open quotation mark)
Restore window	Ctrl+F5
Select an entire row	Ctrl+Shift+right arrow
Select block that includes all cells with data	Ctrl+Shift+8
Select cells from active cell down one screen page	Shift+PgDn
Select cells from active cell to left edge of current row	Shift+Home
Select cells from active cell to top of current column	Shift+PgUp
Select entire column	Ctrl+Shift+down arrow
Select multiple cells	Shift+F8
Shift to another Excel window	Shift+F6
Show serial number corresponding to current date	Ctrl+;
Start Function Wizard	Shift+F3
Start Macro sheet	Ctrl+F11
Start spelling checker	F7
Sum the cells immediately above	Alt+=
Switch to another open software program	Alt+Tab
Toggle bold on and off	Ctrl+2
Toggle italics on and off	Ctrl+3
Toggle standard toolbar display on and off	Ctrl+7
Toggle strikethrough on and off	Ctrl+5
Toggle underline on and off	Ctrl+4
Underline selected text	Ctrl+U

WHAT..?

Speak Like a Geek: The Complete Archive

A sure-fire way to sound good at cocktail parties in Redmond, Washington.

absolute reference   A reference that doesn't change when it's moved or copied. (See *relative reference*.) You make a reference absolute by preceding it with a dollar sign ($), as in C3.

active cell area   The area of cells that will be affected by your commands or changes. A heavy border surrounds the cell or group of cells.

active cell indicator   The bold outline that shows where you are on the worksheet. It marks the cell that will be affected by your commands or changes.

address   The location of a cell or a group of cells. Takes the form B3, where B is the second column and 3 is the third row, or R3C2. Also called a reference.

argument   The part of the equation that's not an operator. How's that for a bum definition? Okay, it can be a constant, function, name, cell reference, or value.

Auditing toolbar   A group of buttons that simplify the auditing process.

block   Any group of cells. Often a block gets a name, and becomes a *range,* because it's a place you go to again and again. A simple "group of cells" is too fleeting to get a name.

cell   A place on the worksheet grid; the intersection of a column and row.

cell reference   The address that describes the location of a cell. See *address*.

click   What you do with a mouse to an object on your screen. Click is that satisfying sound made by the button on your mouse when you press it. To click a word or a cell or anything else, position the mouse pointer (which is usually shaped like an arrow) over the object of your affections and press the left mouse button. Sometimes you'll double-click, and sometimes you'll right-click (click the right mouse button instead of the usual left mouse button).

Close button   The third button (the X) in the upper-right corner of your screen. It closes the application, but it won't put the toilet seat down.

constant A number or text entry that you type directly into the formula (as opposed to something like a cell reference, with which you tell Excel where to find its own numbers or text).

cursor The blinking line or square that shows where you are on the spreadsheet. Sometimes it happens to be in the same place as the *active cell indicator*, but that's only a coincidence.

data points Sales figures, profit numbers, expenses, staff size, market size, saturation percentages, or anything else that can be represented numerically on a chart or database.

database A list of data arranged in columns. It's basically any table to which you can assign a name.

database workbook The workbook that contains your database list; used in the AutoTemplate feature.

dependent Any cell that descends in whole or part from a specified cell; used in the auditing feature.

dialog box A box Excel displays to ask you for more information; usually contains options related to the current function.

direct dependent Any cell that descends in whole or in part from the active cell; used in Auditing.

direct precedent The first ancestral line of the formula in the active cell; used in auditing.

equation You learned this in the third grade, right? Something equals something else, except that in Excel, you don't know what it equals until you hit the Enter key. You might also call it a formula.

external reference A reference to a cell or cells in other another workbook; used in formulas.

factor One of the elements of a formula; a value, reference, name, operator, or function. Yeah, you're right. It's the same thing as an *argument*.

field In a typical Excel *database* list, each column of the list is a new field.

field buttons When you create a pivot table, the column labels in your data list become field buttons.

folder A section of your hard drive in which you store your files. (Folders were called subdirectories in older versions of Windows and in DOS.)

format The display characteristics you assign to an item, or the thing you put your feet on when you drive. We forget which.

formula A mathematical computation that involves multiple factors and results in a new value. Pretty much the same thing as an *equation*.

formula bar   The line just above the column headers; Excel displays the contents of the active cell here, so you can edit them.

frame   The box that appears around an *object* when it's active.

function   A prebuilt *formula*; functions are what give Excel all its power.

graphic   A chart, graph, map, drawing, or picture.

graphic report   A chart, graph, or table.

group   You can subdivide categories of data and group the subdivisions together. Africa or Europe might be a category, for example, and all the separate countries in each location can be grouped together.

icon   A picture symbol used by Windows to represent an application or task.

indirect dependent   Any cell that descends in any way from a direct descendent of the active cell; used in auditing.

indirect precedent   A cell that is any part of the entire ancestral line of the formula in the active cell; used in auditing.

internal reference   A reference to another cell on the same worksheet; used in formulas.

keyboard shortcut   A combination of keys you can use to avoid using the mouse. For example, Ctrl+V is the keyboard shortcut for pasting an object into your spreadsheet.

label   Text. Not numbers. Okay, maybe numbers and text together. The word *label* also refers to the heading at the top of a column, when you're working with databases.

legend box   The box on a map or chart that describes the graphic symbols being used.

link   The process that connects one or more workbooks with shared data. Linking is better than copying because when you change the source cells in one document, Excel automatically updates them in the second document.

list   The information in a database, arranged in columns with a label at the top of each column. Pivot tables use database lists as the source for their data.

macro   A series of keystrokes. Excel records them so that you can replay them at will.

main menu bar   The second line from the top of your Excel screen. It displays the names of menus, which contain groups of related commands. When you click a word on the menu bar, a pull-down menu appears.

Maximize button   The second button in the upper-right corner of your screen. It toggles between full-screen and window view.

Minimize button   The button in the upper-right corner that looks like an underscore character. It reduces the program to a button on the Windows taskbar at the bottom of your screen.

Name box   The box at the left end of the Formula bar where you name your ranges.

object   Any graphic you place in your worksheet. This can be a drawing, an imported picture, a map, or a chart.

operator   Any of the mathematical symbols that tell a formula what to do. The operators are + (add), − (subtract), / (divide), * (multiply), % (percent), ^ (exponent), and the equivalencies: = (equal), <> (not equal), > (greater than), and < (less than).

page field   A separate worksheet page that contains some fields of a pivot table's data. You can direct the pivot table to break certain fields out onto page fields so that they can be displayed one at a time.

pivot table   A table you create to show interactive relationships between many kinds of things. A pivot table enables you to drag columns and rows back and forth.

pivot table control   The buttons you use to click and drag columns or rows to other locations. Excel creates these buttons from the row and column labels in your data.

pivot table data   All the summarized data out in the middle of the table.

pointer   The onscreen mouse indicator. It changes shape according to your task and the phase of the moon. Normally, though, it's shaped like an arrow.

precedent   The first ancestral line of a formula. Used in auditing.

pull-down menu   A menu that drops down when you select a word on the Main Menu.

range   A cell or a block of cells identified by either a name or an address.

range name   The English-language name that identifies a particular range. (French and Spanish names work, too. But no Chinese names unless you know how to Romanize them, like this: Hau Bu Hau?)

record   In a typical Excel list, each row of the list is a new record.

reference   The name or address of a cell or a range.

relative reference   A reference that doesn't change when it's moved or copied. (See *absolute reference*.) By default, any reference that you copy is a relative reference.

result   The answer that Excel calculates when you finish entering a formula.

Select All button   The unlabeled square in the upper left corner of your work area (at the intersection of the row and column headers).

selection handles   The small black boxes that appear on the periphery of the frame when you select an object. Click between the selection handles to move or copy an object.

scenario   A set of suppositions you make about your data.

scrollbars   The bars at the right side and bottom of your worksheet with which you move around the worksheet.

shortcut key   A combination of keyboard keys you can use if you dislike using the mouse or menus.

shortcut menu   A quick menu that appears when you right-click an object.

sizing handles   Same thing as a selection handle. Use one to change the size of an object or frame.

source data   Each pivot table is created from an existing database list or from a whole bunch of lists. These lists are the source data for the pivot table.

spreadsheet   A collection of cells arranged in columns and rows.

summary functions   The calculations (summarized, calculated, subtotaled, and grand-totaled) that Excel uses to create a pivot table.

syntax   The rules about where to put the parentheses, commas, asterisks, and operators in an Excel formula.

taskbar   A bar at the bottom of the Windows 95 screen that's visible in all applications. It contains the Start button, buttons that show the other applications you have open, and the current time.

template   A blank workbook that you can use as the basis for a useful document for a specific application.

template workbook   An input form you design.

title bar   The bar across the top of every page that tells you the name of your application.

toolbars   Ribbons of buttons and controls that you can use to circumvent menus, commands, and certain dialog boxes.

value   A number, not text.

vertex   The small square boxes that appear on a free-form object when it's ready for reshaping.

wizard   One of several features in Excel that automate a process, such as creating a chart or a map.

workbook   Multiple *worksheets* combined in a single file.

worksheet   An electronic spreadsheet.

Index

353

Q-R

QUERY

S